DEBATING HUMANITARIAN INTERVENTION

DEBATING ETHICS

General Editor
Christopher Heath Wellman
Washington University of St. Louis

Debating Ethics is a series of volumes in which leading scholars defend opposing views on timely ethical questions and core theoretical issues in contemporary moral, political, and legal philosophy.

Debating the Ethics of Immigration
Is There a Right to Exclude?
Christopher Heath Wellman and Philip Cole

Debating Brain Drain
May Governments Restrict Emigration?
Gillian Brock and Michael Blake

Debating Procreation
Is It Wrong to Reproduce?
David Benatar and David Wasserman

Debating Climate Ethics
Stephen Gardiner and David Weisbach

Debating Gun Control
How Much Regulation Do We Need?
David DeGrazia and Lester H. Hunt

Debating Humanitarian Intervention
Should We Try to Save Strangers?
Fernando R. Tesón and Bas van der Vossen

DEBATING HUMANITARIAN INTERVENTION

Should We Try to Save Strangers?

FERNANDO R. TESÓN
AND BAS VAN DER VOSSEN

OXFORD
UNIVERSITY PRESS

Oxford University Press is a department of the University of Oxford. It furthers the University's objective of excellence in research, scholarship, and education by publishing worldwide. Oxford is a registered trade mark of Oxford University Press in the UK and certain other countries.

Published in the United States of America by Oxford University Press
198 Madison Avenue, New York, NY 10016, United States of America.

Library of Congress Cataloging-in-Publication Data
Names: Teson, Fernando R., 1950– author. | Van der Vossen, Bas, 1979– author
Title: Debating humanitarian intervention : should we try to save strangers? /
Fernando R. Teson, Bas van der Vossen.
Description: New York, NY : Oxford University Press, 2017. |
Series: Debating ethics | Includes bibliographical references and index.
Identifiers: LCCN 2017004866 (print) | LCCN 2017026190 (ebook) |
ISBN 9780190202934 (online course) | ISBN 9780190202927 (pdf) |
ISBN 9780190202910 (paperback) | ISBN 9780190202903 (cloth)
Subjects: LCSH: Humanitarian intervention—Philosophy. | Humanitarian
intervention—Moral and ethical aspects. |
BISAC: PHILOSOPHY / Ethics & Moral Philosophy. |
PHILOSOPHY / Political. | PHILOSOPHY / Social.
Classification: LCC JZ6369 (ebook) | LCC JZ6369 .T43 2017 (print) |
DDC 341.5/84—dc23
LC record available at https://lccn.loc.gov/2017004866

Paperback printed by WebCom, Inc., Canada
Hardback printed by Bridgeport National Bindery, Inc., United States of America

CONTENTS

PART II HUMANITARIAN NONINTERVENTION

By Bas van der Vossen

DEBATING HUMANITARIAN INTERVENTION

Introduction

FERNANDO R. TESÓN
AND BAS VAN DER VOSSEN

THIS VOLUME EXAMINES THE ETHICS of humanitarian intervention. We use the tools of modern analytical philosophy—in particular, modern just-war theory. Our arguments are necessarily abstract, but they bear on a moral issue of the greatest practical importance—namely, whether and under what conditions governments can start wars for the ostensibly benign purpose of saving human lives. Fernando R. Tesón argues that some humanitarian interventions are morally permissible. Bas van der Vossen argues that humanitarian interventions are almost always morally prohibited.

We define humanitarian intervention *as the international use of military force to defend persons from attacks, in their own territory, by their own rulers or other groups.*[1] Writers sometimes use the concept of humanitarian intervention loosely to denote any war to save persons from atrocities, including those committed by armies in the course of war. An intervention to

1. We use the term "attack" as shorthand for "severe rights violations." We will not address intervention to save people from natural disasters like earthquakes or tsunamis, although our discussion will apply *mutatis mutandis* to these humanitarian crises.

save such victims could be humanitarian as well. But here we use of term "humanitarian intervention" narrowly to denote a war by a state or states to defend persons who are being attacked in their own territory by their own government or other groups. In Rwanda in 1994, groups of Hutus perpetrated a genocide against the Tutsis.[2] These Hutu groups massively attacked other groups within the territory of Rwanda, and the Rwandan government at the time encouraged the crimes. The group that now calls itself ISIS is not a state but, rather, a proto-state, a group that aspires to be a state. ISIS's notorious atrocities against civilians take place in territories that it controls.[3] A war to save persons from ISIS is also a war to assist those who are fighting ISIS, and so it is, indirectly, an intervention in a civil war. A similar situation transpired in Libya in 2011, where the action by the United Nations–authorized coalition, while explicitly aimed at saving civilians, was at the same time a decisive intervention in that country's civil war.[4]

THE JUSTIFICATION OF WAR

War is the most terrifying and destructive form of human violence. Your authors agree that any analysis of the ethics of war must begin with the strongest presumption that it is prohibited. But most people also think that some wars can be justified.[5]

2. For an account, see Gérard Prunier, *The Rwanda Crisis: History of a Genocide* (Columbia University Press, 1997).
3. See http://www.ibtimes.com/isis-atrocities-iraq-syria-labeled-genocide-us-house-representatives-vote-2336535.
4. See http://www.theatlantic.com/international/archive/2016/04/obamas-worst-mistake-libya/478461/.
5. Pacifists are the exception. It is certainly possible to hold the view that all wars are wrong in principle. This view is known as absolute

The task of a theory of war is to identify precisely when war is justified—that is, to specify the rare but important cases that defeat the presumption against war.

Much has been written about war.[6] Like our predecessors, we distinguish three sets of norms that govern war. The rules of *jus ad bellum* specify when states[7] may use armed force. Those rules define *just cause* for war. The rules of *jus in bello* specify *how* states and others may permissibly fight. In principle, the rules of *jus in bello* apply to all combatants, whether or not they have a just cause (although the two sets of rules are related in important ways). The third category is *jus post bellum*. These

pacifism. For a defense, see Michael Allen Fox, *Understanding Peace: A Comprehensive Introduction* (Routledge, 2014), 126–127. Another view is contingent pacifism, which holds that wars are not wrong in principle, but that actual wars cannot possibly meet the requirements for justification. See Larry May, *Contingent Pacifism: Revisiting Just War Theory* (Cambridge University Press, 2015); and the critique by Jan Narveson, *Notre Dame Philosophical Reviews*, December 12, 2015, at http://ndpr.nd.edu/news/63253-contingent-pacifism-revisiting-just-war-theory/.

6. Modern analytic philosophers have revived just-war theory. In addition to Michael Walzer's classic, *Just and Unjust Wars: A Moral Argument with Historical Illustrations,* 4th ed. (Basic Books, 2006), recent book-length treatments include Cécile Fabre, *Cosmopolitan War* (Oxford University Press, 2012); Jeff McMahan, *Killing in War* (Oxford University Press, 2009); Frances M. Kamm, *Ethics for Enemies: Terror, Torture, and War* (Oxford University Press, 2011); David Rodin, *War and Self-Defense* (Oxford University Press, 2003); and Larry May, *After War Ends* (Cambridge University Press, 2015).
7. We use the term "states" to include other political groups, such as those that either aspire to be states, or those that constitute an ethnic minority within the state, and so on. Perhaps a proper term would be "collective political non-state actors."

are the rules that govern the behavior of victorious states *after* the war, in particular in the vanquished nation's territory.

Since this book deals with the topic of when it is permissible to go to war for humanitarian reasons, we focus almost exclusively on the question of *jus ad bellum*. We will occasionally touch on *jus in bello* and especially *jus post bellum* issues to the extent that they bear on *jus ad bellum*, on the permissibility of humanitarian intervention.

As a starting point, we may say that a war is just if it meets the following conditions:[8]

1. The war has a just cause. A just cause consists in stopping or preventing the violation, backed by lethal force, of persons' rights to life and physical integrity (in brief, repelling or preventing attacks against persons).
2. The commander[9] intends the just cause either as an end, or as a means to some other end, or, perhaps, as a foreseen side effect.
3. The war stands a reasonable chance of succeeding by military means that do not breach *jus in bello* requirements.
4. The war is a necessary means to pursue the just cause while minimizing casualties.
5. The war is a proportionate response to the wrong it seeks to remedy.
6. Neither the war's occurrence nor the way it is fought should threaten the establishment of a just peace.

8. We adapt this formulation from Cécile Fabre, "War Exit," *Ethics* 125 (2015): 631–652, 632–633, although we depart from it on a couple of points.
9. By "commander" we mean here the person who starts the war. The commander usually will be the political leader of a state, the commander-in-chief.

A just humanitarian intervention is a subspecies of just war. Humanitarian intervention is a war characterized by a specific just cause: the defense of persons in a foreign territory attacked by their own government (or other groups) in that territory. Adapting the above definition, we define a justified humanitarian intervention as follows:

1. A just cause for armed intervention is defending persons against attacks by their own government or other groups in their territory.
2. The intervener intends to defend the victims either as an end, or as a means to some other end, or (perhaps) as a foreseen side effect.
3. The intervention has a reasonable chance of succeeding by military means that do not breach *jus in bello* requirements.
4. The intervention is necessary to defend the victims while minimizing casualties.
5. The intervention is a proportionate response to the wrongs it seeks to remedy.
6. Neither the intervention nor the way it is fought should threaten the establishment of a just peace.

We have left key terms in this definition ambiguous. We will clarify them in the course of our respective arguments, and much will turn on the specific ways in which these terms are filled out. Fernando Tesón thinks that these conditions can sometimes be satisfied. Bas van der Vossen denies this: in the real world virtually no humanitarian intervention will satisfy these conditions.

International wars can aspire to be legitimate only if they fall into one of three kinds. The first is *national self-defense*, a war to counter armed aggression. The second is *collective self-defense*, a war to assist *other* states in countering armed aggression by third states or other armed groups. And the third is *humanitarian intervention*, the subject of this study. A humanitarian intervention is typically a war to defend persons attacked in their territory *by their own government or other political group.*[10] Both collective self-defense and humanitarian intervention take place in *another state's* territory. So we can say that national self-defense is a war to repel the aggressor in *our territory*; it is a defense of persons, my compatriots and myself, against the foreign attack. Collective self-defense is a defense of persons in another state's territory against a third party, a *foreign* attacker. And humanitarian intervention is a defense of persons in another state attacked by their own government (or other groups) in their territory.[11]

Your authors take different approaches on precisely what are citizens defending in wars of national and collective self-defense. Fernando Tesón thinks that what just warriors defend is exclusively a matter of persons and their rights. Bas van der Vossen thinks that there can be something beyond individual rights, an idea of self-determination or sovereignty (whether self-determination can be derived from

10. We say "typically" because, as Fernando Tesón explains in chapter 2, he accepts the permissibility of *proportionate* action to redress lesser evils. Thus, an intervention to restore democracy will be permissible only *if* proportionate. Many oppose pro-democratic intervention. We think that such opposition stems from the fact that, as Van der Vossen explains, these interventions are likely to be disproportionate.
11. Our terminology differs from the standard international law terminology. Article 51 of the UN Charter calls national self-defense *individual* self-defense. We adopt the term "national self-defense" because, to us, individual self-defense is the one regulated by the criminal law—that is, the right of an *individual* to defend herself against unjustified attacks.

individual rights is a separate matter). The different understandings of self-determination by the authors, as well as the weight they assign to it, affect their views on humanitarian intervention. Another central difference between the authors is that Van der Vossen thinks that military interventions are highly unlikely to achieve their humanitarian objectives, while Tesón is more optimistic on this count. As a consequence, Van der Vossen believes that humanitarian intervention is almost always a bad idea, whereas Tesón supports it in a wider range of cases.

HUMAN RIGHTS VERSUS SOVEREIGNTY?

The literature on humanitarian intervention is huge.[12] As a rough overview, it is fair to say that legal scholars are hostile

12. For an update up to 2005, see the bibliography in Fernando Tesón, *Humanitarian Intervention: An Inquiry into Law and Morality,* 3rd. ed. (Transnational, 2005). Since then, book-length treatments include Alex J. Bellamy, *Responsibility to Protect: The Global Effort to End Mass Atrocities* (Polity Press, 2009); James Pattison, *Humanitarian Intervention and the Responsibility to Protect: Who Should Intervene?* (Oxford University Press, 2010); Timothy W. Crawford and Alan J. Kuperman, *Gambling on Humanitarian Intervention: Moral Hazard, Rebellion and Civil War* (Routledge, 2006); Aidan Hehir, *Humanitarian Intervention: An Introduction,* 2nd. ed. (Palgrave Macmillan, 2013); Tony Brems Knudsen, *Humanitarian Intervention: Contemporary Manifestations of an Explosive Doctrine* (Routledge, 2010); Terry Nardin and Melissa S. Williams, eds., *Humanitarian Intervention,* Nomos vol. 47 (New York University Press, 2006); Michael Newman, *Humanitarian Intervention: Confronting the Contradictions* (Columbia University Press, 2009); Don E.

to humanitarian intervention unless authorized by the United Nations Security Council;[13] philosophers are generally favorable to humanitarian intervention in certain cases;[14] and political scientists are more or less divided.[15]

There are, of course, important differences among these groups. Some think that humanitarian intervention is always morally and legally impermissible (with the possible exception of Security Council–authorized intervention). Others believe that humanitarian intervention should be legally banned but morally permissible in some cases. The intervener, in those cases, would engage in civil disobedience, as it were. Others think that the strictures of just-war theory determine permissibility in the legal and moral sense. Each position allows one to think (like Van der Vossen) that those strictures are rarely met, or (like Tesón) are less pessimistic and thus sympathetic to a more interventionist position in defense of victims of tyranny.

A general theme in the literature (and an important reason why the topic fascinates scholars) is that the principle of

Scheid, ed., *The Ethics of Armed Humanitarian Intervention* (Cambridge University Press, 2014); Brendan Simms and D. J. B. Trim, eds., *Humanitarian Intervention: A History* (Cambridge University Press, 2011); Katariina Simonen, *The State Versus the Individual: The Unresolved Dilemma of Humanitarian Intervention* (Martinus Nijhoff, 2011); and Thomas G. Weiss, *Humanitarian Intervention*, 3rd. ed. (Polity Press, 2016).

13. The standard legal view can be found in Steve Ratner, *The Thin Justice of International Law: A Moral Reckoning of the Law of Nations* (Oxford University Press, 2015), 292–301.
14. All the modern just-war writers discussed in this volume accept the permissibility of humanitarian intervention in some form. Even Michael Walzer accepts it in extreme cases.
15. For a sympathetic view, see Weiss, *Humanitarian Intervention.* For an unsympathetic view, see Crawford and Kuperman, *Gambling on Humanitarian Intervention.*

state sovereignty, central to the Westphalian world order, can clash with the principle that persons are entitled to fundamental human rights. The traditional norm of sovereignty requires governments to tolerate, to a degree, ordinary human rights violations in other states. Yet human rights are violated daily across the world. Governments and other groups suppress speech, persecute religions, torture prisoners, discriminate against women and minorities, and more. On this traditional view, these misdeeds should be addressed by the victims themselves by whatever means they have at their disposal, including, at the limit, revolutionary violence. Military interventions by outside states to remedy these violations are, as a general rule, prohibited, in part because they tend to be counterproductive (they lead to worse human rights violations) and in part because they destabilize whatever regional or global stability may obtain at that time and place.

As a result, the traditional view has been that state sovereignty must be respected unless the violations "shock the conscience of mankind."[16] Genocide and crimes against humanity are reasons, in principle, to disregard state sovereignty. Theories of intervention have noticeably evolved since the traditional version was put forth. It is no secret that international law protects states and especially incumbent regimes. The rise of the human rights movement in the twentieth century subjected the traditional view to a considerable strain. People increasingly felt that the principle of sovereignty could not be properly justified if, to paraphrase Samuel Johnson, it amounted to no more than "the last refuge of scoundrels." That is why scholarship and practice moved increasingly to allow exceptions to the traditional noninterventionist rule.[17] Novel cosmopolitan theories

16. See the references in Tesón, chapter 2, this volume.
17. For a useful overview, see Thomas M. Franck, "Interpretation and Change in the Law of Humanitarian Intervention," in

proposed a different boundary between sovereignty and human rights, one that was more permissive of intervention. Even the law, usually so slow to adapt, moved in that direction, as we shall see here.

However, in the wake of Iraq and Libya, the general sentiment was that the cosmopolitan position had perhaps gone too far. The authors of this volume represent, in a way, two common positions on humanitarian intervention. Bas van der Vossen claims, roughly, that the softening of sovereignty has gone already too far and that further expansions of the right to intervene are unwise and undesirable. Fernando Tesón, in contrast, thinks that the law as it stands is still too protective of tyrants, and that the international norms should move cautiously in the direction of permissibility. More precisely, your authors approach the puzzle in different ways. Van der Vossen is skeptical that military intervention will improve things, unless the violence and deprivation are extreme. Tesón thinks that it is always possible to argue that a particular intervention is justified. Part of Tesón's argument is that the very idea of humanitarian intervention as posing a tension between sovereignty and human rights is misconceived: all just wars are about human rights, about defending persons. For Tesón, the norm of sovereignty as such—that is, conceived as a freestanding deontic principle that protects states above and beyond the rights and interests of its subjects—can never be a reason against intervention.

One relatively unexplored issue is a comparison between justified revolutionary violence and justified humanitarian intervention. Under the influence of writers like Michael

Humanitarian Intervention: Ethical, Legal, and Political Dilemmas, ed. J. L. Holzgrefe and Roberto O. Keohane (Cambridge University Press, 2003), 204–231.

Walzer, most people believe that the threshold for justifying intervention is higher than the threshold for justifying revolution. The authors differ on this question as well. Tesón rejects the mainstream view and argues that the threshold for both is identical. Van der Vossen's arguments imply that the traditional view is to be upheld, mostly on consequentialist grounds.

The authors agree that humanitarian intervention, like any war, must satisfy principles of proportionality. A war is proportionate if it does not cause excessive damage. This simple formulation, however, conceals many complexities that the authors address in their respective contributions. It is tempting to say that a (benign) foreign intervention will often upset social and political structures, and that therefore an intervention has additional costs than other forms of war. But this cannot be decided in advance. A war in national self-defense can also upset social and political structures, as exemplified by World War II. On the other hand, a humanitarian intervention may carry a low cost, as exemplified by France's overthrow of Jean-Bedel Bokassa in 1979. Whether any war satisfies proportionality can only be decided by evaluating the facts on the ground, as well as more distant effects that can reasonably be traced to the war.

HOW TO EVALUATE INTERVENTION

A key part of the discussion in this book concerns how—or perhaps, *when*—tomorally evaluate interventions. Your authors disagree on the applicable standard of permissibility for humanitarian intervention. Van der Vossen thinks that the standard should be evidence-based—that is, the morality of a humanitarian intervention should be evaluated *ex ante*, when the commander contemplates the invasion. This excludes judging an intervention by its outcomes. Many people evaluate wars by whether they worked out or not. The Second World War turned out well, and so (it is said) it was the right thing to do. The Iraq war turned out badly, therefore (it is said) it was the wrong thing to do. Van der Vossen challenges that *ex post* view. Tesón, in contrast, thinks that an evaluation of the permissibility of intervention rests centrally on outcomes.

The hard question, and we both think the much more important question, is whether the *decision* to go to war was right *at the time it was made*. Here the same disagreement resurfaces: Fernando Tesón thinks that decisions to intervene to save lives can sometimes be right. Bas van der Vossen is much more skeptical and would support a rule that strongly discourages commanders from making these calls.

The authors have a more subtle or philosophical difference as well. Tesón thinks that a permissible intervention must have a just cause and satisfy proportionality. He rejects a pure evidence-based standard of permissibility. If the commander is negligent he deserves scorn, but that will not affect permissibility. On the other hand, if a commander makes the evidence-based right decision but things turn out disastrously, it is hard to conclude that the intervention was permissible. Van der Vossen takes a more radical stance and thinks that such a position is untenable. According to him, whether a commander may permissibly act must be determined exclusively *ex ante*. And judged *ex ante*, these decisions are almost always wrong, as they are saddled with unacceptable risks.

The authors try to apply their ideas to the issues of the day. At various junctures, they illustrate how their normative proposals can bear on events such as the Iraq war, the Libyan war, the war against ISIS, the Syrian war, and others, past and present. This is not a legal treatise, so our ambition is not to establish precedents in favor or against the permissibility of humanitarian intervention. Rather, our purpose is to try to see how abstract conceptions of rights, harm, coercion, and intention can be operationalized in real combat, with real people and real victims.

THE INTERNATIONAL LAW OF HUMANITARIAN INTERVENTION

International law generally prohibits the use of force in international relations. Article 2(4) of the United Nations Charter reads:

> All Members shall refrain in their international relations from the threat or use of force against the territorial integrity or political independence of any state, or in any other manner inconsistent with the Purposes of the United Nations.

Lawyers differ in their interpretation of this rule. Everyone agrees that the article prohibits many offensive wars that were lawful in the past, such as wars of conquest or annexation. Everyone also agrees that the article prohibits wars to enforce treaties or judicial or arbitral decisions, or to enforce even legitimate claims that states may have. If state A violates a treaty it has with state B, state B may not use force as a response.[18] Territorial claims illustrate the breadth of the prohibition. Argentina claims that the Falkland/Malvinas Islands belong to Argentina and not to the United Kingdom, the current administrator. But when Argentina invaded the islands in 1982, the general reaction was to condemn the invasion. Even if Argentina has a superior territorial claim, it may not enforce

18. Article 2(3), UN Charter.

that claim unilaterally; it has an obligation to settle the territorial dispute by peaceful means.

Yet article 2(4) does not prohibit all uses of force. Everyone agrees that the prohibition has two exceptions: self-defense (article 51, UN Charter) and force authorized by the UN Security Council (Chapter 7, UN Charter). Beyond that, scholarly opinion and practice are divided, and especially with respect to humanitarian intervention.

Does the Charter allow humanitarian intervention? Let us start, once again, with a point of agreement. As it stands at present, international law allows humanitarian intervention when authorized by the UN Security Council in response to severe humanitarian crises, such as ethnic cleansing, crimes against humanity, or genocide. This position has been solidly established by the 2005 United Nations Summit, which in relevant part reads:

> [W]e are prepared to take collective action, in a timely and decisive manner, through the Security Council, in accordance with the Charter, including Chapter VII, on a case-by-case basis and in cooperation with relevant regional organizations as appropriate, should peaceful means be inadequate and national authorities are manifestly failing to protect their populations from genocide, war crimes, ethnic cleansing and crimes against humanity.[19]

This paragraph represents the legal counterpart to the philosophical shift, discussed earlier, away from a nearly absolute enforcement of state sovereignty and toward a more robust protection of individual human rights. It was included in the final declaration of the summit after intense lobbying by NGOs

19. UN General Assembly 2005 Summit Report, para. 139, at http://www.un.org/ga/59/hl60_plenarymeeting.html.

that insisted the international community adopt as a norm the report entitled *The Responsibility to Protect*, drafted by an independent commission under the auspices of the Canadian government.[20] The report strongly urged softening the prohibition on intervention by positing a responsibility on the part of the international community to intervene when individual states failed to uphold the human rights of their subjects.

While, in a formal sense, UN General Assembly resolutions are not legally binding, the fact that the governments of all nations adopted this particular resolution by consensus may elevate it to customary law.[21] Alternatively, we can say that the resolution does no more than restate the standard view that the Security Council can authorize force for virtually any reason, and that would include force to stop genocide and similar crimes. Nevertheless, it is widely agreed that the acceptance of at least the language of the ICISS Report did represent somewhat of a shift in norms—away from the state as the primary focus of international law and (somewhat more) toward a focus on the individual.

Perhaps the thorniest point of controversy concerns whether *unauthorized* humanitarian intervention is legally permissible. This issue has given rise to a heated controversy for the last thirty years or so. Space prevents us from reviewing all the positions that have been advanced in this regard.

20. International Commission on Intervention and State Sovereignty, *The Responsibility to Protect*, 2001, at http://responsibilitytoprotect.org/ICISS%20Report.pdf, For a comprehensive discussion, see Alex Bellamy and Tim Dunne, eds., *The Oxford Handbook of the Responsibility to Protect* (Oxford University Press, 2016).
21. For a view of what counts as genuine customary law, see Fernando R. Tesón, "Fake Custom," in *Reexamining Customary Law*, ed. Brian Lepard (Cambridge University Press, 2017), 86–110.

Suffice it to say that a majority of legal scholars answer in the negative: unauthorized humanitarian intervention is unlawful, a violation of article 2(4). Some dicta by the International Court of Justice support this noninterventionist view.[22] But a sizable minority of scholars dissent. To them, the principle of state sovereignty does not protect genocidal regimes, and the international community has a right to use force to stop massacres when the Security Council fails to act (whether paralyzed by veto or for some other reason). Paragraph 139 of the 2005 Summit (assuming it is good law) does not help much, because it simply confirms that the Security Council may authorize force to stop these crimes. It would be a stretch to interpret that paragraph *a contrario sensu* as excluding unauthorized intervention. The text simply addresses what the United Nations may do; it does not mention the rights that individual states may or may not have when facing genocide in neighboring states.

A point repeatedly brought up by supporters of humanitarian intervention like Tesón is that a failure to intervene often leads to unjust results. Because of this, in a recent book, Steven Ratner has argued that international law, while at present outlawing unilateral humanitarian intervention, should move toward accepting a rule allowing it in appropriate cases.[23] In contrast, critics of humanitarian intervention like Van der Vossen remind us that many interventions have failed to achieve their humanitarian goals, and that therefore the world would benefit by adopting a prophylactic legal prohibition. And

22. See International Court of Justice, *Military and Paramilitary Activities in and against Nicaragua* (Nicaragua v. United States of America). Merits, Judgment. I.C.J. Reports 1986, p. 14, para. 268: ("the use of force could not be the appropriate method to monitor or ensure such respect [for human rights]").
23. See Ratner, *The Thin Justice of International Law*, 298–301.

the requirement of proper authorization can play an important role in this.

An examination of state practice likewise yields ambiguous results. There are cases, old and new, where interventions that had the intent or the effect of saving persons from massacre were (arguably) explicitly or implicitly approved by the international community.[24] Proponents of humanitarian intervention take those precedents as supporting its legal permissibility; critics simply retort that all those were violations of the law, that the reaction of other states was ambiguous at best, and that governments have repeatedly taken a stance against humanitarian intervention.

This disagreement about of the value of humanitarian-intervention precedents unearths a deeper jurisprudential problem. The legal interpretation of text and precedent will depend on the jurisprudential assumptions of the interpreter. Frequently, legal scholars and courts who reject the lawfulness of humanitarian intervention present themselves as legal positivists. To them, the language of the United Nations Charter is clear: the only exceptions to the prohibition in article 2(4) are defensive force and UN Security Council–authorized force. They think that the precedents invoked by supporters of humanitarian intervention are in reality violations of the law. True, they say, sometimes the rest of the world is slow in condemning those interventions for a variety of political reasons. But the rise of the human rights movement means only that the proper authority, the Security Council, should pay more attention to protect populations from these crimes, just as the *Responsibility to Protect* report says. It does not mean that the ban on the *unilateral* use of force has been weakened in any way.

24. See Tesón, *Humanitarian Intervention*, esp. chapters 8 and 10.

In contrast, many defenders of humanitarian intervention embrace a sort of natural-law approach. To them, the text and the precedents on *jus ad bellum* are too vague and imprecise. As a result, they must be interpreted, as Ronald Dworkin would say, in their best possible light. Text and precedent should be read in light of the best theory of just war we can muster. And if we do so, humanitarian intervention can be justified as a way to counter the worst abuses of tyranny. The noninterventionist position, on this view, not only rewards tyrants but also rests on an impoverished theory of law.

In any case, these positions pose a wrong dilemma. Even if the natural lawyer is correct that the law should incorporate moral reasoning, it does not follow that humanitarian intervention is lawful. Nor does a commitment to legal positivism imply condemning such military operations. Consider the many historical precedents that seem to support humanitarian intervention. Modern cases include India's intervention in East Pakistan, 1971; Tanzania's intervention in Uganda, 1979; France's intervention in the Central African Empire, 1979; and NATO's intervention in Kosovo, 1999.[25] And World War II itself can be read as a humanitarian effort, at least in part. The task of the lawyer is to determine whether this line of precedents creates a new exception to the prohibition of force. Custom may be defined as convergent practice over time that eventually is backed by a general opinion that criticizes deviation, praises, compliance, or both. In game-theoretical terms, a customary norm emerges when states identify the salient features of a situation as equilibrium points. An initial coordination game

25. These and other cases are extensively discussed in Fernando R. Tesón, *Humanitarian Intervention*. For an interesting account of the origins of humanitarian intervention, see Gary J. Bass, *Freedom's Battle: The Origins of Humanitarian Intervention* (Vintage, 2009).

turns later, when states insist on compliance, into an iterated prisoner's dilemma.[26] Moreover, the practice is often far from robust: it is contradictory, spotty, or unclear. Diplomatic history does not present itself in the form of neatly patterned norms: we have to *interpret* history in order to draw normative lessons.

But this does not mean that the right answer is the permissibility of humanitarian intervention. A central aim of this book is to present to our readers two contrasting ways to understand and, if need be, to reform international law. Bas van der Vossen thinks that the weight of moral reasons counsels opposing humanitarian intervention. Fernando Tesón thinks that the weight of moral reasons supports humanitarian intervention in appropriate cases. In this sense, we both think that philosophy has a proper place in the analysis. In positivist language, our task is to evaluate what the international law on intervention ought to be (if not what the law currently is). In the language of natural law, evaluating the morality of intervention is a key part of interpreting and understanding the real import of the international legal prohibition of force. Either way, the critic of humanitarian intervention does not have to deny the importance of morality in evaluating the law on intervention. And the case for intervention does not rest on the rejection of legal positivism. Both have the resources to express their support or skepticism about humanitarian intervention.

We believe that the legal materials are sufficiently indeterminate to allow one to argue for and against the permissibility of humanitarian intervention. Having said this, the question of what precise legal norm to adopt is extremely complex, for many reasons. First, when designing new norms policymakers

26. See Fernando R. Tesón, *A Philosophy of International Law* (Westview, 1998), chapter 3.

should be aware of the dangers of noncompliance. International law is replete with rules that are just cheap talk that no state obeys, except opportunistically. Second, the law creates its own incentives. This means that the law of humanitarian intervention should not necessarily track the morality of humanitarian intervention. Someone may agree that humanitarian intervention is morally permissible in some cases but still support a per se prohibition of humanitarian intervention. The state that decides to invade and stop genocide would be akin to someone who commits civil disobedience for the sake of a higher moral cause.

PART I

A DEFENSE OF HUMANITARIAN INTERVENTION

FERNANDO R. TESÓN

1

Humanitarian Intervention as Defense of Persons

I ARGUE THAT SOME HUMANITARIAN interventions are morally permissible.[1] As we saw in the introduction, humanitarian intervention is the international use of military force to defend persons from attacks, in their territory, by their own rulers or other groups.

JUS AD BELLUM: JUST CAUSE FOR WAR

Of the requirements listed in the introduction, the most important is just cause. The just- cause requirement is essential in the

1. I refine my previous general defense of humanitarian intervention in Tesón, *Humanitarian Intervention*; "The Moral Basis of Armed Humanitarian Intervention Revisited," in *The Ethics of Armed Humanitarian Intervention*, ed. Don E. Scheid (Cambridge University Press, 2014), 61–77; "The Moral Structure of Humanitarian Intervention," in *Contemporary Debates in Applied Ethics*, A. I. Cohen and C. H. Wellman, eds. (Wiley-Blackwell, 2014), 391; and "The Liberal Case for Humanitarian Intervention," in *Humanitarian Intervention: Ethical, Legal, and Political Dilemmas*, J. L. Holzgrefe and Robert O. Keohane eds. (Cambridge University Press, 2003), 93–129.

sense that it has priority over the other conditions.[2] Thus, an intervener has the right intention when he intends the just cause, the necessity and proportionality requirements are measured in relation to the just cause, and the success condition means that justified wars must realize the just cause.

According to a popular view, the only justified war is in response to aggression. This view classifies wars into defensive and offensive wars. States may permissibly fight in response to aggression; this is a *defensive* war. By the same token, *offensive wars*—that is, wars that are not in response to aggression—are presumptively impermissible. The gist of the view is that there is something unique about aggression that authorizes states to wage war in self-defense. It is unreasonable to ask a state that is wrongfully attacked not to react, given that most of the time such a state cannot seek protection from a higher authority. Moreover, it would be irrational to prohibit self-defense anyway, since victims of aggression will continue to react regardless of what philosophers say. So wars in self-defense are in principle justified. On this popular view, other wars are offensive because they are not responses to attacks and are, for that reason, presumptively impermissible.[3]

On this view, humanitarian intervention is an offensive war because it is not in response to aggression. The state that is the target of intervention has not attacked the intervener; therefore, the latter cannot permissibly wage war. Say the government of

2. See Thomas Hurka, "Liability and Just Cause," *Ethics and International Affairs* 21 (2007): 199.
3. Michael Walzer defended this view, which he calls "the legalist paradigm"; see Walzer, *Just and Unjust Wars,* 58–62. Allen Buchanan calls this position "the Just War Norm"; see Allen Buchanan, "Institutionalizing the Just War," *Philosophy and Public Affairs* 34 (2006): 2–38. Most international lawyers endorse this view as well.

state A is committing atrocities against its own citizens. On the traditional view, this is of course terribly wrong and one would hope that the victims would have the wherewithal to resist. But the wrongness of the atrocities does not generate a permission for foreign armies to intervene, because in that case state B, the intervener, would be attacking state A without state B's having itself suffered any attack by state A. The war waged by state A, then, would be a presumptively impermissible offensive war. On this view, a humanitarian intervention is much harder to justify than a war of national self-defense because such justification must defeat the justificatory reasons that the target state has for exercising *its* self-defense.

Both critics and supporters of humanitarian intervention treat these two types of war as essentially different. Cécile Fabre defines humanitarian intervention as "a humanitarian war against a sovereign political community" over which that agent lacks jurisdiction.[4] The implication is that humanitarian intervention differs *in kind* from national self-defense. In national self-defense, persons fight for their own rights; in humanitarian intervention, they fight for the rights of others. Similarly, David Rodin writes that humanitarian intervention is antithetical to self-defense: "if there is a right of humanitarian intervention, then it is because the moral basis of the right of national defense can in certain circumstances be justly overridden, not because the right of humanitarian intervention is, in some sense, an application of those moral considerations."[5] Michael Walzer is particularly firm: states are the arenas of self-determination from which in principle foreign

4. Fabre, *Cosmopolitan War*, 166.
5. David Rodin, *War, Aggression, and Self-Defence* (Oxford University Press, 2003), 131. See my reply, "Self-Defense in International Law and Rights of Persons," *Ethics & International Affairs* 18 (2004): 87–91.

armies are excluded.[6] And Allen Buchanan thinks that while institutions should make room for humanitarian intervention, what he calls the Just War Norm—that is, the norm that only authorizes war only in response to aggression—should be preserved.[7]

This traditional distinction, however, cannot resist scrutiny. To see why, we must dig deeper into the concept of just cause. The mainstream view concedes that wars in self-defense are justified. But defense of who and what? A natural response is: defense of the state, the state that is attacked. But surely the state matters because it is inhabited by persons. The state is an artificial creation that is supposed to serve the individuals who created it. And territory matters because it belongs to persons, privately or held in trust by the state.[8] As Michael Walzer argued in his classical treatise, aggression is a crime because the aggressor forces men and women to abandon their projects and fight for their survival.[9] The state, then, must be disaggregated into its components, human beings. This approach is in line with normative individualism: individuals, not states, are the proper objects of moral concern. The moral standing of the state is entirely parasitic on the rights and interests of persons.[10]

6. Michael Walzer, "The Moral Standing of States: A Response to Four Critics," *Philosophy and Public Affairs* 9 (1980): 209–229.
7. Buchanan, "Institutionalizing the Just War," 2–38.
8. See Fernando R. Tesón, "The Mystery of Territory," *Social Philosophy and Policy* 32 (2015): 25.
9. Walzer calls it the tyranny of war; see *Just and Unjust Wars*, 31.
10. Notwithstanding her differential treatment of self-defense and humanitarian intervention, Fabre concurs: humanitarian intervention is a case of the victims' right to enlist third-party help; *Cosmopolitan War*, 172.

Once we disaggregate states, then, it becomes clear that war has *only one general justification: the defense of persons and their rights.* This is the important truth behind the mainstream position: all justified violence is defensive violence. But the proper entity that deserves our defense is the individual and only derivatively, sometimes, the state.[11] If this is correct, there is no reason to confine a justified war to a war of *national* self-defense. A justified war may also be a war in defense of persons in *other* states. A defense of persons in other states may in turn be classified into two kinds. The first is *collective self-defense*. A war in collective self-defense is a war in defense of persons located in the territory of other states that are victims of aggression by a *third* state. When Iraq invaded Kuwait in 1990, the war by the United Nations–sponsored coalition was an act of collective self-defense, a war in defense of others.

The second is *humanitarian intervention*, the subject of this study. As we saw in the introduction, a humanitarian intervention is a war to defend persons attacked in their territory *by their own government or other political group*. If we compare humanitarian intervention with both types of self-defense (national and collective), we see that the three types of war are wars in defense of persons, and as a consequence, all three must meet the conditions specified in the Introduction. Many writers (legal scholars in particular) and governments accept both versions of self-defense but reject humanitarian intervention. Yet, the justification of humanitarian intervention is an application of the same principles that justify self-defense, national and collective. Because the three of them are wars in defense of persons, this differential treatment is arbitrary.

11. If stateless persons are threatened with genocide in the state of nature, then we can justifiably rescue them, even though we would be defending no state. And, in the real world, many states are not worth defending.

One reason why so many think that self-defense is essentially different from humanitarian intervention is that a war in self-defense seems to *strengthen* sovereignty while a humanitarian intervention seems to *weaken* sovereignty. In self-defense, when citizens take up arms against the invader, they are arguably defending their home. When the tyrant takes up arms against the invader who tries to save the tyrant's victims, he likewise *seems* to defend the nation's home (and he will certainly proclaim that to justify the war). But this symmetry is illusory. In self-defense, the defending citizens are defending their life, liberty, and property (whether we want to call this their home or not is a simple verbal choice). In humanitarian intervention, the tyrant is defending *himself* against those who are aiding his victims. To say that the tyrant is defending the nation is to succumb to the statist prejudice that there is something worth defending above and beyond individuals and their rights—what I have elsewhere called The Hegelian Myth.[12] Once we adopt the individualist paradigm, we can dissolve the paradox. When they resist humanitarian invaders tyrants fight for themselves, not for the nation or the people. Because they have rendered themselves guilty of serious crimes, they do not have any defensive rights. They are fighting an unjust war and their moral duty is to surrender. The only reason not to intervene in these kinds of cases is that the intervention will cause excessive damage.[13]

Humanitarian intervention, then, is a case of defense of others. Defense of others is an extension of individual self-defense, well accepted in the criminal law. Persons are entitled not only to defend themselves against unjust attacks but also to defend others who suffer unjust attacks. If Attacker unjustly attacks Victim, Victim is entitled to use defensive force. But

12. See Tesón, *Humanitarian Intervention*, chapter 3.
13. See the discussion of proportionality in chapter 4, this volume.

Third Party is also morally permitted to defend Victim by force. We can say that Attacker's attack on Victim is unjust whenever Victim has a right not to be attacked. So if Attacker attacks Victim and Victim has a right not to be attacked, Attacker becomes liable to be attacked. To be justified, an attack by Third Party against Attacker must presuppose that Attacker has lost its moral shield, as it were. A humanitarian intervention, then, is Third Party's attack against Attacker who is unjustly attacking Victim. Attacker is the government of a state, Victim is the population of that state, and Third Party, coming from a different territory, is the just intervener. Third Party assists Victim (the local population) in his defense against Attacker's (tyrant's) unjust aggression. If a state is entitled to defend its own citizens against aggression, it is also entitled to defend third parties—foreigners—against aggression, even by their own government.

Having said this, self-defense and humanitarian intervention have some differences. One difference, already noted, derives from self-determination or sovereignty. Intervention to protect rights is problematic, it is thought, because people should be allowed to solve their problems by themselves. Foreigners have no business interfering. I discuss and reject this argument in chapter 3. However, there is a potential problem regarding consent by the victims of rights violations to the intervention. This question does not arise in national self-defense, where most of the time the victims themselves fight against the aggressor and consent is presumed. But in humanitarian intervention it is possible that the victims themselves refuse to allow the invasion of the territory or to object to a particular intervener. They prefer to endure the rights violations rather than see the foreign army march into the state's territory.

Another difference merits attention. Thomas Hurka gives the example of the citizens of a nation defending themselves against aggression and thereby causing bad ulterior consequences, such as upsetting regional or global stability. It seems that no one would condemn them despite the expected bad consequences.[14] The situation is intuitively different for a foreign invader, however. If intervening to stop a massacre will predictably cause regional or global instability, many say the intervention is wrong. Intuitively, the fact that, unlike foreign interveners, citizens may use defensive force against an aggressor without regard for further bad consequences marks a difference between self-defense and humanitarian intervention that apparently counts against the permissibility of the latter in some cases. The same intuition operates in the case of a justified revolution when compared with foreign intervention. Critics of the 2011 intervention in Libya point to Libya's subsequent debacle as evidence that the intervention was wrong; but it is far from clear that these same critics would use that same evidence to condemn the *domestic* revolt against Gaddafi. I do not share that intuition, however. In principle, revolution and intervention are subject to the same standards of justification. They both require the same kind of just cause and they both are subject to the same standards of proportionality. I'll explain this doctrine of equivalence in chapter 3.

In summary: The traditional dichotomy between national self-defense as a defensive war (and presumptively justified for that reason) and humanitarian intervention as an offensive war (and presumptively unjustified for that reason) should be rejected. When justified, humanitarian intervention is a war in defense of others, simply because *all* justified wars are wars in defense of self or others.

14. See Thomas Hurka, "Proportionality in the Morality of War," *Philosophy & Public Affairs* 33 (2005): 34–66.

WAR AS PART OF A COERCION CONTINUUM

Humanitarian intervention is a kind of war. The justification of war is part of the larger question of the justification of violence. War is an extreme form of coercion, so the inquiry should start with the more fundamental concept of coercion. When is coercion against others justified? I assume that persons enjoy a presumptive immunity against coercion. This means that any act of coercion against them must be justified. In general, a person's immunity against coercion collapses when that person violates the rights of others. A standard way of putting this is to say that the rights violator becomes *liable* to coercion.[15] Someone who violates the rights of others becomes morally vulnerable to a reaction by the victim or others in response.[16] That coercion against the rights violator may be exercised by the victim herself or by third parties on behalf of the victim. As Kant said, coercion, as a hindrance of someone else's freedom, is authorized against those who have in turn hindered the freedom of others.[17] Rights violation identifies the *kind* of reasons to coerce

15. See Jeff McMahan, "Proportionality and Just Cause," *Journal of Moral Philosophy* 11 (2004): 428–453, 428.
16. It may be objected that coercion can be justified against persons who have not violated the rights of others. The idea is that people become morally vulnerable to coercion in a larger class of cases. But in this chapter I am interested in humanitarian intervention. Rulers become liable to coercion when they have violated the rights of their subjects. My intuition is that coercion is only justified for the sake of justice. This includes a garden variety of acts of state coercion, including taxes. Here I do not address these other cases of justified coercion. It is enough for my purposes that coercion is justified against freedom deniers—those that violate the rights of others.
17. See Immanuel Kant, *The Metaphysics of Morals*, Mary McGregor, ed. (Cambridge University Press, 1991), 6:231.

others. Persons cannot be coerced to gain advantage over them, or to get them to do something for their own good, or to advantage others at their expense, or simply to make a point.

But the fact that someone has violated rights is not a *sufficient* reason to exercise coercion against him, because it might well be that doing so would produce intolerably bad results, such as excessive harm to the offender himself or bystanders, or an increase in the number of rights violations. The harm caused by the coercive act, that is, will be disproportionate (in ways to be determined) to the importance of redressing this particular rights violation. If a villain takes children as hostages and threatens to kill them, the police may not storm the building and kill or capture the villain (to exercise otherwise permissible coercion against him) if the children will predictably die, too. This is true even if the villain has lost his moral immunity against coercion—that is, even if the police have the right *kind* of cause for capturing or killing him.

Now consider war. War is an extremely destructive form of coercion. For this reason, it will often be a disproportionate means to redress rights violations. The burden of a theory of humanitarian intervention is to establish with the best possible approximation when the moral urgency to redress rights violations will justify a *military* intervention, which is the most extreme form of coercion. Because the extreme violence of war will frequently cause excessive harm, the rights violations that constitute the just cause for war must ordinarily reach a high level. But this should not obscure the fact that war should be placed in the continuum of permissible coercion against rights violations. A violation of the rights of persons who have not otherwise lost the immunity against coercion is never permissible. If an outsider could stop or redress the violation at an acceptable cost, his interference would be permissible. This is why the assertion that intervention is impermissible against lesser wrongs, stated in this bald form, is false.

Only *disproportionate* intervention is impermissible against lesser wrongs. (My position here is purely formal. It does not rely on a particular political theory about what rights people have. Whatever moral rights persons have, their violation is impermissible.[18])

In his treatment of just cause, Jeff McMahan writes: "just causes for war are limited to the prevention or correction of wrongs that are serious enough to make the perpetrators liable to be killed or maimed."[19] Because McMahan is concerned with war in general, and in particular cases of national self-defense, he uses the general notion of moral wrong, the most important exemplar of which is aggression. In humanitarian intervention, that serious moral wrong will be the violation of the moral rights of persons by their own government in their territory. But it is because war ordinarily causes great damage that the rights violation must achieve a high level of severity. Only that level of severity justifies a reaction that kills and maims, because otherwise the killing and maiming will be disproportionate to the seriousness of the wrong it aims to redress.

However, few people are prepared to accept the reverse proposition: *lesser* forms of violence will be justified to redress *lesser* rights violations. McMahan's formulation for the case of war is a special case of the more general principle, namely that *the suppression of wrongs is a just cause for coercion*. That war is justified only to suppress the most serious wrongs is a consequence of the principle of proportionality. Lesser rights violations justify lesser forms of coercion. So to say that in war

18. For a particularly expansive view of the rights whose violation authorizes war, see Fabre, *Cosmopolitan War*, 103–129.
19. Jeff McMahan, "Just Cause for War," *Ethics and International Affairs* 19 (2005): 11.

the perpetrator of a massacre becomes liable to be killed or maimed is a special case of the proposition that rights violators become liable to proportionate *defensive action*. If the violation of rights is less egregious, then the victims and those who assist them are entitled to use coercion short of war.

But this does not necessarily mean that the rights violator necessarily retains his immunity not to be killed. Consider: Is war to suppress lesser rights violations prohibited because in these cases the rights violator has *not* become liable to being killed? Or is war prohibited in those cases because the war would be disproportionate generally—that is, it would kill innocents and cause devastation generally? These dilemmas arise in justified revolutions. Are the revolutionaries entitled to kill the tyrant who oppresses them but does not commit massacres? If the answer is yes, provided that killing does not cause excessive damage, then the same is true of foreign intervention that kills the tyrant. In other words: it seems that run-of-the-mill oppressors are liable to be killed, but that we balk at the prospects of foreign interventions because of their intolerable moral costs. It is not out of concern for the tyrant that foreign armies should exercise restraint. An answer to this problem must distinguish between justified harm to the tyrant and justified harm to others. I shall discuss them in chapter 4.

For now, I observe that the same principle of proportionality that bans military interventions in most cases—namely the expectation that the intervention will do more harm than good—also *authorizes* action that remedies the wrong *and* causes more good than harm in the relevant sense. Proportionate actions will sometimes be non-coercive, such as economic sanctions, but sometimes will be coercive and even result in the killing of the rights violator and, unfortunately, in the collateral deaths of persons that are not liable to be attacked. The requirement is that the action, coercive or not, be proportionate. If the action is coercive, of course, it will satisfy the proportionality requirement less often.

If these lesser actions have no further costs, the intervention would have been proportionate and thus justified. But critics point out that such a condition is seldom met in practice.[20] The intervener does not know that escalation will not occur, turning an initially justified act into an unjustified full war. This epistemic barrier is the reason why these actions should not be undertaken. If the 2003 war in Iraq had ended right after the overthrow of Saddam Hussein, it would perhaps have been plausibly justified as humanitarian intervention. But most people think that because the intervention triggered a long and protracted conflict in the region, the war was ultimately unjustified.[21]

I agree with the objection. I think the epistemic worries support the requirement that only a very serious violation of rights justifies military action. (I discuss this requirement in chapter 2.) A military intervention to remedy a lesser wrong runs a very real risk of escalating into a full war or other forms of violence, such as widespread insurgency or military intervention by another power. But that should not obscure the matter of principle: *if* the moral gain justifies the moral cost, the intervention will be justified. This is consistent with blaming the intervener for not having known, at the time of the decision, that the intervention would satisfy proportionality.

In the study of humanitarian intervention it is essential to specify the kind and gravity of rights violations that may occur in different societies. For purposes of simplification, I classify morally objectionable regimes into three categories, with the

20. See Bas van der Vossen, this volume.

21. I discuss the Iraq war in the part I appendix, this volume.

caveat that reality is much more complex than the classification suggests, and so many regimes will fall in between:

1. *Genocidal tyrants* are governments or proto-governmental groups that perpetrate or have perpetrated massacres or morally equivalent crimes—what we may call The Great Crimes. These regimes have unleashed acts of genocide or crimes against humanity against all or part of the population. Some historical examples include the Third Reich circa 1943–45, the Ottoman Empire circa 1915, Cambodia's Pol Pot regime in the 1970s, the Rwandan Hutus in 1994, Pakistan in 1971, the regime of Emperor Bokassa in the Central African Republic, Iraq's Saddam Hussein at various points during his rule, the current Syrian regime, and as I write these lines, the Islamic State for Syria and Levant and the government of Syria. The UN-sponsored World Humanitarian Summit identified, in May 2016, populations at immediate risk in Yemen, Syria, Iraq, and Nigeria.[22]
2. *Ordinary tyrants* are governments that oppress their subjects short of massacre. These include all governments that fare on the higher end in the Freedom House rankings (the higher the ranking, the worse the regime).[23] Typically, these governments suppress civil and political freedoms, oppress women and minorities, deny freedom of expression[24] and religious freedom, persecute

22. Global Centre for the Responsibility to Protect, *Atrocity Alert,* No. 4, May 25, 2016, at http://www.gaamac.org/blog/atrocity-alert-a-weekly-update-by-the-global-centre-for-r2p/#.V0W1TGNTaLU.
23. See Freedom House, *Freedom in the World 2016*, at https://freedomhouse.org/report/freedom-world/freedom-world-2016.
24. Freedom of expression is reportedly at its lowest level in twelve years; see https://freedomhouse.org/report/freedom-press/freedom-press-2016.

dissidents, and engage in torture. They also perpetuate themselves in power by denying elections or staging sham elections. As of this writing, examples include North Korea, Sudan, Chad, Central African Republic, Russia, China, Algeria, Libya, Egypt, Angola, Congo, Iran, Kazakhstan, Belarus, Uzbekistan, Turkmenistan, Saudi Arabia, Myanmar, Cuba, Vietnam, Ethiopia, Somalia, and Zimbabwe.

3. *Kleptocrats* are governments that *steal* from their subjects.[25] These governments generally respect the subjects' civil and political rights but blatantly violate their property rights. They disregard the rule of law and enjoy an unlimited power to expropriate land, investment, and capital. Typically, these regimes are sustained by electoral majorities who vote for populist policies that in the medium and long run ruin the country. Examples include Venezuela, Argentina, various other Latin American regimes, and perhaps current Greece. Other cases, like South Africa, are dubious but come close. Needless to say, many kleptocrats are also ordinary tyrants.[26]

Victims of *both* genocidal and ordinary tyranny are entitled to use *necessary and proportionate* force to stop or correct the rights violations. The right to use defensive force is transferable

25. Admittedly, this classification is a gross oversimplification. A more accurate classification would distinguish among genocidal tyrants, ordinary tyrants, and regimes that perpetrate lesser wrongs, of which the kleptocrat is just an example. Here and in chapter 4 I use the kleptocrat as an example of a regime that violates rights but falls short of tyranny as commonly understood.
26. For some particularly distasteful examples, see Leif Wenar, "Property Rights and the Resource Curse," *Philosophy and Public Affairs* 36 (2008): 2–32.

to outsiders. However, foreign help to justified revolutions often will violate the principle of proportionality (in a sense to be specified) and for that reason (but only for that reason) it should be presumptively avoided. Victims of kleptocracy, in contrast, are not entitled to use force, but must resort to peaceful means to redress the violation of their property rights, as the use of force would be surely disproportionate.

In the chapters that follow I will discuss various conditions of legitimacy for humanitarian intervention (with the exception of most *ius in bello* requirements, since these have been profitably examined in an abundant specialized literature[27]).

27. See, *inter alia*, Larry May, *War Crimes and Just War* (Oxford University Press, 2007).

2

Just Cause in Humanitarian Intervention

THE JUST CAUSE IN HUMANITARIAN intervention is *saving persons from rights violations by their rulers or other groups in their territory.*[1] As I explained in chapter 1, the just cause in humanitarian intervention is of the same kind as the just cause in national self-defense. In both cases, the just cause is defensive force. But most writers require a high threshold of gravity of atrocities to justify humanitarian intervention. The common view is that only what I have called *genocidal tyranny* (GT) qualifies as the proper target of humanitarian intervention. The threshold has been described as "conscience-shocking harm."[2] The ICISS Report proposes the following definition of just cause:

> [L]arge scale loss of life, actual or apprehended, with genocidal intent or not, which is the product either of deliberate state action, or state neglect or inability to act, or a failed state situation; or

1. Again, to be clear: in almost all situations that violation must be severe, because any military action must meet proportionality requirements. But it is possible (although rare) that an intervention to stop less severe rights violations be proportionate and thus permissible.
2. Weiss, *Humanitarian Intervention*, 114.

> large scale "ethnic cleansing," actual or apprehended, whether carried out by killing, forced expulsion, acts of terror or rape.[3]

And the UN General Assembly in 2005 adopted an even stricter threshold:

> [W]e are prepared to take collective action, in a timely and decisive manner, through the Security Council, in accordance with the Charter, including Chapter VII, on a case-by-case basis and in cooperation with relevant regional organizations as appropriate, should peaceful means be inadequate and national authorities manifestly fail to protect their populations from genocide, war crimes, ethnic cleansing and crimes against humanity.[4]

In my previous work I suggested that a just cause for intervention is ending severe tyranny or anarchy.[5] This threshold is lower than the ones just quoted, but it is still high. This high threshold is, then, GT.[6] On this view, only GT justifies humanitarian intervention.

3. Report of the International Commission on Intervention and State Sovereignty (2001), p. 32, at http://responsibilitytoprotect.org/ICISS%20Report.pdf (ICISS Report).
4. United Nations 2005 World Summit Outcome, A/Res/60/1, para. 138, at http://www.un.org/womenwatch/ods/A-RES-60-1-E.pdf.
5. Tesón, *Humanitarian Intervention*, 155. Cécile Fabre is an exception: she thinks that intervention may be justified even to protect socioeconomic rights; Fabre, *Cosmopolitan Justice*, 173.
6. Genocidal tyranny encompasses a variety of legally defined crimes: crimes against humanity, genocide, and major war crimes. They are defined by the Rome Statute. See Articles 5–8, Rome Statute of the International Criminal Court, at https://www.icc-cpi.int/nr/rdonlyres/ea9aeff7-5752-4f84-be94-0a655eb30e16/0/rome_statute_english.pdf.

Writers have justified the GT threshold for intervention by invoking the principle of state sovereignty. The ICISS Report, for example, says that an intervention to correct less egregious wrongs (that is, ordinary tyranny) would be impermissible because it would infringe state sovereignty.[7] The idea is that states, as part of their right to rule, have a sovereign right *as against outsiders* to do wrong things within their territory. Or, more precisely, while under international law they may not have a right to violate the internationally recognized human rights of their subjects, when they do so they have immunity against any *force* by outsiders to assist the victims. In that sense, it is sometimes said that states have a "right to do wrong."[8] I take this statement to mean that outsiders cannot legitimately stop rulers from doing wrong, and not literally that rulers have a right to violate the rights of their subjects. On this view, only when those violations shock the conscience of humankind do states forfeit their sovereignty and become vulnerable to intervention. Lesser forms of tyranny, although perhaps condemned by the law of human rights, are within the state's discretion, as it were, and the principle of sovereignty precludes military action to remedy those wrongs.

Sometimes this idea is couched in the language of self-determination. Michael Walzer, for example, writes that "the state is presumptively . . . the arena within which self-determination is worked out and from which, therefore, foreign armies have to be excluded."[9] And the ICISS Report reaffirms the importance of state sovereignty as the default norm against which any reaction to governmental wrongdoing

7. ICISS Report, 7–8, 31–32.
8. See, e.g., Bas van der Vossen, "The Asymmetry of Legitimacy," *Law and Philosophy* 31 (2012): 565.
9. Walzer, "The Moral Standing of States," 210.

should be considered. On this view, these lesser wrongs may be addressed by the victims themselves, who have the right to resist, or by the international community by nonmilitary means, such as diplomacy, or even economic sanctions. Only in exceptional circumstances—those that shock the conscience of humankind—may outside military intervention be considered.

I agree that *in most cases* humanitarian intervention requires the GT threshold, but I do not believe that the reason is that state sovereignty protects ordinary tyranny. If ordinary tyranny were protected by state sovereignty, then outsiders would not be entitled to pressure the offending regime to change its ways through *nonmilitary* means. Suppose that a government suspends constitutional guarantees but does not commit massacres. If one agrees that democratic neighbors are entitled to put diplomatic pressure on this authoritarian regime, then one does not really believe that, as against outsiders, the regime may validly suspend constitutional guarantees.[10] If one thinks that nonforcible diplomacy is permissible to get a government to respect human rights, then one does not really endorse Walzer's thesis that the state is the arena for self-determination and for that reason it must be respected by outsiders.[11] For imposing nonmilitary sanctions on an authoritarian regime is hardly consistent with the principle of respect for self-determination. It is false, then, that governments have, as against outsiders, a sovereign right to oppress and that they lose that sovereign shield only in the exceptional case where they perpetrate massacre. This is consistent with accepting that *war* in most cases requires something like the GT threshold.

10. Occasionally governments invoke their sovereign right to oppress, but that position is discredited today.
11. While Walzer's initial concern was military intervention, he makes it clear that nonforcible interference would be impermissible as well; Walzer, "The Moral Standing of States."

Furthermore, the view is mistaken that only GT makes the perpetrator liable to be killed or maimed. Without developing a general theory of defensive action, I claim that *victims of genocidal or ordinary tyranny and their foreign allies have the right, at the very least, to use the force necessary to end those wrongs, provided that use of force complies with the principles of proportionality*. It is therefore incorrect to say that GT is the only wrong that makes the perpetrator liable to be killed or maimed. If killing or maiming the tyrant is the only way to end ordinary tyranny—say, because the tyrant remains defiant and resists attempts to capture him—then killing or maiming him can be justified. Foreigners who assist these victims may perform these defensive actions as well. It is just that in many cases a foreign invasion will predictably violate the principle of proportionality.[12]

Further elaboration of this idea may profitably borrow from Christopher Finlay's recent analysis of *revolutionary* violence.[13] Finlay rejects the view that lethal force may not be used against lesser wrongs (he calls them "Political Rights") by invoking the notion of *conditional threats*. The idea is simple. Think of a government that prohibits public criticism of its actions. Each subject has a general right to resist by, at first, simply disobeying the prohibition—say, criticizing the government in public. If

12. I thus agree with James Pattison that this danger, the danger of causing excessive damage, and not sovereignty, is the main reason for requiring a high threshold for humanitarian intervention; Pattison, *Humanitarian Intervention and the Responsibility to Protect*, 22. See also Eric Heinze, "Commonsense Morality and the Consequentialist Ethics of Humanitarian Intervention," *Journal of Military Ethics* 4 (2005): 168–182, 172.
13. Christopher J. Finlay, *Terrorism and the Right to Resist: A Theory of Just Revolutionary War* (Cambridge University Press, 2015), chapter 3.

the tyrant then uses lethal force to enforce the prohibition, the subject has a right to resist by lethal force, by application of the general permission the subject has to use force against those who try to kill him. It turns out, under this analysis, that a violation of a lesser right is, when closely analyzed, also a threat of lethal force. Finlay summarizes his view:

> So, at the very least, we can say that those who resist an oppressive government that seeks to force them into a retreat by means of conditional threats are not prohibited a priori from continuing to resist. Even at the risk of facing escalation by other parties, they have a prima facie right to resist in the first instance using means proportionate to the Political Rights they seek to defend or secure; should things deteriorate into a direct confrontation with armed repression they then have a right of self-defence that is likely to cover necessary uses of lethal violence.[14]

Now, Finlay's analysis applies to revolution. Subjects are entitled to revolt just in case they are faced with a violation of their rights to life and limb, or with a violation of lesser rights backed by threats. In chapter 3, I will argue that, if this analysis is correct, it applies equally to the evaluation of humanitarian intervention, subject of course to the various tests of proportionality.

The reason humanitarian interventions can be problematic is *not* that ordinary tyranny is a lesser wrong than genocidal tyranny (although of course it is). They can be problematic because of the *uncertainty of escalation* that would result in the killings and destruction typical of war, and in the possibility of instability after the intervening forces have withdrawn. The reasons for adopting the GT threshold for armed intervention are essentially *epistemic*. The intervener does not control all the

14. Ibid., 66. Finlay, following McMahan, thinks that subjects may even use preemptive violence.

variables, and hence can never be sure that the intervention will not cause excessive damage. The 2003 war in Iraq, which in my judgment could be defended initially on humanitarian grounds, was severely criticized precisely because it triggered an array of bad consequences, many of which should have been anticipated by the Bush administration.[15] However, it cannot be assumed that this epistemic barrier can never be overcome. In the 1994 Haitian incident, the threat by the United States was sufficient to restore the constitutional government. The forgotten 1983 intervention in Grenada, which brought a long period of democracy and prosperity to the island, likewise avoided escalation while realizing the just cause.

THE GREEN BUTTON EXPERIMENT

If this is correct, the GT threshold is required as a general rule, not because of the importance of state sovereignty or because the offending ruler does not deserve the harm that is coming to him, but because initiating a war to remedy lesser wrongs is almost always a *disproportionate* response to those wrongs. In the nature of things, invasions trigger armed responses and many people die as a result. When faced with minor forms of tyranny, states must exercise restraint because of the nefarious consequences of war, and not because of a nonconsequentialist duty to respect sovereignty. The principle of state sovereignty—that is, the idea that governments, as part of their right to rule over a territory, have a putative right to violate the moral rights of their subjects—has nothing to do with the impermissibility

15. For an optimistic *ex ante* view, see Fernando R. Tesón, "Ending Tyranny in Iraq," *Ethics and International Affairs* 19 (2005): 1–20. For a reassessment, see the Appendix, this volume.

of intervention in these kinds of ordinary tyranny. Let me show this by positing, in the best tradition of moral philosophy, an outlandish thought experiment: I call it the Green Button Machine.

A state is violating the rights of its subjects. I, a foreigner, own a fabulous machine activated by a green button. By pressing the button I can instantly discontinue all rights violations. The green button will not harm anyone, nor alter anyone's personality, nor will it have other undesirable consequences. It will not turn persons into different ones, nor alter their psyches or beliefs. It will simply block rights violations. Pressing the green button, I suggest, is morally justified. More: I cannot imagine reasons why anyone should not press the button. If pressing the button is permissible, then there is no independent normative value in state sovereignty. The costlier the means to end the offending practice, the less permissible those means will be (which is why pressing the green button seems right), but not because the offending practice embodies anything inherently valuable. In international relations, diplomatic pressure—unlike war—is permissible to end rights violations because it is less costly. And war will be impermissible because it is too costly, not because of the principles of sovereignty or nonintervention.

Costless intervention is *always* permissible against a government that violates the moral rights of its subjects. This is true even if the government in question is considered legitimate by some general standard of legitimacy.[16] The United States incarcerates millions of persons for morally innocent behavior. Suppose we had the Green Button Machine available.

16. See Loren E. Lomasky and Fernando R. Tesón, *Justice at a Distance: Extending Freedom Globally* (Cambridge University Press, 2015), chapter 7.

Pressing the button would have *only* the effect of freeing these unjustly incarcerated persons. There would be no other cost, to anyone. It seems to me that we may—indeed, must—press the button. The only reason we have an obligation to refrain from going *beyond* the button to address this problem is that violent means would cause more harm than good (harm and good here are normatively qualified, as we will see in chapter 4). Consider states that violate the rights of their citizens as a matter of course. Egypt, for example, seriously curtails speech and political activities.[17] It would be folly to invade Egypt to remedy this, but not because Egypt has a right to oppress as long as it does not massacre people, nor because the Egyptian problems should be addressed solely by Egyptians. Rather, invading Egypt is wrong because it would violate the requirement that war be proportionate. Again, outsiders can use proportionate means to pressure Egypt to enact liberal reforms, and for the same reason, if we had the Green Button Machine available, we could permissibly use it to end Egypt's right violations.

This means that the permissibility of humanitarian intervention should be judged by application of a general theory of war, and not by positing a default principle of state sovereignty that bars intervention unless the government forfeits that sovereignty by perpetrating sufficiently severe rights violations. Governments do not have a right to violate the moral rights of their subjects.[18] When I say that intervention in North Korea is unjustified, what I mean is that it would violate the principle of proportionality. I do not mean that we have an obligation

17. See https://freedomhouse.org/report/freedom-world/2015/egypt.
18. As McMahan writes: "This objection [self-determination] is often specious . . . when the intervention is desired by the victims of governmental persecution"; McMahan, "Just Cause for War," 13. See also Tesón, *Humanitarian Intervention*, chapters 3 and 4.

to tolerate North Korea's violations of the rights of its subjects. On the contrary, outsiders *have* a just cause for intervening in North Korea. That cause is saving the victims of Kim Jong's despotism. But outsiders do not have a just cause for *war*, because the costs of war are morally prohibitive. If diplomacy would cause the North Korean regime to change its ways at an acceptable cost, then diplomacy or economic sanctions would be justified for that purpose. North Korean sovereignty has nothing to do with it.

Bas van der Vossen dismisses the Green Button experiment because, he thinks, it leaves out precisely what is most serious about war.[19] In real life, we don't press any buttons; rather, armies invade and cause great harm. And this uncertainty about the extent and gravity of the harm makes interventions impermissible. By guaranteeing that there will be no bad consequences, the Green Button Machine hypothetical assumes away the truly problematic feature of war. Leaving aside that such worry applies not only to humanitarian intervention but also to all wars (see chapter 3), this criticism misses the point about the Green Button. The point of the Green Button Machine hypothetical is to show that sovereignty and self-determination play no role in the justification of humanitarian intervention. In other words, the Green Button Machine case underscores that (properly weighed) consequences are the paramount factor in establishing the permissibility of an intervention that has a just cause. The hypothetical demonstrates *exactly* the point that Van der Vossen repeatedly makes: the bad consequences of interventions are what makes them problematic.

How just a war may be is a matter of degree. Writers tend to treat the justice of war as a binary issue: either the war was

19. Van der Vossen, this volume.

just or it was not. It was just if it met the specified conditions—to simplify, just cause and proportionality. If the war failed to meet any of these it was unjust. But this ignores that a war may have a just cause, realize that just cause, and fail the proportionality test. The war then will be condemned. But that war would have been even *less* just if it wouldn't have realized the just cause. The war in Iraq exemplifies this. If one thinks, as I do, that removing Saddam Hussein was a just cause, then that cause was realized, even if the ultimate judgment is negative because of the disproportionate bad effects of the war. But having removed Saddam Hussein, one of the worst tyrants of the twentieth century, was commendable nonetheless. In this sense, the war was less unjust than it would have been had the coalition not achieved that objective.

INDEPENDENT AND CONDITIONAL JUST CAUSES

Military interventions are sometimes justified to end tyranny. Severe rights violations are major wrongs, and they provide a just cause for waging war against the perpetrator in order to save the victims. Following Jeff McMahan and Robert McKim, I call this the *independent just cause* for humanitarian intervention.[20] The independent just cause is the defense of persons attacked by their government. Realizing the just cause—that is, saving these victims—is the obligation of the intervener once it has started the war for that reason. But can the intervener who starts the war with a just cause pursue ends *other* than the realization of that cause? These other

20. See Jeff McMahan and Robert McKim, "The Just War and the Gulf War," *Canadian Journal of Philosophy* 23 (1993): 502–506.

ends can be quite diverse. The intervener may want to deter future acts of tyranny or may want to punish those responsible for the crimes. The intervener may also try to remedy *lesser* wrongs in that society, such as religious, racial, or gender oppression, or suppression of speech. Finally, the intervener may seek self-regarding goals, such as favorable trade treatment or regional hegemony. These other causes have been called *conditional* causes.[21] The question is whether a successful just intervener may permissibly pursue causes beyond the independent just cause—the cause that justified intervention in the first place. This issue is highly topical in light of current events. In reaction to the atrocities perpetrated by ISIS, many voices have called for military intervention against the group.[22] But it is widely acknowledged that the probability of recurrence of the atrocities is high. If so, it seems that any intervener should do *more* than just rescue the victims, and this may mean pursuing goals other than those that justify the armed intervention.

Answering that question requires making a few distinctions. Conditional causes differ in kind, and should not be lumped together. Assuming the intervention is justified by the presence of an independent just cause, such as a massacre of civilians, I distinguish three categories of conditional

21. See Hurka, "Liability and Just Cause," 199.
22. See Jeff McMahan, "Syria is a Modern-Day Holocaust. We Must Act," at https://www.washingtonpost.com/news/in-theory/wp/2015/11/30/syria-is-a-modern-day-holocaust-we-must-act/; and Fernando R. Tesón, "The Case of Armed Intervention against the Islamic State of Iraq and Syria," *The Independent Review* 21 (2016), at http://www.independent.org/publications/tir/article.asp?a=. Here's President Obama: "We will go after ISIS until it is destroyed," at http://www.cnn.com/2016/03/23/politics/obama-argentina-brussels-attacks/.

causes: causes *endogenous* to the independent just cause; causes that are morally worthy but *exogenous* to the independent just cause; and *self-regarding* causes.

CONDITIONAL CAUSES ENDOGENOUS TO THE INDEPENDENT JUST CAUSE

These causes are formally distinct from the independent just cause but are intimately related to it. In a humanitarian intervention, the endogenous conditional cause is the *need to prevent future rights violations*. This is deterrence, broadly understood. Generally, it is permissible for the intervener to pursue these causes because their realization is necessary to the realization of the independent just cause. This is a corollary of two just-war conditions listed in chapter 1. Under the necessity condition, a war, to be just, must be the necessary means to pursue the just cause while minimizing casualties. If the just cause is stopping a massacre, then the need to *deter* future massacres is endogenous to it. Similarly, the requirement of reasonable probability of success requires in most cases doing more than rescuing the victims. An intervention to stop a massacre would not be successful if the massacres are likely to recur (although that depends on how one defines success).

This family of conditional causes, then, are deterrence-based. Scholarly discussions of deterrence-based conditional causes have used the criminal punishment analogy.[23] In these cases there is a criminal, the tyrant, and there are other potential criminals, current or would-be tyrants elsewhere. We must distinguish, as is usually done in the criminal law, between *specific* and *general* deterrence. The tyrant is liable

23. See Hurka, "Liability and Just Cause"; and the response by Kamm, *Ethics for Enemies,* 136–141.

only to the harm that he deserves for his crimes. If his crimes are genocide and oppression of women, then he deserves the harm justified by his committing genocide plus the harm justified by his oppressing women, but no more. He is liable to be harmed for oppressing women (so, I contend in chapter 4, it is false that ordinary tyrants are immune to harm). But it is unjust to visit on the tyrant more *harm* than he deserves solely for the sake of deterring *other* tyrants.[24] Excessive violence against the tyrant for general deterrence purposes is impermissible.[25]

Three deterrence-based causes suggest themselves: disarmament, regime change, and punishment.

DISARMAMENT

If disarming the perpetrators is necessary to prevent future crimes, then the intervener is justified in doing that. Once a government has perpetrated a massacre, disarming it by force,

24. This is an issue of narrow proportionality that I discuss in chapter 4, this volume.
25. Thus, I deny that there are morally acceptable ways to deliberately punish someone more than he deserves. Compare Kamm, *Ethics for Enemies,* 138–141. Kamm also denies that we have a right to punish a criminal more than he deserves, but allows that it might sometimes make sense to do it. Kamm may be right that Hurka's punishment analogy, as such, does not show the permissibility of imposing on the offending regime more deliberate harm for the sake of a conditional cause. But I cannot see why it wouldn't be permissible to impose on the offending regime the harm for which it has become liable by virtue of the lesser wrong. This is tantamount to inflicting on the offending regime exactly the harm it deserves. This harm is additional to the harm justified by the independent just cause, the greater wrong.

and thereby incapacitating it for future massacres, becomes a legitimate goal of war.[26] Of course, the various proportionality requirements apply to it. Thus for example, following the Gulf War, the UN Security Council mandated a complete disarmament of the Iraqi regime.[27] In the Congo, the United Nations has likewise pursued the disarmament of the Democratic Forces for the Liberation of Rwanda, as an effort to pacify the region following the 1994 genocide and subsequent ethnic conflict.[28] Disarmament is not free of problems, however. If the regime that perpetrated the massacre is left in place, that regime will need the power and the means to maintain law and order (or else the society will drift into anarchy), and there is the danger that it will use that power to turn against its subjects once again. In 1991, the coalition that defeated Saddam Hussein (who had already rendered himself guilty of massive crimes) decided to leave him in power.[29] Saddam subsequently conducted massacres against Shiites and Marsh Arabs.[30] In these kinds of cases, regime change may be necessary to prevent the recurrence of the massacres, but conceivably the just cause may be realized without having to overthrow the regime. For example, one of the current issues in the negotiations to end the civil war in Syria is whether or not the Al Assad regime should be allowed to remain in power. This regime is undoubtedly guilty

26. Both Hurka, "Liability and Just Cause," 201, and McMahan, "Just Cause" agree that disarmament is linked to the independent just cause. See the discussion in chapter 4, this volume.
27. UN Security Council Res. 687 (1991).
28. See http://allafrica.com/stories/201409260360.html.
29. See George H. W. Bush and Brent Scowcroft, "Why We Didn't Remove Saddam," *Time Magazine*, March 2, 1998.
30. See http://www.independent.co.uk/news/world/saddam-drains-the-life-of-the-marsh-arabs-the-arabs-of-southern-iraq-cannot-endure-their-villages-1463823.html.

of major war crimes.[31] Yet effective disarmament may conceivably lead to pacification of the region, with guarantees against future massacres, while also leaving Al Assad in the presidential palace. This may be morally repugnant, but we must bear in mind that the justice of the war is judged by the various proportionality rules. If removing Al Assad from power will make the region unstable and increase the risk of war and future massacres, then disabling him from perpetrating crimes while allowing him to remain in power might turn out to be the second-best solution. Similarly, Emperor Hirohito was allowed to rule Japan even though he was arguably responsible for the war crimes committed by the Japanese during World War II. These examples show that at least in some cases the realization of the just cause does not require a change of the regime, but simply a neutralization of its killing capacity. But I think that disarmament of a criminal regime is justified even if the chances of future crimes are relatively low. The intuitive view of disarmament has been well put by Thomas Hurka: "even if disarmament that is not a response to active planning cannot by itself justify war, it can be permitted once another, independent justification for war is present."[32] If this is the case, then disarmament falls in the category of morally worthy causes exogenous to the just cause, discussed later in this chapter.

REGIME CHANGE

Regime change (the overthrow of the tyrant) will be justified whenever it is necessary to realize the just cause and thus secure a just peace, provided it satisfies the proportionality

31. See Ben Taub, "The Assad Files," *The New Yorker*, April 18, 2016, at http://www.newyorker.com/magazine/2016/04/18/bashar-al-assads-war-crimes-exposed.
32. Hurka, "Liability and Just Cause," 204.

requirements. If the genocidal regime is left in place and the likelihood of recurrence of the massacres is high, then the independent just cause would not have been realized and the war would not have had a just end. Leaving the perpetrator in power, with the tanks and guns ready to renew the attack on civilians, is a betrayal of the purpose for which the war was fought in the first place.

Writers have cast doubt on the propriety, morality, or wisdom of regime change following a humanitarian intervention. Michael Reisman, for example, writes that regime change is almost always a bad idea. He distinguishes humanitarian intervention from regime change. Humanitarian intervention is "a short initiative, aimed only at stopping massive and ongoing human rights violations." In contrast, regime change is "future-oriented . . . conducted to change the structure and/or personnel of a government."[33] The first is a *surgical* intervention, where the intervener invades, saves the victims, creates safe zones for them, and withdraws. In contrast, an intervener that overthrows the regime stays well after having saved the victims. In some cases, a surgical intervention will realize the just cause. If the regime surrounds an ethnic group with the intention of exterminating them, an intervention that saves them and deploys troops to protect them would have realized the just cause without changing the regime. Or, a surgical intervention may save the victims and succeed in deterring the regime from perpetrating future crimes. But in other cases, only deposing the perpetrators will achieve the just cause. If the justice of the war depends on the realization of that cause, then an intervention that leaves the tyrant in a

33. W. Michael Reisman, "Why Regime Change Is (Almost Always) a Bad Idea," *American Journal of International Law* 98 (2004): 516–525, 517.

position to renew his crimes is unjustified, because the just cause would not have been realized. Regime change, then, is future-oriented in the narrow sense that it aims at preventing the recurrence of the rights violations, and it is justified precisely in such case. Reisman characterizes regime change as an act conducted to change the structure or personnel of a government, but that is an under-description in humanitarian intervention cases. The case I am addressing here is that of an intervention that changes political structures or personnel *to prevent future rights violations*, and I claim that in those cases regime change is *pro tanto* justified. (I discuss interventions later, including those that involve regime change, where the intervener seeks to achieve non–just-cause-related goods such as ending political oppression.)

Reisman does not say that regime change is morally wrong, but that it is a bad idea. This suggests that his reasons for opposing regime change have to do exclusively with the bad consequences that might ensue. He worries that regime changers are likely to err in the choice of the new regime, that the task of changing the regime may be too onerous for the changers, that civil rights at home may suffer, that local populations may not tolerate the outsider for a long time, and that resistance may lead to greater violence.[34]

Suppose these worries are justified in a particular case. Then, regime change would be impermissible simply because it would cause more harm than good. *It would violate the various principles of proportionality* discussed in chapter 4. In that case, the intervener should exercise the restraint required to comply with the proportionality requirement. Maybe it should leave the criminal regime in place and promote measures to curb its aggressive behavior, or maybe it should encourage the

34. Ibid., 522–523.

democratic opposition to act. The point here is that there is no independent principle that bars regime change if it is necessary to realize the just cause, including prevention of future massacres. If the intervention has a just cause and overthrowing the regime is necessary to prevent recurrences of the crimes, then that action is permissible, provided it does not cause more harm than good. I would go further: sometimes the intervener will be justified to overthrow a regime for the wrongs it has already committed.[35]

Reisman says that *regime change* is almost always a bad idea, but he does not say that *humanitarian intervention* is almost always a bad idea. The implication is that in many cases where intervention, as a surgical action that saves lives, is a good idea, but regime change, as a permanent interference with civil society, is not. Reisman apparently endorses an intervention that saves the victims but rejects, in those cases, the subsequent change of a regime that is prepared to renew the massacres. It seems to me that such intervention would have been a partial failure, since the victims who were saved or other future victims would be now vulnerable to a renewed attack by the tyrant. It would have saved the victims temporarily, but it would not have fully realized the just cause because it would not have brought about a just peace. In this context, a just peace is the state of affairs where the rights violations that justified the intervention in the first place are not likely to recur. Moreover, I think that the cases where the humanitarian

35. I argued this point with respect to Saddam Hussein, in Tesón, "Ending Tyranny in Iraq," 1–20. *Contra*, Kenneth Roth, "Was the War in Iraq a Humanitarian Intervention?, *Journal of Military Ethics* 5 (2006): 84–92; and Pattison, *Humanitarian Intervention and the Responsibility to Protect*, 173–176. These authors think that humanitarian intervention is permissible only against ongoing atrocities.

intervention does *not* require regime change are less frequent than Reisman thinks. In most cases, the perpetrators must be defeated militarily and removed from power if the just cause is to be honored.[36] The ends of the war may require toppling the regime. It seems unlikely that keeping Pol Pot or Emperor Bokassa in power would have been consistent with realizing the just cause in those cases.

Yet, the distinction between surgical humanitarian intervention and regime change presents a difficult puzzle. Is a surgical humanitarian intervention—one where the intervener goes into the territory, saves the victims, and quickly leaves—*permissible*? If one takes the position that a humanitarian intervention is permissible only if it fully realizes the just cause, then the answer in many cases—namely those where the realization of the just cause requires regime change—seems no. An intervention that temporarily saves the victims but leaves the perpetrator in power or fails to disarm him, or otherwise leaves intact the means and the strength of the perpetrator to finish the criminal job, cannot be considered successful. On the other hand, the intervention would have saved these victims here and now, and it is hard to conclude that such action has no moral value (always, of course, subject to proportionality). For consider: What should we say to the victims themselves, those who desperately hope that the foreign army will save them? We would tell them something like this: "Look, we can save you but we won't do it because we need to withdraw quickly, and that means the criminal regime is likely to strike again. Since we cannot prevent this, we do not intervene." This sounds strange, to say the least. On the other hand, there is a lot to be said for the view that a

36. This raises issues about the consent of the victims of rights violations. See Fabre, *Cosmopolitan War*, 177.

humanitarian intervention is just if and only if it realizes the just cause or, if *ex ante,* the probabilities of realizing the just cause are sufficiently high.

Consider a humanitarian intervention to save the victims of ISIS. Suppose we know that a surgical intervention will save ISIS's current victims, but the full eradication of ISIS is militarily and politically impossible, as many (I think wrongly) argue.[37] Is such an intervention permissible? Michael Walzer says no. He says that any solution must secure a just peace. But I am not at all sure that the surgical intervention, one that saves these victims here and now, is morally impermissible, at least if such surgical action is likely to satisfy the various principles of collateral proportionality (the harm done in the course of the war; see chapter 4). This is Jeff McMahan's view: an intervention in ISIS is obligatory, he thinks, to end the genocide that ISIS is perpetrating in the territory.[38]

I think McMahan is correct on this point. In my view, this difficulty can be addressed in the following way. We should not think about the justice of intervention exclusively in binary terms. The intervention that rescues victims from genocide will be *perfectly* just if it also establishes a just end, such as preventing recurrence. But an intervention that only rescues the victims yet fails to prevent recurrence will be *partially* just, provided it otherwise complies with the strictures of proportionality. Put differently, the difficulty or even impossibility of securing a just peace should not be an absolute bar for humanitarian intervention. This is because it might be morally urgent to rescue these persons here and

37. See Michael Walzer, "What Kind of War Is this?" *Dissent*, December 3, 2015, at https://www.dissentmagazine.org/blog/france-us-uk-air-strikes-isis-just-war-theory; and my reply is in Tesón, "The Case for Armed Intervention against ISIS."

38. McMahan, "Syria Is a Modern-Day Genocide."

now. To say to these persons that we are not going to rescue them simply because we do not have the wherewithal to prevent their government's future crimes sounds hollow. Now, this surgical intervention must comply with proportionality. If rescuing these victims will cause more harm than good in the relevant sense, then it should not be done. But a state of affairs other than a just peace will not always be a violation of proportionality. There is a logical space between the absence of a just peace and the occurrence of excessive harm in the intervention. This is why the eighth condition for the justice of humanitarian intervention stated in chapter 1 merely stipulates that neither the intervention's occurrence nor the way it is fought should threaten the establishment of a justified peace. It does not *mandate* the establishment of a just peace in all cases, precisely because of the moral plausibility of some surgical interventions. To take again the ISIS example, perhaps it is justified to rescue the *present* victims of ISIS's atrocities, as McMahan says, even if it is difficult or impossible to establish a just peace in the region.

That difficulty aside, if the intervener has a just cause for humanitarian intervention, regime change is justified if necessary to realize that just cause. If regime change is not necessary to realize the just cause, then whether or not to depose the government should be judged by the strictures of a doctrine of proportionality. In some cases, regime change is likely to trigger bad consequences of such magnitude that restraint will be indicated. But in those cases, restraint will not be mandated by any principle of respect for sovereignty or communal integrity. It will be indicated, instead, by a (normatively qualified) consequential calculus. If the intervener can depose the tyrannical regime at an acceptable cost, it seems permissible to do so. (I will have more to say about this in my discussion of proportionality in chapter 4.)

PUNISHMENT AND THE QUESTION OF EVIL

Punishing the individual perpetrators is also a conditional cause linked to the realization of the independent cause. However, this goal is less closely related to the realization of the just cause than is disarmament or regime change. To the extent that bringing the criminals to trial, Nuremberg-style, fulfills appropriate deterrence or retributive functions, then it should be permissible for the intervener to do so. However, in some situations the intervener's best decision may be *not* to bring the perpetrators to justice. There is an extensive literature on transitional justice that addresses this topic.

Whether or not bringing the members of the criminal government to trial is conducive to realizing the just cause is highly dependent on local conditions. In some cases, prosecuting the perpetrators is necessary to pacification; in some other cases, it is not. And the punishment of genocidal rulers raises the same issues as criminal punishment in general. Whichever theory justifies criminal punishment—for example, negative retributivism (the view that it is never permissible to punish an innocent even if this achieves deterrence, but it is permissible to under-punish for deterrence or other reasons)—will also apply to the justification of war crime trials after an intervention.[39]

I should say here that culpability, and hence retribution, plays a distinctive role in humanitarian intervention. In these kinds of cases, the tyrant is a culpable aggressor. The literature on war uses the concept of unjustified threat. This idea is broad enough to include culpable and non-culpable aggressors, and for that reason is, I suppose, theoretically sound. But a non-culpable tyrant is unimaginable. Contrast this with cases of self-defense against aggression. Perhaps in some of those

39. See the discussion in Hurka, "Liability and Just Cause," 204–205.

cases the idea of non-culpable aggressor is plausible. Perhaps the aggressor honestly believes he has a just cause. Perhaps he has fallen prey to the security dilemma and honestly but falsely believes that his neighbor is about to invade. But it is highly implausible to think of a domestic tyrant as a non-culpable aggressor. Typically, the tyrant torments unarmed civilians. He has the monopoly on power, the tanks and weapons. He uses this power to cowardly attack those who cannot defend themselves. It is virtually impossible to imagine a tyrant that merely poses a non-culpable unjustified threat.

Talk about mere unjustified threats glosses over the fact that tyrants are *evil*. To say that Hitler, Saddam, or Pol Pot posed unjustified threats is to seriously under-describe them. They were evil rulers, whether they were merely opportunistic or acting out of evil maxims.[40] I am aware that mention of evil is not fashionable in academic circles, and perhaps that is why the rather aseptic talk about threats has prevailed in the literature on war. But in humanitarian cases we must enhance the concept of just cause by adding the importance of fighting evil. It is far beyond the scope of this essay to offer a full theory of moral evil. But whatever the ultimate explanation, there is no question that fighting evil is a central component of any action to combat tyranny.

MORALLY WORTHY EXOGENOUS CONDITIONAL CAUSES

Regimes that perpetrate massacres frequently violate a range of other human rights such as religious freedom, freedom of

40. I make the distinction in Fernando R. Tesón, "Targeted Killing in War and Peace: A Philosophical Analysis," in *Targeted Killings: Law and Morality in an Asymmetrical World*, ed. Claire Finkelstein, Jens Ohlin, and Andrew Altman (Oxford University Press, 2012), 403.

expression, or gender or racial equality. May the intervener seek to remedy these wrongs, or must he confine himself to realizing the independent just cause? The intervention is justified because the genocidal regime has made itself *liable* to attack by having attacked the victims. Now, suppose that the government is also guilty of the lesser wrong of oppressing women. Presumably, a military intervention would not have been justified to liberate women because it would have violated the proportionality requirement. Liberation of women is not an independent just cause, for proportionality reasons. Suppose the humanitarian intervention succeeds in stopping or preventing genocide. May the intervener *then* force political reforms to end the oppression of women? Strictly speaking, doing so would not be part of realizing the just cause, as the intervener would have realized the just cause by stopping the genocide and preventing future crimes.

The analysis of this type of conditional cause, the remedy of lesser wrongs, requires distinguishing among three different situations.

In the first case, state A is ruled by an autocratic regime that, among other things, oppresses women. The regime unleashes a genocide against an ethnic minority. State B invades state A and stops the genocide. The state A regime surrenders after military defeat, the fighting stops, and state B becomes the occupier. May state B enact reforms that liberate women? I would think that the answer is yes. Once the regime has been defeated, there is no reason not to try to improve the institutions of the defeated state by enacting reforms. The reason why this is permissible is that the war has ended. The coercion that the occupier needs to enact the political reforms that liberate women is the coercion required by *peacetime governance*. If so, liberating women will comply with the principles of proportionality, and will therefore be morally permissible.

The second case is like the first, but here the regime does *not* surrender after the genocide has stopped. Because the regime is defiant, the liberation of women requires *further* fighting, with the attendant moral costs. If liberating women is not an independent just cause, then the intervener, all things being equal, may not prosecute the *war* for that purpose. The requirement of proportionality takes over. This means that the predictable death and destruction of war cannot be justified for the purpose of liberating women, simply because in that case the war will do more harm than good. The fact that the war was originally justified to stop genocide does not entitle a *continuation of the war* once the genocide has been stopped. The idea is, then, that conditional just causes cannot be just causes *for renewing a war* that has ended. The intervener may not prosecute the war only for the purpose of liberating women once the independent just cause has been realized. It may be that prosecuting the war against the offending regime is justified, as we saw, for deterrence or other reasons centrally connected to the independent just cause—preventing genocide. But if deterrence has been achieved, further combat, with its known miseries, should not be permissible.

In these kinds of cases, pursuing the liberation of women is justified as part of *jus post bellum*. Once fighting has ended, the occupier is entitled to promote and enact liberal reforms such as ending women's oppression. But then, liberating women would not be a cause for war; it would be a permissible action *after* the war. The peacetime coercion exercised then by the occupier would be the one needed for just *policing and enforcing* of laws. This coercion will, in the great majority of cases, satisfy any applicable proportionality requirement.

The third case is more complex. I suggested that prosecuting the war *only* to free women is unjustified and, conversely, that freeing women *after* the war is justified. But the hard question is this: Can the remedy of lesser wrongs *count in the calculation of proportionality* for the purpose of justifying the war in the first place? The situation would be something like this: state A is committing a massacre and also oppressing women. An intervention by state B will *simultaneously* save the victims of massacre and liberate women. Now, to be just the intervention must be for a just cause *and* should (roughly) cause more good than harm. During the intervention to stop a massacre, the intervener may inflict *lesser* harms on those responsible for the oppression of women in order to liberate the victims of that oppression. This is a corollary of the analysis above, that proportionate coercion is permissible against those who violate the rights of others. The major violence entailed by war is permissible against the major violence exerted by the perpetrator of massacres. War would not have been permissible against these same persons only in response to their oppression of women, but minor forms of coercion would have been permissible. So, if the intervener defeats the criminal rulers on the battlefield, it can then bloodlessly detain them or perform other acts that discontinue the oppression of women without killing or maiming the oppressors.

More difficult is the question of *harm to bystanders* in the pursuit of conditional causes. Suppose a tyrant is committing a massacre and also oppressing women. An intervention is justified to stop that massacre. Assume that the morally acceptable collateral harm of the intervention to stop the massacre is X. But his oppression of women is also a just cause for *coercion* (but not war) against the tyrant. Assume that the morally acceptable collateral harm of an intervention to end the oppression of women is Y, where $Y < X$. This means that a military intervention (in the absence of massacre) *only* to end oppression of women would not be justified, since it would cause X harm, which is excessive. However, once the intervention to stop the massacre succeeds, it is permissible for the intervener to liberate women at an additional cost of Y. The total morally acceptable cost of stopping the massacre *and* freeing women is X + Y. The intervener has ended *two* tyrannical practices and has not exceeded the permissible moral cost of doing so. He would have exceeded the permissible moral cost had he started a *war* for the purpose of ending the oppression of women, because in that case the cost of X would have been too high. But the Doctrine of Double Effect (to be discussed in chapter 4) authorizes a lesser collateral harm to remedy a lesser wrong. That doctrine does not apply only to massacres. If the intervener does not exceed the permissible moral cost of this latter action, then he may act.

In summary, I can see no reason why the intervener who has a just cause should be disabled from pursuing other humanitarian causes that constitute lesser wrongs.[41] As McMahan says, "[t]here is no reason to suppose that only the good effects specified by the just cause can count in the assessment of wide proportionality."[42] This is particularly true in the case of humanitarian intervention, the purpose of which is to end tyranny. The oppression of women is part of the broader phenomenon of tyranny. The massacre threshold is required in a particular case because of proportionality concerns. Ordinary tyranny in many cases does not justify military intervention, even though the offending regime is morally liable to be removed. Intervention is banned because the required military action would cause too much damage. But if the regime perpetrates a massacre that provides the independent just cause in this case (because now the need to prevent the massacre will

41. McMahan used to disagree (see his "Just Cause for War"), but has now joined the consensus. See now McMahan, "Proportionality and Just Cause," 428–453.
42. McMahan, "Proportionality and Just Cause," 437. I discuss proportionality in chapter 4, this volume.

justify the damage contemplated by the military intervention), then the intervener may *simultaneously* put an end to *other* tyrannical practices.

As I indicated, any further action must meet the proportionality test *with respect to those lesser wrongs*. Hurka's discussion illustrates some of the difficulties here. He claims, for example, that assuming the United Kingdom had a just cause for war in the 1982 Falklands/Malvinas war (responding to aggression), presumably it would . . . not have been permissible for Britain to remove the junta after they invaded the Falklands, since the invasion did not itself license that regime change."[43] This seems correct, but the question is why not, given that the crimes of the military junta were very serious. Is it because the change of regime would have necessitated further fighting? Or is it because the regime change was properly left to the Argentines themselves? What if the removal of the junta would have been bloodless? It would seem that in that case regime change would have satisfied the proportionality test, unless one posits some intolerably bad consequences that would have flown from the precedent of the United Kingdom's removal of the junta. Hurka encapsulates his doubts here by stating that "there are no decisive arguments for recognizing the third type of conditional cause, but there are also no decisive arguments against doing so."[44]

I think part of the reason why Hurka hesitates here is that he is comparing the just cause of *aggression* with the cause of remedying *lesser* human rights violations. In the Falklands/Malvinas war, the Argentine regime was guilty of aggression, and it was also guilty of serious human rights violations. The aggression justified, say, a proportionate response

43. Hurka, "Liability and Just Cause," 207.
44. Ibid.

in self-defense by the United Kingdom. Such response was unrelated to the tyrannical nature of the Argentine regime. The question, then, was whether or not the United Kingdom would have been entitled to extend its self-defense war into a humanitarian war. I think the answer is no, but not because the junta was morally immune to violence aimed at ending its tyrannical practices. The human rights abuses of the Argentine junta were sufficient to justify *proportionate* action for removal. They were not sufficient, however, to justify a full British invasion of Argentina, because that would *not* have been proportionate.

That does not mean that *a regime that has rendered itself guilty of ordinary tyranny is not liable to be removed.* The regime is liable to proportionate action to end its tyrannical practices. In particular cases (maybe a great majority of cases) of ordinary tyranny, the proportionality calculus fails. And this means it is impermissible to remove the regime (but, as I will argue in chapter 3, if intervention is impermissible in that case, so is revolution!). Whether or not the regime should be removed, all things considered, depends on such calculus, including whether removal is required for the establishment of a just peace.

Another reason for counting morally worthy conditional causes in the proportionality calculus is that if the aggregate relevant *harm* caused by the intervention counts to render a verdict of injustice, then the aggregate relevant *good* caused by the war should likewise count in the verdict of approval. This is true even if realizing that good would not have justified the intervention in the first place. Take again the 2003 war in Iraq. If it is fair game to calculate the harms that the intervention triggered in order to condemn the war, then it is fair game to calculate the benefits that the intervention brought about in order to defend the war (assuming just cause). Even in the case of Iraq, where most observers say that the 2003 war was unjustified, it is surely fair game to count the improvement, if any, of Iraqi political institutions in the proportionality calculus (even if such improvement would not have constituted an independent just cause).

We can summarize the foregoing discussion by saying that every act of coercion must have an acceptable moral cost. So, imagine that a tyrant is committing genocide. The intervener can start a war because war's expected damage is an acceptable moral cost given the enormity of genocide. If the intervener can liberate women by acts of coercion short of war, then he can permissibly act, because in that case he will incur acceptable moral costs. The general principle, then, is that, assuming a just cause, every act of violence must have an acceptable moral cost at the time the act is performed.

SELF-REGARDING CONDITIONAL CAUSES

The final category of conditional causes is quite common. Suppose state A is perpetrating genocide. The prime minister of neighboring state B is in the middle of a difficult presidential reelection battle. She correctly predicts that invading state A and stopping the genocide will secure her electoral victory. She then invades, stops the genocide, and subsequently wins reelection. Has the requirement of just cause been satisfied?

Some writers answer in the negative. In the just-war tradition, the intervener must have purity of motives, a pure right intent. I address right intent later in this chapter. Here, I simply observe that the existence *vel non* of a just cause is independent of the intention of the intervener. The ongoing genocide in our example is a just cause for war in an objective sense. As I explain in chapter 4, the type of intention by the intervener will have a strong bearing on the moral judgment of *her*, but will not have such a strong bearing on the justice of the intervention. The desire to win reelection is not a just cause. But the intervener intends stopping genocide as *a means* to win reelection, and stopping genocide is a just cause for intervention. The permissibility of the intervention is not affected by the fact that the intervener has an ulterior, self-regarding motive. India's intervention in Bangladesh in 1971 was justified to stop the ongoing genocide against the Bengalis, even if India might have had ulterior motives of achieving hegemony in the Indian peninsula or, more likely, stopping the flow of refugees into India.

However, self-regarding motives may affect elements of proportionality. The fact that the intervener is primarily concerned with her own domestic electoral prospects may make her lose sight of the just-war requirements and may turn an initially just war into an unjust one. And, unlike the conditional causes discussed in the previous two sections, the realization of the self-regarding cause does not count at all in the calculation of proportionality. Prosecuting the war in excess of what proportionality allows for the sake of winning reelection at home is, of course, impermissible (but what if winning reelection is a condition for saving the intervener's country from a terrible tyrannical future?). The only point here is that the self-regarding conditional cause does not turn an otherwise permissible intervention into an impermissible one. But by the same token, no amount of additional violence is justified for the purpose of realizing the self-regarding conditional clause. Thus, once the intervener stops genocide, she may not prosecute the war, with its attendant additional moral cost, just for the purpose of winning reelection (maybe she wants to impress voters at home with television images of the triumphant army entering the capital). If the permissible harm of stopping genocide is X, then X is all the harm the intervener is allowed to cause.

A NOTE ON THE SUCCESS CONDITION

The intervention must have reasonable chances of success. Success is defined as the realization of the just cause. Whether the intervention is successful, therefore, can only be determined by looking at the facts. In an empirical study of seventeen cases, Taylor Seybolt concluded that, when success is measured by lives saved, most of these interventions have been successful.[45] Critics of humanitarian intervention are often too quick to emphasize failures in realizing the humanitarian objective. They point to Somalia, Iraq, and Libya, and they are certainly right in doing so, as these high-profile cases underscore the dangers of intervening and the importance of responsible planning. But these critics systematically overlook the successful cases, such as Grenada, East Pakistan, Tanzania, Panama, Central Africa, Kosovo, and East Timor, to cite just a few, where interventions did succeed. I think part of the reason for this imbalance is that successful cases do not make headlines. No one visits Grenada to find out whether or not the lives of Grenadians were improved following the 1983 intervention that removed the thuggish military officers who machine-gunned their way into power.[46] No one stops to ascertain whether Panama is better off without Manuel Noriega. Nor are

45. Taylor B. Seybolt, *Humanitarian Military Intervention: The Conditions for Success and Failure* (Sipri, 2007), 270. Surprisingly, Bas van der Vossen cites Seybolt for the *contrary* view, using Somalia as an example of failure. Somalia was indeed an intervention that failed, but this is not true of many of the other cases that Seybolt examines.

46. Grenadians call the anniversary of the U.S. intervention "Thanksgiving Day"; see http://aglobalworld.com/holidays-around-the-world/grenada-thanksgiving-day/.

CNN cameras flocking to see if the life of Kosovars is better after NATO prevented the ethnic cleansing there.

In short, the success of a humanitarian intervention is an empirical issue. It is as false to claim that they are all successful as it is to claim they are all failures.

RIGHT INTENT

The requirement of just cause (attack against persons) raises the question of right intent. Must those who start a war of humanitarian intervention *act on* the humanitarian motive for the war to be justified?[47] Traditional just-war theory has required right intent—that is, a certain mental state on the part of the intervener. Here is Thomas Aquinas: "For it can happen that even if war is declared by a legitimate authority and for a just cause, that war may be rendered unlawful by a wicked intent."[48] Similarly, Alex Bellamy claims that right intention is pivotal to the permissibility of intervention.[49] The idea is that a necessary condition for the justification of humanitarian intervention is

47. I do not consider here whether right intention should be a *definitional* requirement for humanitarian intervention. My discussion in this chapter accepts that an intervention can be right even if started for the wrong reasons, and that intent speaks to the blameworthy of the intervener.
48. Thomas Aquinas, *Political Writings*, ed. R. W. Dyson (Cambridge University Press, 2002), 241.
49. Alex J. Bellamy, "Motives, Outcomes, Intent, and the Legitimacy of Humanitarian Intervention," *Journal of Military Ethics* 3 (2004): 227. See also George R. Lucas Jr., "From *Jus ad Bellum* to *Jus ad Pacem*: Rethinking Just War Criteria for the Use of Military Force for Humanitarian Ends," in *Ethics and Foreign Intervention*, ed. Deen K. Chaterjee and Don E. Scheid (Cambridge University Press, 2003), 72–96, 87.

that the intervener acts out of humanitarian reasons, at least in part. On the traditional view, if a government's preeminent reasons or motives are nonhumanitarian, the intervention will not be humanitarian, and should not be evaluated under the doctrine of humanitarian intervention, even if the doctrine is deemed valid. The use of force will be something else (self-defense, for example) and it should be judged accordingly. The ICISS Report concluded, more realistically, that mixed motives in state action are a fact of life, and therefore they are not enough to disqualify an otherwise legitimate intervention, provided the primary purpose is to halt or avert human suffering.[50]

The issue was hotly debated during the wars in Iraq and Afghanistan. Many thought that George W. Bush, for example, did not really intend to liberate Iraq from Saddam Hussein but, rather, to achieve something else, such as destroying the elusive weapons of mass destruction or, even worse, grabbing Iraq's oil. Because any of those motives revealed the real intent of the intervener, the invasion of Iraq, it was thought, could not possibly *count* as humanitarian intervention.[51]

This simplistic view does not do justice to the complexity of the relationship between intention and permissibility of action. Such complexity has been underscored by the important work of F. M. Kamm, among others. Space limitations prevent me from addressing the intricate aspects of right intent, so I will limit myself to distinguishing, following John Stuart

50. ICISS Report, 35–36.
51. I discuss the issue of categorization in Fernando R. Tesón, "Ending Tyranny in Iraq." Helen Frowe also thinks that the issues of categorization and permissibility are different; Helen Frowe, "Judging Armed Humanitarian Intervention," in *The Ethics of Armed Humanitarian Intervention*, ed. Don Scheid (Cambridge University Press, 2014), 96.

Mill, between two concepts of intent: *intention* and *motive*.[52] Mill wrote:

> The morality of the action depends entirely upon the intention—that is, upon what the agent wills to do. But the motive, that is, the feeling which makes him will so to do, when it makes no difference in the act, makes none in the morality: though it makes a great difference in our moral estimation of the agent, especially if it indicates a good or a bad habitual disposition—a bent of character from which useful, or from which hurtful actions are likely to arise.[53]

Intention covers the contemplated act, what the agent wills to do. I see a person in distress, decide to rescue her, and do it. The action is an act of rescue. I intended to rescue the person, I committed to doing it, and I did it. In the simplest case, intention covers the willed act and the willed consequences of the act. Intention, then, implies not only desire to do something but also commitment to doing it. This involves believing that the act is under the agent's control.[54] If I intended to rescue someone but failed to do so—say, because I didn't put in enough effort, or I was clumsy or otherwise mistaken in my choice of means—then you could say, perhaps, that mine was not an act of rescue. In the case of humanitarian intervention, this requirement translates into the reasonable prospects of victory. The intervener must reasonably believe that he can succeed in stopping the massacre. To intend X implies direct

52. I draw freely from Tesón, "Ending Tyranny in Iraq."
53. John Stuart Mill, *Utilitarianism*, ed. Roger Crisp (Oxford University Press, 1998), 65n2.
54. Here I follow Michael Ridge, "Mill's Intention and Motives," *Utilitas* 14 (2002): 54.

connections between my willing X, my commitment to doing X, and my doing X.

By contrast, a *motive* is a further goal that one wishes to accomplish with the intended act. I rescued the person in danger. But suppose I did it because I wanted to appear as a hero in the local newspaper. I had an ulterior motive. This motive is not part of the class of actions called "acts of rescue"; only the intention is. It makes sense for you to say that my act of rescue was good (it saved a life), but that I am not a particularly admirable person, since my motive was self-interested, not altruistic. In introducing this distinction, Mill showed that intention is more important than motive in evaluating action (as opposed to evaluating persons). The concept of intention fulfills a double role: it allows us to characterize the act, to say that the act belongs to a class of acts, such as acts of rescue; and it allows us, correspondingly, to praise or criticize the act under the moral principles that apply to that class of acts, acts of rescue.

The upshot is that someone may will X either as *an end in itself* or *as a means to another end, Y.* If stopping a massacre is an independent just cause for war, then it is justified to start a war that would stop the massacre, even if the intervener has a further motive Y (say, grabbing oil). It is not against usage to say that the intervener intended X: he intended X as a means to achieve Y. The 2003 Iraq war may have been unjustified for a number of reasons, but not because the coalition lacked the intent to liberate Iraq. The coalition *willed* the overthrow of Saddam Hussein, probably not as an end in itself but in pursuit of other ends. In the worst scenario, the coalition intended to liberate Iraq as a means to achieve some other non–just-cause-related purpose. So, when the agent intends the just cause (defending the victims of massacre) as a means to achieving a further motive (securing economic benefits), the act of saving the victims is justified, even if the intervener's motive may be such that it would not have justified the war. As Mill pointed out, the existence of a questionable motive may be a reason to criticize the *agent*, but not a reason to criticize his *act*. This is the sense of intent used in the criminal law: juries are called to determine the *mens rea*—that is, whether the accused had the intent of committing the crime. This is the Millian sense of intent. For the criminal law, too, the motive for the crime (say, the criminal's rage of jealousy or his desire to feed his family) rarely excuses the crime.[55]

55. James Pattison disputes my claim (in "Ending Tyranny in Iraq") that the coalition in Iraq had a humanitarian intent, namely the intent of removing Saddam; Pattison, *Humanitarian Intervention and the Responsibility to Protect*, 173–176. But he overlooks my definition of intent, which is the intent to perform an action even if that is a *means* to bring about something else. On this definition, it is plain that the coalition intended to overthrow Saddam as a means to whatever else they wanted to achieve. Pattison's argument, it seems to me, is different, and it has nothing to do with intent. He does not (and cannot) really question that the coalition intended to remove Saddam. Rather, to him, removing Saddam was not a just cause; see esp. 175. See also the discussion in the Appendix, this volume.

3

Intervention and Revolution

The Equivalence Thesis

IT IS WIDELY HELD THAT violent revolution can be justified to end tyranny. It is equally widely held that foreign intervention is *not* justified just to end tyranny. Intervention is justified, if at all, in a much narrower range of cases—perhaps to halt massacre or genocide, but not to end ordinary oppression. On this view, state oppression may be sufficient to furnish internal revolutionaries with a just cause for violence, but simultaneously insufficient to generate a just cause for outside parties to do the same.

This chapter challenges that view. It advances instead the *equivalence thesis*: the just cause for humanitarian intervention is *exactly* the same as the just cause for revolution, and both are subject to principles of proportionality. The cases where humanitarian intervention is impermissible while revolution is permissible are those where the intervention will be disproportionate while the revolution will not be. Their differential moral status, then, does not depend on a difference between their respective just causes. As I explained in the first two chapters, war, like any form of violence, is justified only to defend persons and their rights. The traditional view (call it the *nonequivalence thesis*) suggests that remedying rights violations justifies violence, but only by *some* people (the victims' compatriots) and not others (outside interveners). This is arbitrary and unjust.

Writers who favor domestic revolution (and reject foreign intervention) appeal to the value of *political self-determination*. The idea is that the body politic has a collective right to determine its own destiny without outside interference. This idea requires further elaboration.

At the outset I suggested that sovereignty is not a freestanding principle of political morality. The term "sovereignty" is notoriously vague. At the very least, sovereignty can be understood in two senses. The first is *internal* sovereignty, which denotes the *government's* right to rule and the corresponding duty of citizens to obey. It is also called authority. The second is *external* sovereignty, which denotes the immunity of the state and the government against foreign intervention. Subjects are entitled to revolt against their government just in case that government reaches a threshold of tyranny. Theorists differ on what that threshold may be. Some think there is an obligation to obey unjust commands of otherwise just regimes; others take a more permissive view of the right to resist. In contrast, foreign intervention is presumptively impermissible. Only when the government violates human rights severely, it is thought, may outsiders intervene. External sovereignty, on this mainstream view, is much stronger than internal sovereignty. Foreigners should not try to end ordinary tyranny. They may only intervene by force to end tyrannical behavior that shocks the conscience of humankind. The nonequivalence thesis is the flip side of the asymmetrical view of sovereignty: because international sovereignty is stronger than internal sovereignty, foreign violence to end tyranny is excluded in many cases where domestic violence to end tyranny is not.

External sovereignty, in turn, is usually cashed out in terms of *political self-determination*. External sovereignty is stronger than internal sovereignty precisely because, it is thought, the *body politic* has a collective right to determine its own destiny without outside interference. It is unclear, on this view, whether political self-determination requires a democratic pronouncement by the people. Some versions of self-determination would validate undemocratic processes as legitimate instances of political self-determination.

This distinction between internal and external sovereignty has placed revolution in a sharply different ethical place than it has foreign intervention. The idea is that political self-determination imposes a bar on intervention that does not operate in the case of a justified revolution. A revolution, it is thought, is an instance of political self-determination from which foreigners are excluded. Military support for a revolution is presumptively impermissible even if the revolution itself is justified. The general sense is that revolution *advances* self-determination whereas intervention *undermines* self-determination. Perhaps surprisingly, until recently there was no systematic treatment of the ethics of revolution.[1]

Here I will not offer a full theory of revolution. Instead, I claim that the just cause for intervention, considered in itself, is *the same* as the just cause for revolution. That just cause is *tyranny*, defined as rights violations that have achieved a level of gravity that justifies proportionate force in response. I therefore deny that humanitarian intervention, per se, requires a higher permissibility threshold than a justified revolution. To be sure, often foreign intervention to help just revolutionaries will be

1. See now Finlay, *Terrorism and the Right to Resist*. Allen Buchanan has written two important articles trying to fill some gaps: Allen Buchanan, "The Ethics of Revolution and Its Implications for the Ethics of Intervention," *Philosophy & Public Affairs* 41 (2103): 291–323; and "Self-Determination, Revolution, and Intervention," *Ethics* 126 (2016): 447–473.

impermissible. But that is not because the offending regime is not tyrannical enough, nor because states have a collective right of political self-determination, but because intervention, but not revolution, will in many cases violate principles of proportionality.

Writers differ on the moral threshold for revolution. Some authors are hostile to revolution altogether. None other than Kant thought that revolution was impermissible because it contradicted the idea of a lawful constitution.[2] David Copp has argued that a state is legitimate just in case it provides certain essential services.[3] Copp does not address revolution specifically, but if violent resistance is impermissible against a legitimate state, and if a legitimate state is one that provides essential services, then revolution against a state that provides essential services is impermissible, no matter how tyrannical that state may otherwise be.

The dominant view, however, is that revolution is justified to end tyranny. Here's John Locke:

> In all States and Conditions the true remedy of *Force* without Authority, is to oppose *Force* to it. The use of *force* without Authority, always puts him that uses it into a *state of War*, as the Aggressor, and renders him liable to be treated accordingly.[4]

2. See Kant, *The Metaphysics of Morals*, 95–98. For a defense, see Katrin Flikschuh, "Reason, Right, and Revolution: Kant and Locke, *Philosophy and Public Affairs* 36 (2008): 375–404.
3. David Copp, "The Idea of a Legitimate State," *Philosophy & Public Affairs* 28 (1999): 3–45.
4. John Locke, "An Essay Concerning the True, Original, Extent, and End of Civil Government" [1689] [Second Treatise], in *Locke: Two Treatises on Government*, ed. P. Laslett (Cambridge University Press, 2003), para. 155.

For Locke, tyranny generates a state of war between tyrant and subjects, where the tyrant is the aggressor. The subjects are entitled to respond to this aggression by force.

Consider a typical case of ordinary tyranny: The government has suspended constitutional guarantees, jailed dissidents, and denied democratic elections. Most theorists would say, with Locke, that revolution, understood as *violent* resistance against this government, is morally justified. Christopher Finlay has improved on the Lockean view by introducing the idea of conditional threat, already mentioned in chapter 2. Subjects are entitled to resist by force just in case the government suppresses their rights by threatening lethal force, provided the principles of proportionality are satisfied. For Finlay, then, revolution is justified to counter violations of rights other than life and limb, simply because those lesser rights, too, collapse into a threat to life and limb.[5]

Michael Walzer is even more permissive. He writes that "[g]iven an illiberal or undemocratic government, *citizens are always free to rebel*, whether they act on that right or not, and whether they believe themselves to have it or not."[6] For Locke, the government has to be tyrannical to justify the people's taking arms against it. For Walzer, the illiberal or undemocratic nature of the regime suffices to justify revolution. The dominant view, then, is that subjects may revolt against a tyrannical regime (Locke) or even against an illiberal regime (Walzer). For Walzer, at any point in time when the government ceases to be a liberal democracy, citizens are entitled to revolt by violent means to restore liberal institutions. Allen Buchanan

5. Finlay, *Terrorism and the Right to Resist*, 66. Finlay expressly avoids the question whether his standard for justified revolution is available to justify humanitarian intervention; see also p. 6.
6. Walzer, "The Moral Standing of States," 215 (my emphasis).

has proposed a stricter standard for revolution. To him, revolution is justified when the revolutionaries seek to end what he calls Resolute Severe Tyranny. This is "a regime that persistently violates some of the basic human rights of large segments of the population, is extremely authoritarian (that is, wholly undemocratic), and is utterly impervious to efforts to reform it."[7]

The flip side of this view is equally important: people do *not* have a right to rebel against a liberal democracy, or at least against a regime that is not sufficiently tyrannical. This may be because a liberal-democratic government is the one institution that can be deemed to have been consented to by subjects, or because it is the only institution that respects their moral rights. Political violence is not permissible merely to change the government's personnel, or improve economic conditions, even to end governmental corruption. In the words of John Rawls, "we are to comply with and do our share in just institutions when they exist and apply to us."[8]

In spite of their differences on the proper standard for revolution, most writers agree that the bar for foreign intervention is higher than the bar for revolution, as I noted. The right to revolt against tyrannical or illiberal regimes does not transfer to outsiders. Foreigners may not force an illiberal regime to become liberal; only the citizens can do that. Writers explain this asymmetry in various ways. Following Walzer, Ned Dobos argues that "a people's right to a state that

7. Buchanan, "Ethics of Revolution," 296. In this article, Buchanan implicitly seems to accept the same threshold for humanitarian intervention: both are permissible to confront Resolute Severe Tyranny. I am not sure, however, if he means that standard as a necessary or a sufficient condition for a justified revolution.
8. John Rawls, *A Theory of Justice* (Harvard University Press, 1971), 334.

expresses their culture can plausibly be said to extend sovereignty to at least some illiberal governments, and therefore to impose at least some limits to humanitarian intervention."[9] Other views rely squarely on state sovereignty or political self-determination as freestanding moral principles.[10] Massimo Renzo thinks that political self-determination places significant constraints on foreign intervention.[11] Many condemn the Iraq war, for example, in part because they decry attempts by the United States and others to force democracy on presumably unwilling populations.

As anticipated, I dissent from this view. I claim instead that the just cause *as such* (without considering consequences) for justified revolution and justified intervention is the same Lockean standard, *tyranny*, defined as a severe violation of the moral rights of persons.[12] I thus defend the equivalence thesis—that is, a symmetrical conception of just cause. The fact that *both* revolution and intervention are subject to the principle of proportionality has several corollaries. One is that, assuming just cause, there is no reason to think that armed force by outsiders will be impermissible in a much larger number of cases than armed force by revolutionaries. It all depends on the consequences. Foreign intervention will be impermissible in cases where revolution is permissible because often the former will violate the principle

9. Ned Dobos, *Insurrection and Intervention: The Two Faces of Sovereignty: A Theory of Just Revolutionary War* (Cambridge University Press, 2011), 29.
10. See, for example, ICISS Report, 31, at 4.
11. Massimo Renzo, "Political Self-Determination, Revolution and the Limits of Military Intervention," unpublished manuscript.
12. Cécile Fabre takes a similar view, although she gives more weight than I do to self-determination considerations; see Fabre, *Cosmopolitan War*, 135–141.

of proportionality while the latter will not. The higher threshold for humanitarian intervention is usually justified because experience shows that, in many cases, armed intervention has deleterious consequences that revolutions may not have. If foreign intervention in the Syrian civil war would make things worse than allowing the two sides to fight it out, then intervention would be prohibited while revolution might still be justified. But by the same token, sometimes revolution will be impermissible. If the Syrians' rebelling against Al Assad would make things worse, then revolution might be impermissible as well. Moreover, sometimes revolution will be impermissible while intervention will not be. In 1979 France bloodlessly deposed Bokassa, the self-proclaimed Emperor of the Central African Empire. A domestic revolution might have been much costlier, given the disparity of forces between the warring sides. Another corollary is that intervention against ordinary tyranny is justified only *if* it complies with proportionality. Because military interventions against ordinary tyranny will often be disproportionate, many of those will be impermissible. Assuming the just cause of ending tyranny, the reasons for *not* resorting to arms in *both* cases—revolution and intervention—then, are entirely based on the consequences of war. There is no independent principle such as self-determination, or the right to a state of one's own, or communal integrity, or sovereignty that bars intervention independently of the consequences.

Bas van der Vossen's position, too, illustrates the persistence of the prejudice against intervention and in favor of revolution. He writes that the morality of intervention "negotiates the tension between two opposing points. On the one hand, there is the moral impetus to try and prevent humanitarian crises." On the other hand, military interventions invariably impose risks of harm on people that are normally impermissible." To him, "[t]he lesser-evil rationale identifies an acceptable way of balancing these two threats—one from within the country experiencing the crisis, the other from without posed by the intervener."[13] This distinction between internal versus external threat prejudges the issue against foreign intervention. An internal *revolution* is also a threat that must be measured against the threats posed by the government against which the revolutionaries are taking up arms. Yet, a revolutionary threat is not an external threat. So, the proper balance should be between the threat posed by the rescuers (internal or external) and the threat posed by the villain who attacks the victims. Also, the fact that most revolutions are started by a minority of people, often against the preferences of the majority, further diminishes the differences between revolution and intervention.[14]

I argued in chapter 1 that a just war is best understood as a particularly intense instance of justified coercion in defense of persons. People are entitled to use defensive force against those who violate their rights. This general idea is equally applicable to civil wars. Despite fiery nationalist rhetoric, there is nothing essentially different between justified revolution and justified intervention. Both consist of defensive force against tyranny. In principle, therefore, the strictures of just war theory apply to both. A justified revolution must abide by *jus ad bellum, jus in bello*, and *jus post bellum*. Civil war is, too, an extreme form of coercion to counter tyranny. The mainstream view has resisted this logic, however, by appealing to values or considerations that supposedly establish a decisive moral difference between revolution and intervention. Those considerations stem from the ideas of sovereignty and self-determination.

13. Bas van der Vossen, chapter 7, this volume.
14. See Allen Buchanan, "Self-Determination, Revolution, and Intervention," 447–473.

Writers have defended this idea, however called, that peoples or nations have a collective right to decide political matters among themselves without foreign interference, in various ways. It is important to distinguish among them in order to understand how they affect the permissibility of humanitarian intervention.

On first approximation, the nonequivalence thesis (the moral asymmetry between revolution and intervention) is hard to explain. As we saw, if state A unjustly attacks state B, state B may permissibly use defensive force. But by the same token, if state A attacks *the citizens of state A* , state B can equally use defensive force against state A on behalf of the victims, the citizens of state A. Standard accounts of self-defense allow for the permissibility of the defense of others. Proponents of asymmetry think that defense of others may be banned, even if proportionate and even if the victims request help, in situations where, for some reason, perpetrator and victim form a community, or a political society, or a people from which outsiders are excluded. It is this idea that I reject.

THE RIGHT OF SELF-DETERMINATION

There are essentially two versions of political self-determination. One is the *nationalist* version. On this view, citizens are entitled to battle their differences in a political arena from which foreigners are excluded. States, or peoples, have a collective right of communal integrity that foreigners must respect regardless of what happens inside the arena.[15] The second is the *voluntarist* version. It rejects nationalism

15. Walzer, "Moral Standing," esp. 210.

and relies instead on more plausible ideas of social contract and group agency. On this view, political self-determination is grounded in some form of political consent. Only voluntary states have the right of self-determination. Viewed in this way, it is thought, it makes sense to talk about a group's having aims and purposes. The aim is gauged by consulting the organization and coordination among members of the group through accepted procedures within the group. Unlike nationalists, voluntarists do not endorse just any political result within the group. Voluntarists may accept the Lockean insight that no one has natural political authority over anyone else, and that therefore the only legitimate authority is delegated authority. This delegation agreement, or social contract, establishes the procedures for adopting political decisions (such as legislative procedures), and also establishes the limits that those political decisions must observe. A government that violates the social contract is illegitimate. But a legitimate government has full rights of self-determination, which means that foreigners are excluded from its political space.

NATIONALISM

Michael Walzer and Ned Dobos have defended the asymmetrical view grounded in a nationalist understanding of self-determination. Walzer distinguishes between internal and external legitimacy. According to Walzer, a state is *externally* legitimate when it represents the political life of its people—when there is a cultural fit between government and people. By this he means that the government reflects in some sense the political forces, the history, and the values of the population over which that government rules. For Walzer, citizens are bound to one another in a kind of Burkean contract; they are not, however, bound to obey their government. Citizens are free to reject the government; strictly speaking, they have no political obligation to the regime.[16] (In passing, this contradicts Walzer's statement, quoted earlier, that the regime has to be illiberal to justify revolution.) Citizens are entitled to reject their government and, presumably, to overthrow it by force, for any number of reasons. However, this right of subjects to reject their government does not extend to foreigners. Foreigners are not in a position to deny the reality of the "union of people and government." States, even unjust states, enjoy external legitimacy, even if they are domestically illegitimate. For Walzer, the state is the arena where the political process unfolds, where people fight for liberty. It is this arena that foreigners have a duty to respect. This right of citizens to a state that reflects their culture is crucial for the asymmetrical concept of legitimacy: the reasons for citizens to disobey their government, whatever they are, do not affect the obligation by foreigners to respect that government. But the people's right to a state of their own collapses in cases of massacre or genocide. In those cases, Walzer claims, the fit between people and government is no longer apparent, and the shield against intervention collapses as well.

Ned Dobos slightly amended Walzer's asymmetrical theory. People have a right to a state of their own, as Walzer claims. But Dobos does not think that such a collective right should prevail over *any* other right, except the right not to be massacred. Dobos's reformulation reads:

1. Not all internationally ratified human rights enjoy moral priority over (or even parity with) the right to a state that expresses one's culture *and*;

16. Ibid., 210–213.

2. The latter should be honoured unless its infringement is necessary to defend more important or more fundamental human rights.[17]

It follows that the threshold for legitimate humanitarian intervention need not be as high as massacre, because intervention may be justified to uphold human rights that are more important than the people's right to a state of their own. But the rationale for asymmetry is the same for both authors. People have a right to a state that reflects their own culture. Citizens may revolt to uphold their standard human rights in a manner that is consistent with maintaining their collective right to a state of their own. Many foreign interventions aimed at defending such standard human rights may deny citizens a state of their own. Therefore, only the vindication of rights that are morally more important than the right to one's own state can justify humanitarian intervention.

I have elsewhere criticized Walzer's theory of legitimacy and intervention.[18] Many of those criticisms apply to Dobos as well. Essentially, the idea of communal integrity is a fantasy—especially in the case of tyrannies. In a tyrannical state, the government has turned *against* the people, so the mere fact that a majority supports the tyrant does not make him legitimate with respect to the oppressed minority. The political arena that

17. Dobos, *Insurrection and Intervention*, 35–36. In passing, it is unclear what these internationally ratified human rights would be, given the deep differences among international actors on the matter.
18. Tesón, *Humanitarian Intervention*, 81–89; Lomasky and Tesón, *Justice at a Distance*, 187–190. See also McMahan, "Just Cause for War," 13 (self-determination objections to humanitarian intervention are often specious).

Walzer defends is nothing more than a contingent alignment of forces that, in cases of tyranny, does not represent anything worth defending. The implication of Walzer's theory of communal integrity is that tyrants come from the cities and neighbors of the community, and so they are part of the culture in a broad sense, at least as long as they refrain from perpetrating massacres. This is simply blaming the victim. On this view, the tyrant can resist foreign intervention aimed at ending his crimes by simply showing that those crimes are as part of the culture as the hapless folk languishing in prison.

Here I add a more fundamental criticism. There is no such thing as an individual right to a state that expresses one's own culture, and consequently, there is no collective right to such a state. Hence, states do not have rights to nonintervention on grounds of protecting culture. The difficulties with the nationalist view are many. One is the status of those members of the population who do not endorse the tenets of the culture. If culture is the foundation of the state, as the nationalist position would have it, then cultural dissenters are not, in a moral sense, members of the state. If a society has an authoritarian culture (which can only mean that a majority of its members are authoritarians), then liberal dissenters are out of luck. They can be legal citizens, of course, but if the reasons that a given state X is legitimate are cultural ones, then someone who does not share the culture fails to share in the reasons that make her a member of state X. She is not a full citizen, as it were, since peoplehood is defined by a trait she does not possess. The idea that culture defines membership is dangerous because it easily leads to exclusion, discrimination, and ethnic conflict.

The putative people's right to a state that expresses their own culture, despite stirring nationalist rhetoric, is profoundly illiberal. It is not a right against a state but a right *to* a state. It is unconcerned with the legal and moral rights of individuals but, rather, with asserting a new sphere of political power—often more oppressive than the one left behind. To say that *the state* has the power to express the people's culture is to endow the state with the power to impose the culture on the unwilling. This putative right of the people is a recommendation for political and religious intolerance. It masks the ambitions of political entrepreneurs who claim to speak for the culture regardless of whether or not they have been properly elected, and regardless of the views of minorities and individuals who do not endorse dominant values. To require that the state express a culture is to recommend pogroms, deportations, discrimination, and ethnic cleansing.

The right of the people to a state of their own is suspect for yet another reason. Many people think that just as individual autonomy is a value, so group autonomy is a value; just as persons pursue individual projects, so groups pursue collective projects; just as persons seek the private good, so groups seek the collective good. But the analogy does not hold, except metaphorically. Surely groups can have value for their members. Groups can facilitate the achievement of goals that cannot be achieved individually. But this value of groups holds as long as they are *voluntary*. Groups are importantly disanalogous to individuals. An individual has a mind that makes plans and weighs options, alternatives, values, and goals. She may err, of course, but her error will be the result of her considered judgment about how she desires to pursue her personal project, how to lead her life on her own terms. Groups, on the contrary, do not have minds. They are collections of individuals in which some cooperate but others dominate, exploit, and prey on others. When an individual forms a life plan, she acts freely (with the usual caveats and exceptions). When a ruler devises a plan for society, he coercively enrolls others in his projects, whether his projects are shared by many or few. More often than not, a right to a state of one's own masks the desire to coerce others in morally impermissible ways.

If these conclusions are sufficiently repugnant to warrant rejection of the nationalist view of states' right to nonintervention, we cannot appeal to the nationalist view to support the nonequivalence thesis. The nationalist claim is that (1) people have a right to a state that expresses their culture, (2) the state has therefore a collective right to enforce that culture, and (3) for those reasons humanitarian intervention, but not revolution, is banned. If the premises are false, however, the conclusion cannot follow.

VOLUNTARISM

Voluntarism improves over nationalism because it grounds state legitimacy and hence self-determination on individual rights, not on any metaphysical or moral standing of collective entities. Voluntarists, unlike nationalists, narrow the range of legitimate collective entities (as only voluntary entities have moral standing, and so rights against intervention). Voluntarists do accept that groups have ends, interests, or projects that are not conceptually reducible to individual ends, interests, or projects.[19] The conjunction of those two ideas (that voluntary or consensual states are legitimate and that groups can have collective aims) suffices, they think, to ground political self-determination. Under the voluntarist view, revolution is justified when the government breaches the terms of the social contract. Foreigners, in contrast, are not parties to that contract and cannot validly enforce it.

Before replying to voluntarism, it is worth noting that the voluntarist premises do not entail the power of group leaders to

19. See Christian List and Philip Pettit, *Group Agency: The Possibility, Design, and Status of Corporate Agents* (Oxford University Press, 2011).

coercively impose collective ends not sanctioned by the social contract on the dissenters within the group. This means that nonvoluntary collective self-determination—that is, a collectively coerced decision about the cultural identity of a group—is morally suspect. The realization of human ends, including those that can be realized collectively, should in the last analysis be the result of voluntary interaction among free individuals. There are no nonconsensual goods for collectives, nations, or tribes (over and above the goods of persons who constitute the collectivity) that group leaders can permissibly enforce. My claim, then, is normative, not conceptual: the only morally valuable projects are (1) individual projects; and (2) voluntary group projects. Even if we can meaningfully speak of a group project, group leaders cannot permissibly impose that project on dissenters (with the usual caveats and exceptions). In my judgment, self-determination advocates have yet to meet this challenge. There is a reason, then, why *any and all* individual rights are more important than the people's collective right to a state of their own: simply, there is no such collective right. There is no such thing as the general will.

Voluntarism fails for a couple of reasons. First, as A. John Simmons and Michael Huemer have shown, no actual state or other collective political entity rests on consent.[20] Most people in any state, even the most benign, have not agreed to their particular institutions or the exercise of political coercion. So, if voluntarism is the basis of states' right to nonintervention, no real-world states in fact possess such rights. Given this, these rights cannot be invoked in defense of the nonequivalence thesis.

20. A. John Simmons, *Moral Principles and Political Obligation* (Princeton University Press, 1979); Michael Huemer, *The Problem of Political Authority* (Palgrave, 2012). See also the discussion in Lomasky and Tesón, *Justice at a Distance*, chapter 7.

Second, it is doubtful whether voluntarism really supports the nonequivalence view in the first place. For consider: What reason do voluntarists have to reject foreign intervention in aid of the revolutionaries trying to overthrow the government who no longer abides by the social contract? As Locke and many others have argued, an originally legitimate government that turns against its own citizens forfeits whatever standing it had (including its right to nonintervention). There is no reason to think that the subjects of any state have agreed to exclude foreign help when their government tramples their liberties. In other words: whenever a state forfeits its right against internal revolution, it *also* forfeits its right against external intervention. Voluntarism thus favors the equivalence thesis.

PROPORTIONALITY CONTROLS ALL WARS

The implication of this analysis for humanitarian intervention is that there is no *deontological* statist principle (a deontic principle of sovereignty) that can block the right to assist victims of tyranny. Persons have rights, and governments must respect them. Rights violations generate in principle the right to resist and its corollary, the right to request assistance from third parties.

If political self-determination is a specious reason to oppose intervention, we are left with the view with which we started: people have rights. Severe violation of those rights by the government justifies resistance, just as Locke said. There is no political obligation that is not reducible to our duties to respect the rights of others, and there are no collective rights that are not reducible to the rights and interests of individuals. But the intensity of the resistance against tyranny is constrained by the principles of proportionality. Roughly speaking, violent resistance against tyranny will not be justified if it causes excessive damage (in a sense I will explain in the next chapter). This means that, in practice, military intervention with all its destructive and unpredictable consequences will often be wrong. It also means that some humanitarian interventions will be right.

The same justification and constraints apply to foreign intervention to help subjects of a state to resist tyranny. Ending tyranny is a just cause for intervention, just as it is for revolution. But if the intervention, and not the revolution, will make things worse, then revolution will be permissible but not intervention. By the same token, a disproportionate revolution would be morally wrong, whereas a foreign intervention may conceivably comply with the strictures of proportionality. The difference is largely practical and empirical in nature. It is not a deep moral difference.

Consider now a regime that violates rights less severely. Think of a government that respects most rights but suppresses all criticism of the regime (something, perhaps, like present-day Malaysia). What recourse do citizens have in such a case? May they revolt against the regime to restore political dissent? In a way, the question is misleading. In my judgment, citizens in such a society have a right to use *proportionate means* to counter the violation of their right to political expression. This may rule out a *violent* revolution, but not other forms of revolt, such as peaceful demonstrations and additional forms of peaceful civic disobedience. Again: in this case, the reason citizens are not allowed to take arms against the regime is *not* that violation of political speech is not a sufficient just cause for action. Rather, the reason is that the action taken must not cause damage that is excessive in comparison to the realization of the cause.

One can state the general principle as follows: persons are entitled to counter violations of their rights, and this defensive action must be proportionate. This general principle covers revolution and intervention, as well as all other actions, coercive or not, that victims may undertake against those who violate their rights. A victim of a rights violation *always* has a just cause to react, but it does not follow that she has a just cause for *war*. Notice that the flip side is often overlooked: costless (which means nonviolent) revolutions are always permissible to counter rights violations. By the same token, costless interventions are permitted as well.

Someone can agree with the equivalence thesis yet maintain that, as a matter of fact, humanitarian interventions almost always cause more damage than revolutions. Since the equivalence thesis subjects both interventions and revolutions to the same proportionality standards, the practical result is that interventions will be impermissible in the great majority of cases while revolutions will not be. If so, the equivalence thesis will yield the same result as does the standard thesis (of differential permissibility status of each).

This is of course an empirical matter, but a cursory examination of history shows that humanitarian interventions do not necessarily cause more damage than revolutions. Counting casualties alone, consider the following numbers: [21]

Revolutions
American Civil War, 700,000 lives
Spanish Civil War, 500,000
Lebanese Civil War, 250,000
Chinese Civil War, about 8 million
Mexican Revolution, 1–2 million
Ethiopian Civil War, 500,000–1 million

21. These data are from https://en.wikipedia.org/wiki/List_of_wars_by_death_toll.

Biafra war, 1 million
Syrian Civil War, about 300,000–470,000

Humanitarian Interventions
Iraq war (period 2003–2007), about 1 million, more if we count to the present time (2016)
Tanzania's intervention in Uganda, 1,500 lives
France's intervention in Central Africa, bloodless
1989 intervention in Panama, 300[22]
2011 NATO's Intervention in Libya, 115

Of course, this survey is highly unscientific. I consign these numbers simply to dispel the romantic idea that revolutionaries are poorly armed idealistic peasants and students (of the kind we see in *Les Misérables*), while foreign armies are massive war machines that destroy everything in their path. The truth is that civil wars can be as destructive as interventions. And in many countries where a revolution is most needed, the political outcome will not be determine endogenously. In the Middle East, for example, civil unrest will often be a multiparty conflict, a proxy war between the Shia and Sunni powers, Iran and Saudi Arabia. More often, civil wars are particularly destructive because governments crush rebels who failed to secure foreign help on time. At any rate, the judgment must be comparative: Would intervention in this civil war have achieved a just result at a lower cost than an unaided revolution? The answer, of course, cannot be given in the abstract; in my judgment, there is no presumption one way or the other. If there is a presumption against violent humanitarian intervention, then there is also the same presumption against violent revolution.

22. See http://www.nytimes.com/1990/04/01/world/panama-and-us-strive-to-settle-on-death-toll.html.

4

Proportionality in Humanitarian Intervention

THE REQUIREMENT OF PROPORTIONALITY IN war is easy to formulate but hard to apply. The idea is deceptively simple: a war is justified only if the damage it causes is not excessive.[1] Proportionality is a necessary condition for the permissibility of all forms of defensive violence, and the analysis of the general case is applicable to humanitarian intervention as well. The main question concerns both the kinds and the amounts of goods and evils to be weighed in the proportionality calculus. Throughout, we must bear in mind that the intervener must have a just cause, and that the only just cause of an intervention is defending or restoring the moral rights of persons—that is, ending tyranny.[2] An intervention that does not aim at ending tyranny as a means or an end (and, perhaps, as a foreseen side

1. Hurka, "Proportionality in the Morality of War," 34.
2. As I explained in chapter 1, by tyranny I mean the deliberate violation of fundamental rights by rulers or other groups. *Tyranny* is a loaded word, and some will resist using it for cases of lesser rights violations. But I use it here purely for expository clarity. Again, this usage does not imply that all or most wars to end tyranny are justified. Such wars may be impermissible for failure to meet the other conditions listed in chapter 1.

effect) is impermissible unless, of course, it can be justified on some other ground, such as national self-defense.

I showed in chapter 1 that humanitarian intervention is a form of defensive violence. In its crudest form, the principle of proportionality says that the degree of a person's use of defensive force used must be proportional to the degree of force used by the aggressor. A nondeadly threat may only be countered with a nondeadly defense.[3] If humanitarian intervention is a form of defensive force, then, *mutatis mutandi*, the principles of proportionality in national self-defense must govern humanitarian intervention.

The concept of proportionality is obscure because the terms to be measured in the proportionality calculus are hard to quantify. As Michael Walzer noted, "there is no ready way to establish an independent or stable view of the values against which the destruction of war is to be measured."[4] A political leader who decides to intervene for humanitarian reasons, knowing that his decision will cause death and destruction, must weigh factors such as the value of saving lives and the impact of the intervention in the short and long terms. Such a task is often an exercise in comparing apples and oranges, especially given the difficulties inherent in such predictions. How does one measure, say, a thousand human lives against the long-term prospects of a society free of tyranny? What is the amount of sacrifice that the citizens of the liberated state and the citizens of the intervener can permissibly endure for the sake of the realization of the just cause? These and many

3. There is a vast literature on proportionality in the international law of self-defense. See Michael Newton and Larry May, *Proportionality in International Law* (Oxford University Press, 2014).
4. Walzer, *Just and Unjust Wars*, 129.

other hard questions are at the core of the permissibility and the justice of humanitarian intervention.

There are at least three different conceptions of proportionality in humanitarian intervention. The first sees proportionality as the requirement that the intervener use no more force than necessary. The second states that the intervention must be commensurate with the wrong to which it responds. And the third says that the damage inflicted in the intervention not be disproportionate in comparison to the pursued objective.[5] The requirement of necessity is embodied in proportionality. It states that the intervener should not resort to war if a less destructive means can correct the wrong. Using unnecessary force is using disproportionate force. The other two concepts of proportionality are the ones that do the work. One concerns the amount of force that matches the wrong, as it were, and it focuses on the permissible harm that the intervener may cause to the *wrongdoer*. The other one concerns the permissible harm that the intervener may cause to *others* in the pursuit of the just cause.

Following Jeff McMahan, I call these two conceptions *narrow* and *wide proportionality*. [6] A humanitarian intervention must satisfy both narrow and wide proportionality. The harm that the intervener causes the tyrant cannot exceed the degree of liability the tyrant has incurred for his crimes. And the harm the intervener causes to others must meet a much more stringent test of proportionality: when all things are considered, the deaths of non-culpable persons can only be justified as the lesser evil the intervener can cause, given the importance

5. See Dapo Akande and Thomas Liefländer, "Clarifying Necessity, Imminence, and Proportionality in the Law of Self-Defense," *American Journal of International Law* 107 (2013): 566.
6. See McMahan, *Killing in War*, 18–32.

of ending the rights violations. (Characteristically, pacifists claim that this second test can never be satisfied.) Before proceeding, I must mention another classification found in the literature: *ius ad bellum* proportionality and *ius in bello* proportionality.[7] The first one, also called *strategic proportionality*, measures the destruction of the whole war effort against the realization of the just cause. The second, also called *tactical proportionality*, measures the destruction of a particular act of war against the immediate military advantage gained. Unless otherwise stated, in this chapter I focus on strategic proportionality, and leave the study of tactical proportionality to the many excellent treatments in the literature.[8]

NARROW PROPORTIONALITY

Narrow proportionality concerns the harm that the intervener is allowed to inflict to the *wrongdoer*—in our case, the offending regime and those who take up arms to defend it. Surely there are limits to such harm. If the tyrant inflicts great harm on his victims, more intense defensive action is allowed than if that harm is small. The wrongdoer is morally responsible for the wrongs he inflicts, and therefore he becomes liable to suffer harm from the efforts by others to correct his wrongdoings.

7. U.S. legislation has codified the distinction. Department of Defense, *Law of War Manual*, 40, at http://archive.defense.gov/pubs/law-of-war-manual-june-2015.pdf.
8. For the legal approach, see Gary D. Solis, *The Law of Armed Conflict: International Humanitarian Law in War*, 2nd ed. (Cambridge University Press, 2016). For the philosophical approach, Michael Walzer and Jeff McMahan have been influential. Walzer, *Just and Unjust Wars*, 34–50 and Jeff McMahan, *Killing in War*, esp. chapters 1, 2, 3, and 5.

More precisely, an individual who culpably poses a threat of unjustified harm becomes liable to defensive force,[9] and by extension, he becomes vulnerable to humanitarian intervention. The justification of harm to these persons depends on the degree of liability they incur by virtue of their wrongdoing.

Here I must address an important issue in narrow proportionality, already mentioned in Chapter 2. Many writers agree that defensive violence is justified whether or not the aggressor is culpable.[10] They distinguish between desert and liability. The enemy becomes liable to attack only because he poses an unjustified threat to the victim, regardless of whether he deserves the upcoming defensive harm. If, for whatever reason, the attacker is not culpable of posing this unjustified threat, he is nonetheless liable to attack. But in humanitarian intervention I cannot imagine a case where the tyrant non-culpably oppresses people, so for purposes of this essay the distinction is largely irrelevant.[11] The tyrant who severely violates the rights of his subjects is a *culpable threat*. These rulers pose a wrongful threat to their subjects without permission, justification, or excuse.[12]

9. See McMahan, "Proportionality and Just Cause: Comment on Kamm," 433. McMahan calls these conditions agent-related conditions.
10. For a representative treatment, see Helen Frowe, "Equating Innocent Threats and Bystanders," *Journal of Applied Philosophy* 25 (2008): 277–290.
11. I am also agnostic on whether the right of victims and their rescuers forcibly to resist the tyrant is a claim-right, a liberty-right, an act-specific, agent-relative prerogative, or all of the above. See the discussion in Uwe Steinhoff, "Self-Defense as Claim Right, Liberty, and Act-Specific Agent-Relative Prerogative," *Law and Philosophy* 35 (2016): 193–209. For my purposes it suffices that such defensive force is morally permissible provided it complies with the proportionality strictures discussed in the text.
12. McMahan, *Killing in War*, 159.

The offending regime is perpetrating evil acts, and this fact affects the scope of narrow proportionality, because the tyrant deserves to be punished for his crimes. The proportionality restrictions are weaker in the case of culpable threats.[13] In a typical just intervention, he will be apprehended and brought to justice. That is why the logic of war in a humanitarian intervention includes a retributive element that is perhaps less obvious in other forms of war. (In self-defense, for example, it may not be obvious whether or not the presumed aggressor is really an aggressor. When a tyrant violates the subjects' rights to the extent that attracts humanitarian intervention, there is less moral ambiguity about his crimes.)

Subject to the limitation stated below, *in a humanitarian intervention the tyrant is liable to suffer the defensive harm necessary to get him to cease and desist of the rights violations.* In a humanitarian intervention, narrow proportionality collapses into necessity. This is the applicable standard considered separately from wide proportionality—that is, from considerations of collateral harm. If the only relevant harm in an intervention is the harm to which the tyrant is exposed, the test is one of necessity. The limitation is this: the tyrant and his entourage are subject to the necessity test without limits. *His soldiers* are also liable because they pose an objectively wrong mortal threat. They are fighting an unjust war. However, while in principle liable to be killed, they are subject to a test of *limited* necessity. This means that if applying the necessary force to end tyranny means killings a huge number of enemy soldiers, then the intervention may be disproportionate. This limitation may apply, perhaps, because the soldiers may have an excuse for fighting that their leader lacks.

13. Ibid.

The tyrant meets the agent-related conditions that make him liable to defensive harm. He poses an unjustified threat of deadly violence, and in addition, he does so culpably. This is the very definition of rights violation: the regime violates rights and uses force to back that violation. Now, the principle of narrow proportionality says that harm to the offending government must be proportionate to the seriousness of the rights violations perpetrated by that government. This means that the victims and their foreign allies may not inflict on the tyrant a harm that is greater or more serious than the one he causes.[14] I said that the tyrant is culpable. Suppose that on retributive grounds he deserves X harm. But if it is necessary to save his victims to inflict a harm Y, where Y > X, then that increased harm is justified. This is because the victims and their rescuers would be justified to defend themselves even if the attacker were *not* culpable. Because the tyrant is culpable, he may be harmed to the degree he deserves, plus the necessary amount of harm to neutralize his attack, even if the tyrant does not strictly deserve this additional harm.

Let us bring back the three categories of rights-violating regimes listed earlier: genocidal tyrants, ordinary tyrants, and kleptocrats. As I indicated, the genocidal tyrant and the ordinary tyrant are liable to whatever force is *necessary* to get them to desist. This is because in both cases the tyrant violates rights of physical integrity and freedom (by jailing dissidents and so on). In some cases, if the tyrant remains defiant and refuses to relent, he may even be killed. The test is one of necessity. By the same token, those who use force to end tyranny may not kill the tyrant if he surrenders. Critics of the killing of Gaddafi in the streets of Libya in 2011 claimed that the revolutionaries

14. See the discussion in McMahan, "Proportionality and Just Cause," 428–453.

could have captured him and brought him to justice instead.[15] Had Gaddafi remained armed and defiant in the presidential palace, the rebels and their foreign allies could have permissibly killed him in combat. The test of necessity means that necessary force to suppress rights violations is permissible, but also that any force *beyond* what is necessary is impermissible (but necessity may include punishment). The aim of the moral combatant must be to disable the tyrant and force him into submission, "but not do him (1) any mischief which does not tend materially to that end, nor (2) any mischief of which the conduciveness to the end is slight in comparison to the amount of mischief."[16]

But deadly force is not permissible against kleptocrats, even if they, too, back their theft with force. This is the result of applying the common principles that prohibit property owners to kill trespassers. This principle of proportionality is well established in the common law of self-defense. If a ruler unjustly expropriates her subjects' savings, as kleptocrats typically do, then it would seem that the use of deadly force against her would violate narrow proportionality. This is true even if the kleptocrat backs her theft with force. It makes sense to require, in these cases, that people resist the kleptocrat with nonviolent means.[17] For example, the reasonable defensive action by the victim of governmental theft might be to form political coalitions to defeat her in the next elections. And, for

15. For an account, see BBC News Africa: Muammar Gaddafi: How He Died, October 31, 2011, at http://www.bbc.com/news/world-africa-15390980.
16. Henry Sidgwick, *The Elements of Politics* (Macmillan, 1908), 268.
17. As I indicated, kleptocracy is just an instance of a regime that violates rights, short of tyranny. The same considerations of narrow proportionality apply to other lesser wrongs, such as religious discrimination or persecution, and the like.

outsiders, perhaps a justified action in defense of the victims of governmental depredation would be to exert economic or diplomatic pressure on the kleptocrat. Notice that this conclusion is based exclusively on the lesser gravity of the rights violations, and not on considerations of wide proportionality. These latter considerations are *added* to the previous ones. There are reasons of both narrow and wide proportionality, then, not to kill the kleptocrat: her theft does not make *her* liable to deadly violence, and the resort to violence is likely to produce effects out of proportion to whatever good that violence, by restoring property to the rightful owners, might bring. In the case of the kleptocrat, then, the necessity test is inadequate because the rights she violates are less fundamental than the rights that the tyrant violates.

The upshot, then, is that violence against the tyrant (genocidal or ordinary) is not precluded by narrow proportionality. Both kinds of tyrant are liable to the violence that is necessary to stop or correct the violations.[18] In contrast, violence against the kleptocrat is precluded by narrow proportionality. In both cases—tyranny and kleptocracy—considerations of wide proportionality should be added to the calculus. This has two important consequences. First, an intervention to end tyranny may be impermissible because it violates wide proportionality (it will predictably kill too many people or cause further intolerable consequences). And second, considerations of wide proportionality reinforce our intuition that it is wrong to use violence against the kleptocrat: not only does she violate only property rights, but also

18. I do not agree with Thomas Hurka that it is permissible to harm the tyrant in excess of what he deserves (the exception is the extra force needed to save the victims); Hurka, "Liability and Just Cause"; see the discussion in chapter 2.

such violence is likely to have terrible collateral consequences, such as deaths and perhaps the destruction of otherwise valuable institutions. This is why a revolution or an intervention in Cristina Kirchner's Argentina or Dilma Rousseff's Brazil (assuming, without showing, that these were kleptocratic regimes) would have been wrong.[19] On the other hand, a *proportionate* revolution or intervention in Argentina during the rule of the military junta in the 1970s would have been permissible. This may sound excessive to many, but I think that intuitive rejection assumes that the intervention would have violated wide proportionality. If so, the intervention in Argentina circa 1977 would have been impermissible *for that reason*, and not because the military rulers had not become liable for the terrible wrongs they had committed. The same is true of current ordinary tyrants, such as the North Korean regime.

A more difficult issue in narrow proportionality is the harm that the humanitarian intervener is allowed to inflict on the tyrant's *soldiers*—those who fight in the tyrant's defense. I think that such harm is allowed by application of the general

19. For the case of Argentina, See Roger Cohen, "Cry for Me, Argentina," *New York Times*, February 27, 2014, at http://www.nytimes.com/2014/02/28/opinion/28iht-edcohen28.html?_r=0; and "Argentina: A Century of Decline," *The Economist*, February 15, 2014, at http://www.economist.com/news/briefing/21596582-one-hundred-years-ago-argentina-was-future-what-went-wrong-century-decline. For Venezuela, see Moisés Naun, "An Economic Crisis of Historic Proportions," *New York Times*, January 8, 2013, at http://www.nytimes.com/roomfordebate/2013/01/03/venezuela-post-chavez/chavez-will-leave-behind-an-economic-crisis. For Brazil, see "What Has Gone Wrong in Brazil?", BBC, May 12, 2016, at http://www.bbc.com/news/world-latin-america-35810578.

principles that govern permissible killing in war.[20] This extends not only to those who actively commit the rights violations but also to members of the army who unjustly fight the invader. Here again, the harm to such persons cannot exceed the gravity and amount of harm that the tyrant inflicts on the population. The crimes of the North Korean government in principle provide a just cause for intervention. But if an army of 2 million persons is ready to die for Kim Jong-Un and the intervener predicts that those 2 million will die, then perhaps the intervener should not act. There is, then, a difference between the tyrant and his soldiers. The tyrant and his henchmen are liable to necessary force, including lethal force, to get them to desist. His followers are fighting an unjust war and they, too, are liable to being killed. But there is a point where the liability of the ordinary soldiers ends, as it were. Here, the principle of necessity gives way to the need to avoid a catastrophic carnage, even if *each of the victims* of that carnage is liable in principle to be killed in war.

WIDE PROPORTIONALITY: COLLATERAL AND SUPERVENING

Wide proportionality is about the harms to people who are not liable to be harmed. Wars almost always kill and maim bystanders and other persons. Since these persons have done nothing wrong, the justification of harm to them (usually called *collateral harm*) does not depend on their being liable, but on different considerations. As a first approximation, we can say that harm to non-liable persons depends not on culpability but on

20. See the excellent discussion by Fabre, *Cosmopolitan War*, 193–197.

whether inflicting such harm is the *lesser evil*, all things considered.[21] This aspect of war is of paramount importance. It is one thing to use deadly force against a villain. It is quite another to use force against the villain knowing that this will bring about serious harm to innocent persons.

Considerations of wide proportionality can be classified into two types that must be carefully distinguished. The first concerns the deaths of bystanders[22] and destruction of property that occur *in the course of* the humanitarian war. In its effort to end tyranny, the intervener brings about the deaths of persons other than the tyrant's soldiers. Let us call this *collateral proportionality*. The salient feature of collateral proportionality is that the bad effects are causally *close* to the war effort.

The second kind of wide proportionality concerns bad events that occur *after* the intervention but are causally connected to it. The removal of the tyrant may destabilize the region, and this in turn may give rise to renewed war and destruction. Or the intervention may encourage a third power elsewhere to wage an unjust or overly destructive war. Or the tyrant, as a result of the intervention, may be succeeded by someone worse. These kinds of effects enter into the calculus of *supervening proportionality*. The salient feature of supervening proportionality is that the bad effects are causally *remote* (in relative terms) from the war effort. While some criticized the Iraq war for the damage on the ground, most of the criticism focused on what happened after the war. It is commonly thought that the overthrow of Saddam Hussein caused vacuums of power that eventually made the situation

21. McMahan, "Proportionality and Just Cause," 435–436.
22. I use the word *bystander* to denote persons not liable to be killed. The issue is more complicated, however, as we shall see.

worse in the country and the region. I address these two categories in turn.

COLLATERAL PROPORTIONALITY: THE DOCTRINE OF DOUBLE EFFECT

As I indicated, the killing of bystanders is one of the most serious problems in any war and in humanitarian intervention in particular. Virtually any otherwise justified intervention will cause the deaths of bystanders caught in the crossfire. Pacifists have sometimes relied on the moral impermissibility of killing the innocent as a reason to claim that *all* wars are immoral.[23] Indeed, Bas van der Vossen's position in this volume is close to this form of pacifism. The idea is that since the intervener cannot know that his destructive action will be confined to morally permitted targets, then all war is impermissible. A just intervener faces the prospect that the pursuit of the just cause—the end of tyranny—will predictably bring about the deaths of innocent persons. If he could confine his military actions to purely military targets, then the just war would be surgical, as it were: no innocent people would die, and the only issues would be those of narrow proportionality, of what the tyrant deserves (or is liable for). The French intervention in Central Africa in 1979 is a case of this kind. French paratroopers removed the outrageous tyrant Jean-Bedel Bokassa from power. He was arrested and granted asylum in France. Because the intervention was surgical—that is, it did not raise wide proportionality concerns—the only issue was narrow proportionality, what harm were the paratroopers entitled to inflict on Bokassa.[24] The

23. In this sense, Robert Holmes, *On War and Morality* (Princeton: Princeton University Press, 1989).
24. See Tesón, *Humanitarian Intervention*, 238–242.

invaders didn't even have to fire against Bokassa's henchmen, as they quickly surrendered.

Alas, this is a rare case. Surgical humanitarian interventions are uncommon. In the overwhelming majority of cases, armed interventions bring about the deaths of many bystanders. Since these bystanders have not waived their right to life, those deaths are problematic. The intervener faces a dilemma: if he wants victory over the tyrant, he must regrettably cause the deaths of bystanders; if he decides to refrain from killing bystanders, he will lose the war and fail to realize the just cause of ending tyranny. One who upholds an absolute prohibition of killing the innocent must, it seems, reject the permissibility of all wars. She must be pacifist.

It is tempting to resolve this question by reflective equilibrium. If collateral deaths are absolutely prohibited, then we should indeed be pacifists. But pacifism clashes with our intuitions that some wars and revolutions were rightly fought. We *know* that some wars and revolutions are morally justified. Therefore, the absolute prohibition on killing innocents and its corollary, pacifism, must be rejected. This, however, is too easy: maybe the pacifist is right and those wars that we thought justified were objectionable. Perhaps we should revise our intuitions and become pacifists.[25]

Just-war writers have replied to this objection by invoking the Doctrine of the Double Effect (DDE). The DDE distinguishes between *intended* killings and *merely foreseen* killings. It is impermissible to deliberately target innocent persons. The just intervener who decides to aim the guns at bystanders in order to demoralize the tyrant and defeat him is guilty of murder, because he *wills* (directly intends) the bystanders'

25. I happen to endorse this reflective-equilibrium exercise. See the discussion later in this chapter.

deaths. Most people think that this immorality is not cured by the importance of ending tyranny. The DDE suggests that the just intervener who aims the guns at the enemy soldiers while merely *foreseeing* that this action will kill bystanders is on a different moral footing. The bystanders' deaths are not essential to his defeat of the tyrant; he would spare them if he could. Some authors say that in the first case the intervener treats the bystanders as *means* to his goal of ending tyranny, whereas in the second case the intervener does not treat them as means. This intent-based distinction between the two cases is central to the DDE.

It is beyond the scope of this essay to analyze the intricacies of the DDE.[26] For my purposes, a humanitarian intervention will satisfy collateral proportionality if it meets the following conditions (recall that the intervener must always have a just cause):

1. The intervener does not directly *intend* the deaths of bystanders. If he foresees those deaths he must try to minimize them, even at some cost to himself.

26. For a more extended discussion of the DDE, see Lomasky and Tesón, *Justice at a Distance*, chapter 8. F. M. Kamm has consistently taken the position that the requirement of not intending evil cannot be absolute. See F. M. Kamm, *Intricate Ethics: Rights, Responsibilities and Permissible Harm* (Oxford University Press, 2007), 21–24. But I think that for a variety of reasons, it makes sense to require it in humanitarian intervention. An intervener who *wills* evil will not be credible as a liberator of oppressed populations, and this in turn may trigger all kinds of bad consequences that may hamper the intervener's ability to secure a just peace. In this sense, see Lucas, "From *Jus ad Bellum* to *Jus ad Pacem*." I agree with Lucas that a humanitarian intervener should not directly intend evil. But I disagree with him that justice requires that the intervener directly intend the *just cause*.

2. The intervention is materially conducive to ending tyranny. This rule condemns cases where the violence of the war is *unnecessary* to the realization of the just cause.
3. The *urgency* to end tyranny must be *high enough* to compensate for the collateral harm. This condition recognizes that there are degrees of moral urgency, so that not all cases of tyranny will justify collateral harm. The more compelling the cause, the lower the threshold for collateral harm.

The reason why an intervention to end ordinary tyranny will normally be impermissible is *not* that somehow the ordinary tyrant has a right to rule, or that self-determination or sovereignty are bars to intervention. The reason is that in those cases the moral urgency to end ordinary tyranny will not satisfy the permissible threshold for collateral proportionality. In contrast, an intervention to end genocide will normally meet such a threshold, because the moral urgency to end genocide is very high.

The justice of the cause, in other words, informs all moral questions in war. The collateral killings, say, of fifty thousand civilians in order to gain a small military advantage over the tyrant is unjustified because it is *materially* disproportionate. But even a smaller number of collateral deaths may be unjustified if the cause of the war, while just, is not sufficiently compelling. The action will be *morally* disproportionate. There are degrees of moral urgency, and correspondingly there should be degrees of moral permissibility of bad things done in an agent's realization of a moral goal. The upshot is that in order to justify an otherwise impermissible bad effect it is not enough for the agent not to directly intend that bad effect. *Why* he causes the bad effect and how that effect measures (materially and morally) against the good one are decisive factors as well.

So far, I have discussed collateral proportionality as the problem of the deaths of bystanders in a justified humanitarian intervention. There is an additional problem concerning the just *distribution* of harm between combatants and bystanders.[27] Michael Walzer, for example, thinks that soldiers have an obligation to transfer some risk from noncombatants to themselves.[28] But in a humanitarian intervention, the concept of bystander is not granular enough to account for the moral differences among many groups in the population of the target state. There are many kinds of bystanders. Let us assume that most, or virtually all, were victims of tyranny. The intervention has aided them in their revolutionary efforts to end tyranny. They are the primary beneficiaries of the intervention. Therefore, they should bear some of its costs. The intervention is for their sake, and it seems unfair to expect that all or most of the cost of war should fall on the intervener's shoulders. This is an important matter, as shown by current debates surrounding the intervention to combat ISIS. The main reason why the United States insists that the ground troops should be local is that the battlefield is their region, their state, their future. They, the locals, should take up the fight against ISIS on the ground whenever possible. If that is not possible, then a full intervention by others may be called for. But it is reasonable to ask the beneficiaries of humanitarian intervention to bear some of its costs. If this is correct, then it makes a difference in the proportionality calculus.

27. See generally Jeff McMahan, "The Just Distribution of Harm between Combatants and Noncombatants," *Philosophy and Public Affairs* 38 (2010): 342–379.
28. Walzer, *Just and Unjust Wars*, 155–156.

SUPERVENING PROPORTIONALITY

The deaths of bystanders during combat are not the only unintended but foreseen consequences that count in the evaluation of humanitarian intervention. As I write these lines there is a broad consensus of opinion that the 2003 Iraq war was a "catastrophe," and "the worst foreign policy blunder in history."[29] Some voices at the time thought the war was indefensible on collateral proportionality grounds—that is, they thought that the harm that the war itself was causing on the ground was disproportionate. But most observers think that the events that took place *after* the overthrow of Saddam were so bad that they suffice to condemn the war, even if it might have had some initial plausibility. These bad effects include the renewed violence in Iraq, and in particular the emergence of the murderous group ISIS. Some even blame the Iraq war for having caused the civil war in Syria, with its terrible consequences of death and destruction. And the Syrian war, in turn, has triggered a refugee crisis, the consequences of which resonate throughout Europe.

BAD EFFECTS CAUSED BY WRONGDOING AGENTS

The first issue in supervening proportionality concerns the bad effects caused by the wrongdoing of agents *other* than the intervener. A humanitarian intervener, let us assume, justly ends tyranny in another state. The intervention has met the applicable conditions. It had a just cause; the harm to the tyrant was justified (say, he was apprehended and brought to justice); the

29. See http://nationalinterest.org/feature/mistakes-were-made-americas-five-biggest-foreign-policy-11160.

harm to the tyrant's army was proportionate; and the deaths of bystanders, while regrettable, have complied with the strictures of the Doctrine of Double Effect. The intervener temporarily occupies the territory, organizes free elections, and starts building the institutions that will secure liberty and prosperity. Unfortunately, a growing insurgency frustrates these plans. Insurgents start planting bombs against the occupier, the local forces, and the general population. These attacks eventually doom the prospects for stabilization, recovery, and democratization. Among other things, the increased casualties in the intervener trigger an increased opposition to the occupation back home. More and more voices urge the troops to come home and stop meddling in the society that had been liberated from the tyrant but is now increasingly plunging into chaos. Many who welcomed the intervention now express doubts, since the situation on the ground has taken a turn for the worse.

Now these bad effects—the new killing and destruction on the ground and the failure of the rebuilding effort—are directly caused not by the intervener but by the deliberate actions of persons who were on the wrong side of the war and are now on the wrong side of the just peace effort. Are these events sufficient to condemn the war? There are two extreme positions on this issue. One position assigns the entire responsibility for these bad supervening effects to the intervener. The argument is that these killings would not have happened if the intervention had not taken place. But this position faces a difficulty. *Ex hypothesi*, the intervention had a just cause. This means that the insurgents are now fighting an unjust war. Each one of their killings is murder, and their objective—to frustrate the liberation of their country—is likewise unjust. It doesn't matter, on this score, whether they fight to restore tyranny or to defend what they believe to be their national self-determination (say, they oppose both the tyrant and the occupier). They are engaged in an unjust war and their duty is to surrender. So, even if we agree that the insurgency would not have occurred without the intervention, we cannot blame the just intervener for these wrongs, any more than we can blame the policeman who rescues the victim of a villain for attacks subsequently conducted against him and the victim by new villains, attacks that would not have occurred if the policeman had not tried to save the victim.

We may be tempted, then, to adopt the opposite view: the intervener should not be blamed at all for the supervening insurgency. Notwithstanding the force of the objection in the preceding paragraph, this position is also questionable. If an intervener can predict that the intervention to end tyranny will cause more harm than good for that society, including harm deliberately caused by wrongdoers, then plausibly he should not act. The issue is extremely difficult, because the intervener's responsibility depends on the justification available at the moment he is deciding to act. Something as serious as a war imposes on the intervener an obligation to plan as accurately as he can, as I will explain.

The issue is intractable. Nevertheless, following Thomas Hurka, I tentatively suggest a middle position between the two extremes: the intervener has an *attenuated* responsibility for the supervening bad effects caused by others.[30] How attenuated it is will depend on how predictable the deadly insurgency was to an impartial observer at the time. If those effects were predictable, then the intervener is guilty of bad planning and must carry some responsibility for those effects. If, on the contrary, the insurgency was not predictable, then the intervener will have less responsibility for the aftermath. But it is important to make the right objective judgment in these cases: the insurgents are criminals who should have deposed arms, and

30. Hurka, "Proportionality in War," 47.

the intervener fights a just counter-terrorist war against them. This is consistent with saying that the intervener (now occupier) must take the appropriate degree of responsibility if his planning was faulty. If the intervener ignored evidence that bad actors would be enabled by the intervention and would inflict harm that would exceed the permissible harm of the war, then he must be held responsible for having started an impermissible war, even if it is true that those bad actors are themselves liable to harm. Those predictable bad effects count against the justice of the war, because the intervener was negligent in planning the war.

The conclusion in the previous paragraph is predicated on the assumption that the occupier was *unable* to quell the insurrection. If for whatever reason the intervener was *unwilling* to quell the insurrection, then his responsibility is simply the failure to adopt the necessary measures to secure a just peace. The right view in these cases is not that the intervener should not have acted to end tyranny in the first place. The right view is that the intervener should have acted to end tyranny (recall that I am assuming that all the conditions were met) *and* taken all the necessary and proportionate measures to secure the realization of the just cause, the liberation of the population. Failing to build a just peace is a failure to realize the just cause. In some cases, then, the right view is not that the intervener should have done less but, rather, that he should have done more.

EX ANTE OR *EX POST*? PLANNING A HUMANITARIAN INTERVENTION

In chapter 2 I briefly discussed right intent in humanitarian intervention. Here I am interested in the related question of the moral permissibility of a humanitarian intervention in the light of the expected consequences in both collateral and supervening proportionality. The commander invades and then bad things happen. If those bad effects, considered in themselves, are disproportionate, what is the moral status of *the decision to intervene* given that the commander was necessarily uncertain about those effects at the time he made the decision?

Consider a typology suggested by Derek Parfit. He lists three senses of wrongness:

> (1) wrong in the *fact-relative* sense, when this act would be wrong . . . if we knew all the relevant facts;
> (2) wrong in the belief-relative sense, when this act would be wrong . . . if our beliefs about the facts would be true; and
> (3) wrong in the evidence-based sense, when this act would be wrong . . . if we believed what the available evidence gives decisive reasons to believe, and these beliefs are true.[31]

As Jeff McMahan shows, these different senses of wrongness generate Hohfeldian senses of permissibility: (1) what is permissible in relation to the facts, (2) what is permissible in relation to what the agent believes, and (3) what is permissible in relation to the evidence available to the agent.[32]

Let us start with the fact-based standard. A commander decides to intervene to save civilians but the intervention goes

31. Derek Parfit, *On What Matters* (Oxford University Press, 2011), 1:150–151.
32. See Jeff McMahan, "Intention, Permissibility, Terrorism, and War," *Philosophical Perspectives* 23 (2009): 353. McMahan uses Parfit's typology for a different purpose—namely to respond to those who deny the relevance of intention to permissibility.

wrong. Good intentions and good evidence are insufficient to justify such unsuccessful intervention, because permissibility is determined only by what happened. Now, consider the belief-based standard. Say the intervener believes, without sufficient evidence, that the intervention will be successful. That is, he thinks that the intervention will end tyranny and the cost will be morally acceptable. However, he is culpably or negligently mistaken about that, and the intervention fails. Had he taken the trouble to responsibly collect intelligence, he could have known that the war would not succeed. Now, consider the evidence-based standard. The commander responsibly collects the best available evidence. This evidence gives him decisive reason to intervene; however, the intervention goes wrong. Was the intervention permissible at the time it was decreed?

After much thought and several changes of position on this hard question, I have concluded that the *permissibility of an action* depends on the objective rightness of the action, while the *blameworthiness of the agent* depends on his motives and on what he could responsibly know before deciding to act. That means adopting Parfit's number 1 sense of permissibility, the fact-based standard. This position rests on a distinction between the moral status of an event and the moral status of the agent who brings about the event. A humanitarian intervention will be permissible just in case it complies with all the conditions already specified. Imagine that a genocide is afoot in state A. The leader of neighboring state B, without bothering to collect intelligence about the consequences of war, invades and stops the genocide with minimal casualties. He would have acted permissibly, even though he would have acted irresponsibly.

The alternatives are less attractive. Belief-based permissibility cannot be the standard, because what intervener believes may be entirely different from what will happen. His belief that the intervention will be just and proportionate has to be borne by the facts. The remaining standard (a version of which

I previously endorsed[33]) is Parfit's number 3, the evidence-based standard. On this view, permissibility depends exclusively on the responsibly-collected evidence that the intervener has. If that evidence indicates that the intervention will succeed, then he may act. I think this view fails to distinguish between rightness of an action and negligence or culpability of the agent. Here I follow John Stuart Mill's position, discussed in Chapter 2 with respect to right intent. Just as an act can be objectively right even if the agent has bad motives, so can an act be objectively right even if the agent is negligent in collecting the available evidence of the consequences of his decision. Suppose I see a person in distress. All the evidence indicates that trying to rescue her will mean the death of five more people. However, I am foolhardy and rescue the person. Luckily, no one dies. I would say two things: First, the action was objectively right and therefore permissible (all right actions are permissible); second, I should be blamed for my reckless behavior. Imagine that Winston Churchill in 1939 was negligent in his estimation of the consequences of declaring war to Germany, in light of the evidence he had. If that war turned out to be successful (as most people think it did) then Churchill's decision was permissible, even though we should judge him a reckless leader.

The diligence of the agent speaks to his blameworthiness, not to permissibility. When the commander acts on diligently collected intelligence, there are two possibilities that give rise to two corresponding moral reactions to an intervention:

1. The commander acted on his beliefs regarding responsibly collected evidence, that evidence gave decisive

33. See my post The Syrian Bombings and Just War Theory, Part II, at http://bleedingheartlibertarians.com/2017/04/syrian-bombings-just-war-theory-part-ii/.

reasons to intervene, and those beliefs were true. The intervention was successful. The commander acted both non-culpably and permissibly.

2. The commander acted on his beliefs regarding responsibly collected evidence, that evidence gave decisive reasons to intervene, but those beliefs were false. The intervention was unsuccessful. The commander acted *impermissibly* (because right action based on evidence requires the beliefs about that evidence to be true), but *non-culpably* (because he couldn't possibly have known that the evidence was false).

I propose, then, to distinguish three concepts: the *objective wrongness or rightness of an event*, the *permissibility* of the decision to bring about the event, and the *blameworthiness* of the agent in bringing about the event. An act is objectively right or wrong if the facts make it so. All acts that are objectively right are permissible. In addition, the agent who acts responsibly is praiseworthy, whereas the agent that acts irresponsibly is blameworthy.

Say a commander launched an intervention that was indicated in the light of the available evidence. His beliefs were false, however, and the war turned out badly. The intervention was wrong and therefore impermissible (since his beliefs about the evidence were false) but the agent's decision was excusable. We keep both our concerns with outcomes and with justified blame. We can say that the act of intervention was wrong but that the decision seemed (but was not) justified at the time and the agent was not culpable for having performed the wrong act.

The standard I propose yields the combinations shown in table 4.1.

A humanitarian intervention will be permissible only in cases 1 and 3, that is, every time the intervention is successful.

My position does not entail a broad license for commanders to launch interventions, nor does it diminish the importance

Table 4.1

KNOWLEDGE AND PERMISSIBILITY

1. Diligence + success	Objectively right	Permissible	Not blameworthy
2. Diligence + failure	Objectively wrong	Impermissible	Not blameworthy
3. Negligence + success	Objectively right	Permissible	Blameworthy
4. Negligence + failure	Objectively wrong	Impermissible	Blameworthy

of conscientious planning that we should demand of our leaders. Commanders who plan diligently have a much greater probability of success than those who do not. For that reason, people should demand that their leaders plan properly, and should elect leaders who understand the terrible destruction of war. But outcomes are crucial, and sometimes irresponsible leaders get away with having ultimately done the right thing. The idea is that we want to maximize the chances of objectively right outcomes. The reason we object to a negligent commander's launching a war is that we think the war will be probably unsuccessful. But if we could know that the war will be successful, we would grant permission to act.

Bas van der Vossen thinks my view is incoherent because, relying as it does on the fact-based standard, it fails as a guide for practical action. I concede that there is something unsatisfactory in the idea that a successful intervention was permissible despite the fact that the commander couldn't have known that it would be successful. However, it is not strictly true that the fact-based standard gives no guide for action. A diligent commander is much more likely to launch successful (and thus permissible) interventions.

Now let's assume for the sake of argument that Van der Vossen is right and that the fact-based standard of permissibility is incoherent or otherwise mistaken. I think that Van der Vossen's own proposal fails, for three reasons. Recall that he makes two claims: (1) permissibilty must be judged solely by the Ex Ante evidence standard, so outcomes do not figure in the judgment of permissibiliy; and (2) a commander's decision to intervene can (virtually) never satisfy a morally acceptable standard of probability of success. One can accept his first claim without accepting his second claim. I have reluctantly rejected the first claim, but I accept it here for the sake of argument.

First, I am not convinced that the *ex ante* calculation of risk always yields *inaction* as the morally recommended choice. Here's Van der Vossen:

> These operations are fraught with risk, unpredictability, and uncertainty. We never know for sure whether they will succeed, what unintended consequences they will have, whether our means will turn out to be proportionate, whether some other, less violent means were available, or what the consequences would be of the available alternatives. If *ex post* theories fail whenever a situation involves uncertainty, they fail whenever a situation involves intervention.

This observation, however, cannot mean that the recommended action is *not to intervene*. I cannot see why uncertainty about proportionality, unintended consequences, and the like yields inaction as the morally recommended choice. In Van der Vossen's own illustration, the evil dictator is about to kill a hundred villagers. I am not clear whether Van der Vossen thinks that the best choice is to do nothing because the dictator's imminent genocide is uncertain as well. If so, maybe the commander should not act. But if the planned mass murder is certain, then, on Van der Vossen's own description of the alternatives, inaction does not appear as the morally recommended course of action.

Second, I do not agree that the standard of permissibility applies to interventions in the aggregate. Van der Vossen writes:

> Since the point at which interventions become permissible is sensitive to the expected number and quality of outcomes, given the probability required by the success condition, there can be no single value or probability at which interventions are permissible.[34]

But why can't we assign evidence-based probabilities to *each* outcome, considered individually? Why can't a commander reasonably calculate that, given the available evidence, saving 500,000 Tutsis from genocide in Rwanda will cause the deaths of 250 innocent persons and 10 million dollars in damage, taking into account also that the country can be subsequently pacified under United Nations supervision and the like? I do not think that the right standard should be established by the probabilities of success of a future, undefined *series* of interventions that the commander may be called upon to undertake. The commander must evaluate each situation individually, and calculation of risk will be highly contextual. There is no such thing as "humanitarian interventions in general should or should not be permissible."

My third and final reply appeals to reflective equilibrium. If Van der Vossen is right, he should be a pacifist. No war, international or civil, is ever justified. The uncertainties that worry him are present in all wars and revolutions;

34. Van de Vossen, this volume, Chapter 9, p. 11–12.

it is not possible to invoke them *only* to question humanitarian interventions. The Allied decision to fight Germany in 1939 was impermissible, as was the United States declaration of war against Japan in 1941. Abraham Lincoln should not have fought the Civil War, colonized people should not have fought colonial domination, and groups facing tyrants today should similarly refrain from armed resistance regardless of how just their cause may be. On this view, just cause is virtually irrelevant, as it is precisely in those cases when the objection here discussed operates. Worse: on Van der Vossen's view, wars in self-defense are unjustified as well, because the uncertainties about success are equally present there. Victims of aggression must submit to the invaders. To me, this is an unacceptable consequence of the position here discussed. It indicts all wars, past, present, and future, and is implausible for that reason.

The real world lends some support to the standard I propose. A commander that non-culpably launches a disastrous war will be criticized by public opinion, but not as much as if he was demonstrably negligent. Political leaders have privileges of power that carry with them responsibilities for harm done, even for harm that could not have been predicted by them or anyone else. If a commander starts a humanitarian intervention on responsible evidence that the intervention will achieve the just cause—will alleviate human suffering and save the lives of many—and a catastrophe occurs, then that commander will be judged harshly (and unfairly, as I have suggested) by history. The job of commander-in-chief comes with the warning that anyone who gets the job will be judged by results, even if the acts that produced those results were excusable on the available evidence. That a catastrophe occurs is a misfortune beyond the agent's control, but his place in history will be nonetheless tainted. This strongly suggests that outcomes are controlling.[35]

There is another consideration that attracts me to the fact-based view of permissibility. In life we take risks all the time, whether us or others incur the costs of our mistakes. Good statesmanship is, in part, about taking risks when the evidence is insufficient or blurry. That is why we praise Winston Churchill for his decision to go to war. This idea connects with another point that I made earlier. The risks a commander takes should be decisively influenced by the importance of the just cause. This means that the more important the cause, the lower the threshold for collateral and supervening bad consequences. A good leader has more often than not the right intuitions on how to weigh the consequences of her decision given the moral urgency of the goal she seeks. That is why I cannot accept the view that inaction in the face of evil is almost invariably the right course of conduct.

Finally, the view I develop here treats the hopes for the success of the humanitarian intervention as included in the concept of proportionality.[36] The idea is that the success of the intervention is the realization of the just cause. The

35. Why do we admire, in the movies, commandos who launch operations to stop evil villains against all odds? If we really thought that outcomes were irrelevant we should criticize the commandos, since they decided to act when the evidence cautioned restraint. Yet, we all cheer when they succeed, and we admire their courage to take such risks for a good cause. This is because we feel the good outcome made their decision permissible, retroactively.
36. I thus agree on this point with McMahan, Hurka, Coates, and Altman and Wellman, cited by Van der Vossen in chapter 9, note 9.

just cause is saving persons from attack by their government. When the intervention saves those lives, it produces a good: the good of lives saved. Because military interventions very often cause bad results—the maiming and killing of innocents and destruction of property—proportionality dictates that the good of saving lives should outweigh these other bad results. And the permissibility of the intervention will be judged by whether the realization of the just cause outweighs the bad results. This judgment includes a wide range of *ius in bello* considerations—in particular, the obligation of the intervener to minimize casualties and destruction.

5

Further Issues in Humanitarian Intervention

IN THIS CHAPTER I ADDRESS SOME LOOSE ENDS. They are: the intervener-failure objection; the question of right authority; the question of whose consent, if any, is required for intervention; and the problem of institutional design.

THE INTERVENER-FAILURE OBJECTION

Some authors object to humanitarian intervention, not as a matter of principle, but entirely on the ground that commanders invariably fail to realize the humanitarian goal. Bas van der Vossen, for example, grounds his case against humanitarian intervention almost exclusively on the fact that these interventions fail to satisfy the requirement of high probability of success.[1] In support of this view he cites a number of failed interventions, notably Somalia, Iraq, and Libya. These interventions have failed, he thinks, because the intervener is in a bad position to realize the humanitarian goal. State leaders who intervene have, at best, their own national interests

1. See Bas van der Vossen, this volume, esp. chapters 6, 7, and 9.

and, at worst, their own selfish personal (electoral) interests at heart. They have no incentives to embrace the interests of those who are supposed to be the beneficiaries of the intervention. For this reason, leaders who decide to go to war invariably inflate the gains of the intervention and understate or conceal its costs.[2] In addition to perverse incentives, interveners face epistemic obstacles. They do not know enough about the culture and politics of the state they occupy, and as a result they choose poor means to realize the humanitarian goals. Finally, any military operation of this kind requires popular support at home. Should that support falter, the intervener will withdraw prematurely, with the consequence that the humanitarian goal, the just cause, will remain unrealized. There is, in short, a serious public-choice problem inherent in humanitarian intervention—a case of serious government failure. I call it the intervener-failure problem.

One possible answer is to deny such pessimism, at least in this general form. To varying degrees, in the better democracies sometimes leaders are accountable to civic groups that can hold the government to account, particularly in the sense of forcing them to consider the interests of the beneficiaries.

But let us concede that these pathologies occur in any humanitarian intervention. The problem with the argument is that if these public-choice worries invalidate humanitarian intervention they invalidate *any* war and *any* revolution. If one is persuaded by the public-choice concerns one must be a

2. For an examination of the cost issue, see Joseph E. Stiglitz and Linda J. Bilmes, "Estimating the Costs of War: Methodological Issues, with Applications to Iraq and Afghanistan," in *The Oxford Handbook of the Economics of Peace and Conflict*, ed. Michelle R. Garfinkel and Stergios Skarpedas (Oxford University Press, 2010), 275–317.

pacifist, as these concerns are present in any otherwise justified war or revolution. The point here is not that the democratic citizenry is as likely to support a humanitarian war as it is to support a defensive war. Surely this is false: citizens are more prone to support the latter. The point is that public-choice concerns affect both. A manipulative leader can deceive the public in either kind of war, and it is precisely because the public is patriotic that unscrupulous leaders are able to sustain wars for long periods.

Take revolution. One need not be a conservative to heed Edmund Burke's warnings against the destructiveness of well-meaning revolutionaries.[3] Burke's worries about the ills of the French Revolution have been augmented tenfold by the findings of the public-choice literature. Revolutionaries have their own personal interest at heart. The evidence we have is that, with few exceptions, they seek power and wealth above all. One has only to look at the colonial wars, where the symbolic allure of liberating the nation was often a cover for greed and power by revolutionary leaders turned presidents-for-life.[4] Even revolutions that had good outcomes in the long term led to widespread miseries.

Nor is a war in self-defense, as I indicated, exempt from these public-choice worries. People fight to defend their lives and property against the aggressor, but states are states whether they defend themselves or defend others, and I do not see any reason why perverse incentives and most of the other infirmities just mentioned should be absent in a defensive war. For example, a defensive war may be disproportionate and cause

3. Edmund Burke, *Reflections on the Revolution in France* (SMK Books, [1790] 2012).
4. For a gripping account, see George B. N. Ayittey, *Africa Betrayed* (Palgrave Macmillan, 1994).

terrible harm to innocent persons, who will then pay the price for the aggressive adventurism of their own government.

In short, if one opposes humanitarian intervention for government-failure reasons, one has to oppose all wars and revolutions. All organized military operations present an agency problem. Whether it is a fledgling prime minister seeking reelection, a revolutionary leader hungry for power, or a self-determination entrepreneur agitating the masses against real or imaginary foreign oppressors, a perfect or even a minimally satisfactory alignment of incentives will not occur. Therefore, if government failure is a reason to oppose humanitarian intervention, it is also a reason to be a pacifist. Since I do not think most authors who oppose humanitarian intervention, or even any war for this reason, are ready to condemn all revolutions, the objection fails (unless they are ready to turn the other cheek to evil in all situations). Because these authors do not carry the objection to its pacifist logical conclusion, I think they implicitly endorse a sovereignty-based argument of the kind defended by Walzer and others. That allows them to say, again, that self-determination is so important that revolutions, but not interventions, can be legitimate even though these public-choice worries obtain there as well. But if so, the reason to oppose humanitarian intervention is self-determination, not intervener failure.

The objectors make an important point. But the right answer is not to ban attempts at rescuing victims of these atrocities, but to add the agency costs of interventions to the calculus of proportionality.

RIGHT AUTHORITY

Most international law scholars believe that humanitarian intervention is legitimate only if authorized by the UN

Security Council.[5] Unauthorized interventions by states are, they think, illegitimate. There are several reasons for this requirement. One is that the Security Council is supposedly the legitimate authority of the international community. Just as we should summon the police to respond to crime and not become domestic vigilantes, so we should summon the Security Council to authorize military force and not become international vigilantes.

This argument is dubious, for a couple of reasons. First, if an intervention is otherwise permissible, it is hard to see why the failure of the UN Security Council to authorize it would render it impermissible, given the values at stake. And conversely, if an intervention is impermissible, it is even harder to see why the UN Security Council's authorization would render it permissible. For example, if the bad outcome of the 2011 intervention in Libya makes that action impermissible, the fact that it was authorized by the UN Security Council does not change that evaluation.[6]

Second, the world is not a state, and the usual arguments that justify the monopoly of force by the state are almost entirely inapplicable to the semi-anarchical international arena populated by sovereign states. Each sovereign state establishes the monopoly of force in its territory. States have police, courts, and armies, and individual violence is narrowly confined. Sometimes those arrangements fail and states plunge into anarchy, and often the monopoly of force plunges into

5. For a fair description of (what most lawyers believe is) international law, see Ratner, *The Thin Justice of International Law.* Bas van der Vossen also thinks that this requirement may make sense; see his illuminating Giants metaphor, chapter 7, this volume.

6. See Alan J. Kuperman, "Obama's Libya Debacle," Foreign Affairs (March–April 2015), at https://www.foreignaffairs.com/articles/libya/obamas-libya-debacle.

oppression. But the ideal role of the state is to protect citizens against one another and to tame violence under the rule of law, accepted procedures, and constitutional guarantees. The modern state, when it works well, outlaws interpersonal violence by monopolizing force. It prohibits both opportunistic plundering and private retribution, while providing means of redress to those wronged by the aggressive behavior of others.

But the central feature of the international society is precisely that it does not establish a global monopoly of force on any institution. At its inception, the United Nations Charter was meant to create a system of collective security, but its weaknesses are well known.[7] Suffice it to say that international law does not provide a satisfactory remedy for wronged nations, groups, or individuals. To be sure, the international society has made great strides in developing *norms* to curb war. International law has codified in detail the laws that govern combat (*jus in bello*).[8] This is an area of international law that makes a difference in actual conflicts, as the degrees of compliance and enforcement are reasonably high. The *jus ad bellum*, however, is a different story. The United Nations Charter reads *as if* it prohibits most interstate violence and *as if* it empowers the Security Council to respond to aggression on behalf of the international community. Because of this discursive consensus, if today a state invades another for no good reason, observers are more ready to condemn the invasion than they would have been only seventy years ago.

Yet the mechanisms available to actually restrain war are woefully weak. They are certainly much weaker than the

7. For a traditional, sympathetic discussion of the UN system on use of force, see Thomas M. Franck, *Recourse to Force* (Oxford University Press, 2003). For a more critical view, see Tesón, *Humanitarian Intervention*.
8. In the Geneva Conventions.

corresponding mechanisms within a functioning state. Before the UN Security Council authorizes the use of force against a genocidal regime *and* a member is willing and able to act on that authorization, many improbable things have to happen. For one thing, the five permanent members of the Security Council have the right to veto. This means that the Security Council will not authorize force against permanent members or their allies. But more important, while domestic law *obligates* the government to act in response to private violence, international law merely *authorizes* governments to respond to genocide or other criminal behavior. Assuming, against the facts, that the Security Council acts expeditiously in every case of genocide and authorizes the use of force to address those actions, still governments are not *bound* to react. To begin with, only a powerful state (as I write, usually but not always the United States) can act. Unless weaker states can forge a sufficiently powerful alliance (another implausible scenario), they will free-ride on the powerful state. But the powerful state will not act unless its government believes its national interest to be at stake (this, again, is a rosy scenario: politicians will go to war if *their* own interests are thereby advanced, especially their electoral interests). States in a position to respond to genocide can simply decline the invitation.

Because the UN Security Council is not a world government that can effectively protect states and persons against wrongs, states continue to rely on self-help—and war, of course, is the extreme form of self-help. If state A plans to invade state B, state B cannot call the police, for the good reason that (most of the time) there are no police. And if an attacked state wants redress for the destruction caused by the aggressor, it cannot sue the aggressor, for the good reason that (most of the time) there are no international courts of compulsive jurisdiction. If you refuse to pay me the thousand dollars you owe me and I punch you in the nose to "enforce" my rights, my action is reprehensible because I have legal avenues to seek redress (sue you in court and so on). But if a neighboring nation refuses to honor a treaty, most of the time the aggrieved party cannot seek judicial redress. The wronged state is on its own. To be sure, international law prohibits wars to enforce run-of-the-mill treaties, but certainly wronged states can and do resort to various forms of self-help in the form of retaliatory countermeasures short of war. The point here is that self-help is omnipresent and, as a result, given the sobering fact that states and others will continue to commit crimes such as aggression and genocide, war and humanitarian intervention are here to stay, regrettably, for the foreseeable future.

A brief examination of the recent history and the institutional deficiencies of the Security Council reinforces these considerations.

The consensus for the exclusive authority of the Security Council coalesced in the 1990s, a time of optimism after the fall of the Soviet Union when the United States presided over an explosion of global prosperity and freedom, a time of economic and political globalization when, most of the time, international interactions really appeared (perhaps for the first time in a long time) as positive-sum games. There was a general sense then that the stark logic of the cold war had given way to endless possibilities of cooperative behavior for the spread of respect for human rights and democratic rule, and for the expansion of free markets and their attendant prosperity. An important feature of this era was the renewed Security Council. As is known, the Security Council authorized the use of force to address humanitarian crises on various occasions. This led a number of observers, myself included,[9] to express optimism

9. In Fernando R. Tesón, "Collective Humanitarian Intervention," *Michigan Journal of International Law* 17 (1996): 323.

about the use of the United Nations, and the Security Council in particular, as an instrument for the advancement of human dignity and freedom in the world. There was a growing sense that the international community agreed on the values that it should uphold and that the mechanisms in place were an effective tool to promote those values, if necessary, by force. Only rogue states and other recalcitrant dictators remained at the margins. There was a lessened sense of threat and a reinforced belief in the international community not just as a community of minimal interest but also as a community of values.

These hopes were shattered by the attacks of September 11, 2001, and the subsequent events in Iraq, up to the recent surge of ISIS and the terrorist attacks in Europe and elsewhere, and a new and menacing Russia. The ominous sense is that the world has returned, with new actors and new threats, to the zero-sum logic of the cold war. The radical revolt against freedom and reason mounted by terrorism cannot be confronted with the tools developed during the 1990s. However, looking back, I think that with respect to humanitarian intervention, we unduly romanticized the UN Security Council. To be sure, the experience of the nineties was preferable to the deadlock of the cold war. Most important, the Security Council's practice laid to rest the doubts that many had about its legal power to authorize humanitarian intervention under Chapter VII of the UN Charter. Yet, a dispassionate assessment of the practice of the Security Council during that period discloses a number of serious dysfunctions and problems. I have discussed these problems elsewhere, and they include: (1) the Council members often do not have the right incentives; (2) UN Security Council approval does not guarantee success, as the Somalia, Rwanda, and Libya precedents show; (3) the UN Security Council is often plagued by inertia; and (4) The UN Security Council membership suffers from a noticeable moral deficit, as permanent and nonpermanent members alike are themselves oppressive regimes.[10]

Having said this, Bas van der Vossen has a point when he reminds us that "[i]f authorized interveners are generally more likely to operate in morally acceptable ways, if the need to secure international authorization limits the potential for attacks with problematic objectives or using problematic means, then such a rule might be acceptable after all. It might be part of a set of rules that helps avoid interveners becoming threats and make them a source of protection."[11] It may be harder for authorized interveners to abuse, for all kinds of practical and reputational reasons; and therefore perhaps a rule requiring authorization makes eminent sense. This does not mean, however, that the present system, which requires authorization by the Security Council, is the best.

Designing an optimal rule for institutional approval and monitoring of humanitarian intervention would far exceed the scope of this volume. But any proposal should focus on the disinterestedness and transparency of the authorizing body. For the reasons stated, that body cannot be the Security Council as presently constituted. The ideal authorizing body should be a Humanitarian Intervention Council (HIC), an alliance of liberal democracies ranked at the highest level of respect for human rights (for example, states that are lower than 2 in the Freedom House rankings). Governments that contemplate intervention should make an evidence-based case to the HIC, and agree to submit themselves to an evaluation by the HIC after the intervention has taken place.[12] Any institutional

10. See Fernando R. Tesón, "The Vexing Problem of Authority in Humanitarian Intervention: A Proposal," *Wisconsin Journal of International Law* 24 (2006): 762.
11. Van der Vossen, chapter 7, this volume.
12. Here I adapt Allen Buchanan and Robert O. Keohane's proposal for regulating preventive force; Allen Buchanan and Robert

process, therefore, should include *ex ante* approval and *ex post* evaluation. It is also important to codify the principles of just intervention. While I think that the ICISS Report is a valuable starting point, it is, after all, a document written by and for diplomats, and for that reason it is still both too deferential to sovereignty and too unrefined conceptually to be the applicable code. A new text, incorporating state-of-the-art just-war scholarship, should form the basis of such code.

WHOSE CONSENT, IF ANY, IS REQUIRED FOR INTERVENTION?

In previous work I argued that a legitimate intervention requires the consent of the *victims*.[13] Allen Buchanan has criticized this position.[14] He points out that the expression of such consent is almost always distorted and unreliable, and that the intervener would have to make up its own mind about what

O. Keohane, "The Preventive Use of Force: A Cosmopolitan Institutional Proposal," *Ethics and International Affairs* 18 (2004): 1–22. I have several differences with these authors, however. Unlike them, I would not use the Security Council in this process, except perhaps for the possibility of imposing sanctions to interveners who violated the strictures of just intervention. And unlike them, I would not require that the HIC be composed of a "diverse groups of states" but by genuine liberal democracies demonstrably committed to freedom.

13. See Tesón, *Humanitarian Intervention*, and "Ending Tyranny in Iraq."
14. Buchanan, "Self-Determination, Revolution, and Intervention," 448–449. Surprisingly, the criticisms turn Buchanan's position into a *more* interventionist stance than my own. I was concerned in part with common charges of paternalism leveled against the humanitarian intervention doctrine.

the beneficiaries really want. He also thinks that consent would have to include the identity of the intervener as well, a point made also by McMahan.[15] These criticisms are well taken, subject to the appropriate filling with reliable empirical data (thus, McMahan's suggestion that the Iraqis did not want the *United States* to liberate them from Saddam seems to me unproven).

However, whether or not requiring the victims' consent is a good idea, my main point remains untouched: consent is *not* required from anyone else. As against Walzer and others, I deny that considerations of self-determination authorize a majority of the population, or bystanders, or collaborators, to *veto* a humanitarian intervention (to require the consent of the tyrant is too grotesque to be considered seriously).

WHICH RULE IS BEST?

So far I have examined the ethics of humanitarian intervention and have concluded that it is sometimes permissible. But this does not resolve the question of which is the best general *rule* to adopt, in particular for international law. Someone may agree that humanitarian intervention is sometimes permissible but that the international community is better off by adopting a blanket prohibition. Bas van der Vossen, for example, offers a teleological argument to reject humanitarian intervention. A teleological argument "can support rules that prohibit acts that would be beneficial in a particular instance because they are inconsistent with a (teleologically justified) rule that is beneficial in general."[16] Given that he independently believes that the *ex ante* risks of failure (either of failing to achieve success

15. McMahan, "Just Cause for War."
16. Van der Vossen, chapter 9, this volume.

or failing applicable proportionality tests) outweigh the risks of success,[17] we are better off, he thinks, with a blanket prohibition of humanitarian intervention. This means (unfortunately) forgoing interventions that would have been successful in particular cases.

As I see it, this argument is a variation of rule-consequentialism, and fails for the same reasons that rule-consequentialism fails. Let us assume that a successful result is the one that meets the conditions of a just war specified in the Introduction. This result is measured in terms of the vindication of human life, human rights, and similar values. It is a humanitarian value (H). Van der Vossen's teleological argument says that, in a world where tyrants assault H, having the nonintervention (NI) *rule* is justified even if there are some particular cases where intervention (I) would promote H.[18] This is because adhering to NI in the long run will promote H better than a more permissive rule (I), given the perils of intervention. We are better off, in terms of H, not allowing anyone to act.

Moral theorists, however, have shown that rule-consequentialism suffers from serious problems—problems that Van der Vossen's teleological argument inherits. I will mention two.

The first is that rule-consequentialism is either irrational or collapses into act-consequentialism. Let us recast Van der Vossen's thesis as follows: NI, the nonintervention rule, promotes H in the long run better than the rule that sometimes intervention is permissible. It maximizes H. Now, suppose

17. Van der Vossen correctly observes that the notion of success is moralized and not just defined in terms of utility maximization. This point is made in Lomasky and Tesón, *Justice at a Distance*, chapter 8.

18. Thus the title of his essay in this volume, "Humanitarian Noninterventionism."

that a commander who contemplates stopping a genocide in a neighboring country correctly predicts that an intervention (that is, *departure* from NI) will maximize H when all the consequences of the act are computed—not only the rights violations that will occur but also the negative consequence of the erosion of the NI rule. A decision of the commander to refrain from the act out of respect of the NI rule is arguably irrational, because the rationale for NI was the maximization of H in the first place.[19] Put differently, Van der Vossen's NI bans humanitarian intervention. The ban is justified, he tells us, because it maximizes H. But suppose the U.S. government is considering, in April of 1994, whether or not to intervene to stop the impending Rwandan genocide. The intervention, let us assume, is banned under NI. The U.S. government knows, however, that the intervention clearly will maximize H. It seems irrational, even self-contradictory, not to intervene to stop genocide in Rwanda on the grounds that there is a rule justified by its H-maximizing features. This is why moral theorists have said that rule-consequentialism must collapse into act-consequentialism. If the rationale for NI is that it maximizes H, then it must be true that the morally right act is the one that maximizes H, even if it is a departure from the rule. If the departure is codified as an exception to the rule, then the rule-consequentialist rationale collapses into act-consequentialism. If, on the contrary, the rule-consequentialist insists that the rule must be followed even if

19. A clear treatment can be found in John Martin Fischer and Mark Ravizza, *Ethics: Problems and Principles* (Harcourt Brace Jovanovich, 1986), 35–37. The objection in the text does not imply that Van der Vossen is committed to consequentialism strictly defined.

doing so is suboptimal with respect to H, then this is no more than irrational rule worshiping.

The second problem with rule-consequentialism is the problem of *partial compliance*, and it is particularly serious in international law, given the system's notorious enforcement deficit.[20] Van der Vossen's NI maximizes H *only if most agents comply with the rule*—what philosophers call the rule's *acceptance* value.[21] NI is just (it maximizes H) only *when (nearly) everyone in fact refrains from intervening*. Otherwise, NI cannot possibly maximize H, since few are following it. Because governments will likely depart from the rule, especially given international law's lack of enforcement, the NI rule is not only futile; it also fails in its objective of promoting humanitarian values. To illustrate further, consider the example of a ban on secession. Let us agree that such a ban would maximize H if states and groups would generally follow it. We know, however, that groups do not generally follow the ban. Whether a particular secession is accepted or not in the real world depends on who wins on the battlefield or the negotiation. Many actors do

20. Herbert Hart famously wrote that, given its lack of enforcement mechanisms, international law was not really law but international morality. See H. L. A. Hart, *The Concept of Law*, 2nd ed. (Oxford University Press, 1999), 213–237. I don't need to endorse Hart's characterization in order to agree with him that international law suffers from enforcement deficit. An anonymous reviewer has suggested that adopting a prophylactic rule against intervention would be no more irrational than constitutionalism. But this objection overlooks the fact that in a constitutional democracy the problem of partial compliance is a lot less severe, perhaps even minimal, given the robustness of enforcement mechanisms.
21. See Mark Timmons, *Moral Theory: An Introduction*, 2nd ed. (Rowman and Littlefield, 2012), 154–160.

not follow the rule. The rule *would* maximize H if people followed it. Since they don't, by definition then, the rule in the real world does not maximize H.

For these reasons, I think it best to design a rule that permits humanitarian interventions in appropriate cases subjecting them to an effective system of approval that would increase (if not guarantee) the chances for success.

Appendix

The Iraq War

RECENT EMPIRICAL RESEARCH HAS CONFIRMED what most of us suspected: some humanitarian interventions succeed, others fail.[1] Neither optimistic liberal interventionism nor pessimistic realist noninterventionism have carried the day. Taylor Seybolt lists as reasonably successful interventions the protection of Kurds in northern Iraq in 1992,[2] NATO's air operations in Kosovo in 1999,[3] and the intervention in East Timor in that same year.[4] To these I add the 1971 Indian intervention in Bangladesh; the 1979 French intervention in the Central African Empire; the 1979 Tanzanian intervention in Uganda; the 1983 U.S. intervention in Grenada; the 1989 U.S. intervention in Panama; the 1992 ECOWAS intervention in Liberia; and the 1997 UN-authorized intervention in Sierra Leone.[5]

1. See Seybolt, *Humanitarian Intervention*, 84–85.
2. Ibid., 47–52.
3. Ibid., 78–85. See also my analysis in Tesón, *Humanitarian Intervention*, 374–390.
4. Seybolt, *Humanitarian Intervention*, 86–93. In contrast, the interventions in Somalia, Rwanda, and Bosnia were unsuccessful.
5. These cases are discussed in detail in Tesón, *Humanitarian Intervention*, 219–330.

In this appendix I discuss the one case that is problematic for my thesis, the case that has spawned most of the writing on war, academic or otherwise: the 2003 war in Iraq and its aftermath.

In 2005, I wrote an article defending the war in Iraq as humanitarian intervention.[6] I said then that success was essential to an evaluation of the intervention: "Should the Coalition fail to liberate Iraq, . . . to democratize and pacify the Middle East, and to promote liberal democracy in the world, . . . then the judgment of history on the whole effort will be, no doubt, less kind."[7] The aftermath of the war is well known. A prolonged Sunni insurgency and the rise of ISIS have convinced virtually everyone that the war was a bad mistake.

I stand by my view that the overthrow of Saddam Hussein was a just cause for humanitarian intervention, a cause that, moreover, the intervention realized. I believed then, and believe now, that removing Saddam Hussein was a positive feature of the war. But I was then too optimistic about the feasibility of other humanitarian goals, as most of them failed to materialize, which in turn caused the war to be disproportionate. If the bad things that would happen after the war were knowable, then had I known them in advance I should have opposed the war because it would have predictably violated principles of wide proportionality, in particular supervening proportionality.[8] But of course, no one knows the future, and it is easy to

6. Tesón, "Ending Tyranny in Iraq." Those views are restated in Tesón, *Humanitarian Intervention*, 390–413.
7. "Ending Tyranny in Iraq," 12.
8. Other supporters of the Iraq war have subsequently recanted. See Fareed Zakaria, "Iraq War Was a Terrible Mistake," CNN, October 26, 2015, at http://www.cnn.com/2015/10/26/opinions/zakaria-iraq-war-lessons/.

condemn the decision to go to war after all these bad effects are known.[9] But condemn it we must.

Applying the reasoning in chapter 4, I venture the following assessment. First, the coalition had a just cause, ending Saddam Hussein's tyranny, and realized that just cause. Second, the bad aftermath of the war suffices to make it objectively wrong, since it was disproportionate. If this is correct, then the intervention was objectively wrong and therefore impermissible. Third, the evidence suggests that the bad consequences that in fact occurred, such as prolonged insurgency, could have been reasonably anticipated by the interveners. If so, the Bush administration was guilty of bad planning.[10] And fourth, the coalition failed to do things that were necessary to secure a just peace in Iraq. In particular, the withdrawal of troops may have been premature. After commendable efforts to build democratic institutions and rebuild the economy, it is possible to argue that the coalition did not stay the course, although this claim is contested. The evidence seems to show that the Iraqis initially welcomed the intervention, but that the United States

9. A lengthy study concludes that "the law of unintended consequences broke out in Iraq with a vengeance"; Ali A. Alawi, *The Occupation of Iraq: Winning the War, Losing the Peace* (Yale University Press, 2007), 456. Fareed Zakaria asks: "Could Iraq have turned out differently and set a different pattern? If a stable, functioning democracy had been established in the heart of the Middle east, could it have been a model for the region. . . ? Well, if America had made all the right decisions, who knows. But it didn't . . ."; see note 8 above.
10. There is a fierce debate about the role of bad intelligence in the decision to go to war. But that failed intelligence related to Saddam's possession of weapons of mass destruction. Since I think the intervention had a just humanitarian cause, that debate is tangential. There was no failed intelligence on Saddam's crimes.

made several mistakes that doomed the chances for achieving a just peace. Those mistakes included the lack of a clear plan to move the country from dictatorship to democracy, the lack of preparedness to administer the country, the inability to eradicate corruption, and the organization of the new political system on a sectarian basis.[11] If these estimations are correct, then they reinforce the judgment that the war was a mistake because it turned out wrong and because the United States did not adequately plan for the achievement of a just peace. To these flaws we must add the fact that, perhaps, the United States withdrew prematurely and the Iraqi civil society was not strong enough to withstand the onslaught of totalitarian forces.[12]

One difficulty in judging the war is that most of the bad effects consisted in deliberate, unjust killings by agents other than the intervener. As I discussed in chapter 4, this creates a problem in the evaluation of permissibility. It may well be that "the U.S. invasion and occupation of Iraq broke the thick crust that had accreted over the country and the region as a whole, and released powerful subterranean forces."[13] But that thick crust was not a geological fact; rather, it was one of the most brutal tyrannies of modern times, and the subterranean forces were not earthquakes or tsunamis but terrorist groups fighting on the wrong side of the just war, determined to doom the liberation, pacification, and democratization of Iraq. Still,

11. See Adnan Pachachi, "The Road to Failure in Iraq," *New York Times*, April 4, 2013, at http://atwar.blogs.nytimes.com/2013/04/04/the-road-to-failure-in-iraq/?_r=0.
12. See Danielle Pletka, "What Obama Has Wrought in Iraq," *U.S. News & World Report*, June 13, 2014, at https://www.usnews.com/opinion/articles/2014/06/13/iraq-falls-apart-to-isis-after-obama-withdrawal.
13. Alawi, *The Occupation of Iraq*, 456.

the standard of permissibility should be fact based. The war's damage was excessive and impermissible for that reason.

As I indicated in Chapter 4, there is a distinction here between permissibility and responsibility. If the bad effects consisted in deliberate, unjust killings by the enemy, as here, the Bush administration has an attenuated moral responsibility, as I explained in chapter 4. But it is still true that if the administration knew or should have known about these bad effects, then the war was impermissible and the administration should be blamed for that, even if should not be blamed directly for the crimes of the insurgents

Most critics of the war say it was disproportionate and adopt a strict liability standard to judge, retroactively, that the war was a mistake. But the judgment that the war was a mistake is not necessarily a judgment of blameworthiness: to say that A made a mistake in doing X does not mean that it was unreasonable for A to do X. It may simply mean that things went wrong in ways that A could not have predicted. In ordinary language, to say that the Iraq war was a mistake (in the sense that things went badly) is compatible with saying that the decision to go to war was reasonable at the time it was made. However, the war in Iraq was disproportionate and impermissible for that reason, and the U.S. government was guilty of bad planning and open to criticism for that reason. The one thing that must be said in favor of the war is that it had a just cause and realized that just cause. Unfortunately, the price was too high.

The responsibility for what happened in Iraq does not fall only on the shoulders of the Bush administration. Assume the war was impermissible for the reasons I indicated. Still, once the United States was there, it had the obligation to try to achieve a just peace. As we saw, perhaps the United States withdrew prematurely. One of candidate Obama's promises was precisely to end the Iraq war, and surely that promise contributed to his electoral victory. But ending the war cannot mean withdrawing and allowing the enemy to destroy whatever benefits the war might have achieved. That was exactly what happened, so under the principles of *jus post bellum,* the Obama administration bears responsibility, too, for the failure in Iraq. The intervener that removes a tyrannical regime may relinquish by its postwar actions or omissions the justice it may otherwise have claimed in waging the war.[14] The United States' tentative and insufficient reconstruction efforts in Iraq cast a retroactive mantra of impermissibility on the whole effort.

Finally, the Iraqi leaders themselves must bear some responsibility for what happened. The liberation of Iraq was followed by governmental behavior that included corruption and various mishaps in the establishment of a workable peace among the various political and religious communities in the country. It is impossible to say whether better governance would have prevented the bad things that happened (and continue to happen[15]) in Iraq. But a theory of humanitarian intervention must assign a duty incumbent on the local population and its leaders, who after all are the beneficiaries of the intervention, a duty to contribute their share to the realization of the just cause—that is, to the establishment of a just peace. Whether these local failures should or could have been anticipated *ex ante*, before launching the intervention, is hard to say.[16]

14. See Gary Bass, "Jus Post Bellum," *Philosophy and Public Affairs* 32 (2004): 386.
15. See BBC, July 7, 2016, at http://www.bbc.co.uk/news/world-middle-east-36696568.
16. For a discussion of the ethics of the war against ISIS, see Tesón, "The Case of Armed Intervention against the Islamic State of Iraq and Syria."

PART II

HUMANITARIAN NONINTERVENTION

BAS VAN DER VOSSEN

6

A Presumption Against Intervention

WE LIVE IN A WORLD of violence and suffering. As I am writing this, fighting continues in Syria, Iraq, Afghanistan, the Central African Republic, and many other places. These conflicts have claimed hundreds of thousands of lives. In a world like this, it is easy to see the case for humanitarian military intervention. Few people, certainly not me, would think such interventions are never justifiable or could never work.

On the other hand, fighting violence with violence does not have a track record of success. Military intervention is nothing new. As early as 1859, John Stuart Mill warned against what he saw as excessive British military intervention in Egypt and the Crimea.[1] And it's been a staple of countries' foreign policies since. Political scientist Patrick Regan estimates that 175 military interventions occurred in the period 1944 to 1994 alone. Most of these failed, many made things worse.[2]

1. See J. S. Mill, "A Few Words on Intervention," *Fraser's Magazine* 60 (December 1859): 766–776.
2. See Patrick Regan, *Civil Wars and Foreign Powers* (University of Michigan Press, 2002), 29–30. For more discussion, see chapter 11, this volume.

The point of an ethical theory of intervention is to strike a balance between these two points. We want such a theory to identify when military intervention is morally permissible, despite the very serious risks it imposes. Doing this means, I will argue, focusing more strongly than is common on what may be called the *ex ante* perspective within the morality of intervention. Our problem isn't simply identifying what is the best thing that could happen when a humanitarian crisis is going on. Our problem is when is one (when are *we*) justified in deciding to do something about it. Or better, when are we justified in deciding to *try* to do something about it, knowing that trying and succeeding are not always the same thing.

Taking this task seriously means recognizing a presumption against intervention. Roughly speaking, a necessary condition for justified intervention is that the decision to intervene be morally acceptable at the time it is made. (This may sound like a platitude. As we will see, it is everything but.) Given the severe risks involved, and given the strong moral prohibitions against taking such risks, interventions are morally impermissible except in rare or extreme circumstances.[3]

That is only a rough approximation, of course. And it behooves us to keep in mind that these are not all-or-nothing matters. When countries deviate from the presumption against

3. At least at the level of theory, Andrew Altman and Christopher H. Wellman seem to agree: "the deontological constraint should be not be [*sic*] understood as an absolute prohibition but rather as barring the intentional killing of noncombatants unless some extremely high threshold of bad consequences is met and the intentional killing of noncombatants is the only way to avert those consequences"; see Andrew Altman and Christopher H. Wellman, *A Liberal Theory of International Justice* (Oxford University Press, 2009), 209–210, n. 17. As we will see, however, there are significant differences in how we interpret the point.

intervention, they can do so in different ways. Some of these ways will be very risky, others maybe less. So while I will, for ease of discussion, speak of intervention *simpliciter*, and while generally speaking interventions are not morally acceptable, we should remain careful to differentiate between cases that are genuinely different. To find out whether a particular intervention is morally acceptable, we have to look carefully at its particular features, its particular context, and its particular prospects.

The presumption I defend contrasts with a now more popular view, one I will call *interventionism*. According to interventionism, uninvited military action can be justified for reasons like the spreading of democracy and liberalism, the deposing of dictators, and so on. Fernando Tesón thinks the main rationale for humanitarian interventions is to fight tyranny around the world "by peaceful and (when required) by military means."[4] Others agree and claim that there is a moral duty to intervene in countries where human rights are abused.[5] Andrew Altman and Christopher H. Wellman reject what they call the "consensus view," a position roughly similar to the presumption I defend, as too restrictive, claiming that "intervention is permissible even if there is no supreme humanitarian emergency."[6]

These arguments have found fertile soil in policy circles. Barack Obama was the fourth consecutive U.S. president to bomb Iraq for purportedly humanitarian ends, intervened in Libya, Syria, and elsewhere. Supporters of the

4. See Tesón, *Humanitarian Intervention*, 402–403.
5. Kieran Oberman, "The Myth of the Optional War: Why States Are Required to Wage the Wars They Are Permitted to Wage," *Philosophy & Public Affairs* 43 (2015): 255–286.
6. See Altman and Wellman, *A Liberal Theory of International Justice*, 105; and chapter 11, this volume.

international doctrine of *The Responsibility to Protect* see the international community as having not only the responsibility but even the *duty* to protect people around the world.[7] Looking at things from this perspective, it may seem as if the main problems surrounding intervention have to do with the lack of political will to intervene more.[8]

7. See United Nations 2005 World Summit Outcome, A/RES/60/1, p. 30, at http://www.un.org/womenwatch/ods/A-RES-60-1-E.pdf. The doctrine follows the more interventionist report of the International Commission on Intervention and State Sovereignty, *The Responsibility to Protect* (International Development Research Centre, 2001). The duty to intervene is asserted in section 2.29, p. 17. See also Pattison, *Humanitarian Intervention and the Responsibility to Protect,* 3–4. More generally, the ICISS Report described the aim of *The Responsibility to Protect* as to "remove a barrier to effective action" (section 2.5, p. 12). The idea of a *duty* to intervene goes back much further, at least to the aftermath of the first Gulf War. For discussion, see Nicholas Wheeler, *Saving Strangers* (Oxford University Press, 2003), 141. For the claim that there is such a duty, see Bernard Williams, "Humanitarianism and the Right to Intervene," in *In the Beginning Was the Deed: Realism and Moralism in Political Argument,* ed. Geoffrey Hawthorn (Princeton University Press, 2007), 145–153.
8. International lawyers Michael Byers and Simon Chesterman write: "States are not champing at the bit to intervene in support of human rights around the globe . . .. [T]he primary goal must be to encourage states to see widespread and systematic human rights violations as their concern too—as part of their 'national interest'—and to act and act early to prevent them, stop them, or seek justice for them"; see Michael Byers and Simon Chesterman, "Changing the Rules About Rules? Unilateral Humanitarian Intervention and the Future of International Law," in *Humanitarian Intervention,* ed. J. L. Holzgrefe and Robert O. Keohane (Cambridge University Press, 2003), 177–203, 202.

At the limit, these views resemble the kind of notorious interventionism seen during the George W. Bush administrations. Indeed, Tesón has argued that the 2003 U.S. invasion of Iraq "was justified as a humanitarian intervention."[9] Oxford economist Paul Collier thinks that military intervention in countries can be justified to fight global poverty by "fixing" political institutions elsewhere.[10]

Interventionism is to be rejected in all its forms, however. The interventionist view seems to be popular, but it is also irresponsible. Interventionism involves a kind of reckless risk-taking that has no place in an acceptable moral theory of intervention. Or so I will argue.

9. See Tesón, *Humanitarian Intervention*, 392. For a similar view, see Thomas Cushman, "Introduction: The Liberal-Humanitarian Case for War in Iraq," in *A Matter of Principle: Humanitarian Arguments for War in Iraq*, ed. Thomas Cushman (University of California Press, 2005), 2.
10. "[N]on-intervention is simply not ethically defensible in the societies which contain the bottom billion people because many of these states have shown themselves structurally unable to provide or maintain accountable government . . .. [W]e must review or reverse our wholesale opposition to the coup, and to realise, however counterintuitive it may be, that coups and the threat of coups can be a significant weapon in fostering democracy"; see Paul Collier, "In Praise of the Coup," *New Humanist* (March 2009), at http://rationalist.org.uk/articles/1997/in-praise-of-the-coup. Compare Paul Collier, *The Bottom Billion* (Oxford University Press, 2008), 130. For a similar view, see Deepak Lal, *In Praise of Empires: Globalization and Order* (Palgrave Macmillan, 2004); Niall Ferguson, *Colossus: The Rise and Fall of the American Empire* (Penguin, 2005); Cushman, *A Matter of Principle: Humanitarian Arguments for War in Iraq*.

7

Between Internal and External Threats

HUMANITARIAN INTERVENTIONS INVOLVE ONE OR more countries invading the territory of a target state without that state's consent. What sets such interventions apart from plain old invasions is that their stated aims have a humanitarian nature. Humanitarian interventions aim to save the lives of innocent people who would otherwise be the victims of war, rapacious governments, armed groups, and so on.

This aim of saving innocent people is essential to their justification. Interventions employ means that pose the very same dangers they are meant to avert—killing and harming innocent people. Doing so is morally unacceptable unless the greater good of the lives that are saved significantly outweighs the deaths and harms that are caused (if then).[1] In this sense, the very idea of a humanitarian intervention is moralized. What sets humanitarian interventions apart from plain old invasions is the possibility that the violence used is morally justifiable.

Whether an intervention counts as humanitarian, then, depends on whether it lives up to its humanitarian rationale.

1. Throughout I am assuming that other standard conditions of just war are satisfied, such as that the intervention does involve the use of prohibited weaponry, and so on.

This is not the same as saying that interventions must successfully bring about their humanitarian aims. Obviously, it's possible for interventions to be humanitarian yet fail. The point that an intervention's humanitarian rationale matters more than its outcome is a theme to which we shall return.

Saying that interventions have a humanitarian rationale when they purport to bring about a good in terms of lives saved that significantly outweighs the bad of deaths and harms caused is to imply a lesser-evil justification for interventions. Invariably, when military force is used, many people who have a right not to be harmed or killed end up being harmed or killed. Interventions kill citizens, people already trying to defend the victims of the crisis, and other innocent bystanders. Their suffering is unjust unless it can be justified by the prevented unjust suffering of others.

There are many complications here. Most important, not everyone who is killed or harmed as a result of an intervention has his or her rights violated as a result. (Nor does everyone who is a victim of the crisis necessarily have his or her rights violated.) Some people involved will have lost or forfeited their rights against certain forms of harm. If A is in the process of killing B, and the only way to save B is to kill A, one does not violate A's right to life by killing A while rescuing B. By attacking B and threatening B's life, A has become liable to defensive harm.[2]

Many people who die or are harmed as a result of intervention are not liable to be killed or harmed, however. According to most standard theories, the conditions under which people are liable to be killed or harmed are relatively tightly circumscribed. It is not enough, for instance, to be wearing a uniform,

2. I take lesser-evil justifications to be distinct from liability justifications, then. See, e.g., McMahan, *Killing in War*, 27.

be on the battlefield, and so on. One needs to actually be threatening innocent people, be morally responsible for an actual threat, or something similar.[3]

In order for a lesser-evil justification to succeed, the number of people saved must be significantly greater than the number of people who will be harmed as a result of the intervention. This is a consequence of taking seriously the fact that people have rights against being killed or harmed. The job of an ethical intervener is not merely to minimize the total number of lives lost. People's rights constrain our actions, including our actions of rescue. Some ways of rescuing people are morally acceptable, others are not. When interventions infringe upon the rights of others, the moral constraints that those rights pose need to be overridden. And for this, among other things,[4] a significantly greater good has to be in the offing.

INTERNAL AND EXTERNAL THREATS

The morality of intervention negotiates the tension between two opposing points. On the one hand, there is the moral impetus to try and prevent humanitarian crises. On the other hand, military interventions invariably impose risks of harm on people that are normally impermissible. It's not just that there are moral limits to the kind of means we can use to

3. I have argued elsewhere that there must be at least reasonable evidence that one is posing such a threat. See Bas van der Vossen, "Uncertain Rights Against Defense," *Social Philosophy and Policy* 32 (2016): 129–145.
4. Throughout, I assume that additional conditions like necessity and proportionality are part of lesser-evil justifications. I return to some of these issues in chapter 9, this volume.

try and save people. It's also that trying is not the same as succeeding, and sometimes it's better not to try at all.

The fact that humanitarian interventions have a lesser-evil rationale underscores this point. For such interventions to be justified, the threats they undo must significantly outweigh the threats they pose. The lesser-evil rationale identifies an acceptable way of balancing these two threats—one from within the country experiencing the crisis, the other from without posed by the intervener.

These threats center on a number of salient facts about the international system in which we live. Our world is one of separate and largely independent states, which strongly centralize the use of force within their territories. And this means there are great disparities in power between governments and armed groups, which possess large, organized, and sophisticated military forces, and the ordinary citizens who tend to be the victims of humanitarian crises and who typically lack all but very basic means to protect themselves. Under these conditions, military intervention may be the only way to protect innocent people from abusive and dysfunctional governments, militias, and other armed groups.

On the other hand, interventions invariably have to involve the use of rather blunt instruments. The politically favored tool of the intervener is the airstrike or bombing campaign. As we will see, and for structural reasons, these strategic choices are rarely if ever made with an eye to maximally protecting the people in the target state; rather, they aim at protecting lives on the intervener's side. As such, interventions risk imposing excessive harms in light of the good they bring about. Interveners can kill and harm more innocent people than the number of people they save—indeed, they can fail to save people at all. At their worst, they can increase the number of victims in a humanitarian crisis.

Our question, then, concerns the moral constraints on the use of violent and potentially unjustifiable means in pursuit of avoiding the kind of suffering to which interventions are a response. One way to capture this idea is by putting it in teleological terms. The moral rules of intervention have a point. They aim to constrain military action in ways that render people everywhere as safe as they might reasonably expect to be by correctly negotiating the two threats of harm just mentioned.

THE CIRCUMSTANCES OF INTERVENTION

To correctly mediate the internal and external risks described, a good ethical theory must take into account the conditions under which the question of intervention arises. A good ethical theory of intervention provides rules that transform a situation that would, in the absence of such rules, be excessively dangerous into one in which people are as safe as they might reasonably be. The morality of intervention, that is, offers guidance *given* these conditions.

The morality of intervention is not unique in this respect. In his discussion of distributive justice, David Hume identified what has come to be known as the circumstances of justice. To Hume, the circumstances of (distributive) justice include a moderate scarcity of goods and limited benevolence. Because there simply aren't enough goods available for all people to be fully satisfied in their wants, and because people are not motivated to work for the wants of others as they would be for meeting their own, we face a situation of predictable but avoidable conflict over resources. The rules of distributive justice are the solution to this problem. They change a situation of conflict into one of mutual advantage.[5]

5. David Hume, *An Enquiry Concerning the Principles of Morals* (Oxford University Press, 1998), section III, part 1.

To Hume, as to us, then, the rules of justice have a point. A theory of distributive justice fails if it does not resolve the potential conflict created by moderate scarcity and limited benevolence. Similarly, an ethical theory of intervention fails if it does not resolve the tension between internal and external threats. These two opposing sets of conditions present what we may call the "circumstances of intervention." And the task of a theory of intervention is to transform a situation in which those internal and external forces pose threats to people's safety into one where those forces promise them protection.

Consider an example. Many theories hold that intervention is morally justified only if the intervener enjoys a kind of legitimacy or is authorized by appropriate international legal bodies.[6] In one way, this may seem like a puzzling demand. Suppose state A intervenes in state B and saves thousands of innocent people. Why condemn the intervention as unjustified simply because state A didn't first ask some international body for permission? In most other contexts, the morality of force doesn't include a condition like that. If you see person A beating up person B on the street, you can permissibly break up the fight. You don't need to first call the police to ask permission.

However, the circumstances of intervention are different from the circumstances of a street fight. And the difference

6. See Pattison, *Humanitarian Intervention and the Responsibility to Protect: Who Should Intervene?* Also, W. Michael Reisman, "Unilateral Action and the Transformation of the World Constitutive Process: The Special Problem of Humanitarian Intervention," *European Journal of International Law* 11 (2000): 3–18. Compare also the discussion in Allen Buchanan and Robert O. Keohane, "The Preventive Use of Force: A Cosmopolitan Institutional Perspective," *Ethics and International Affairs* 18, no. 1 (2004): 4; and in Allen Buchanan, "Justifying Preventive War," in his *Human Rights, Legitimacy, and the Use of Force* (Oxford University Press, 2010), 280–297.

matters with regard to the morality of using force. Consider the following somewhat fanciful analogy. Suppose there were a species of enormous creatures—call them the Giants. And suppose the Giants are not only much bigger but also much stronger than you and I. As a result, the Giants are much better at stopping violence and conflict. However, and also as a result, when the Giants stop a conflict, they tend to cause more damage than was strictly needed. Perhaps they are merely clumsy. Perhaps they tend to overreact.

Imagine that your neighbors A and B are having a domestic dispute. Let's say that A is beating up B. Is the morality of your intervening on B's behalf the same as when a Giant would intervene? Obviously not. Given that a Giant intervention poses dangers that your intervention does not, we might insist on additional rules for the Giant. Perhaps the dispute would have to be more severe before it's okay for a Giant to come in than it would have to be for you to come in. Or perhaps we'd insist that Giants undergo some kind of anger-management training before sending them in.

In light of these differences, it's at least an open question whether justifiable intervention by states requires international authorization. Countries wielding military force behave more like our imaginary Giants than like you when you intervene in a street fight. If authorized interveners are generally more likely to operate in morally acceptable ways, and if the need to secure international authorization limits the potential for attacks with problematic objectives or using problematic means, then such a rule might be acceptable after all. It might be part of a set of rules that help avoid interveners becoming threats, and instead make them a source of protection.[7]

7. I do not claim here that such authorization is presently morally required. This depends in part on the quality of existing

The possibility arises, then, that certain actions might count as unjustified even though they produce very good outcomes. Suppose a Giant were to intervene in your neighbors' fight and ends up doing, against the odds, a flawless job. We might still have reason to think the intervention wrongful. For even though things turned out well—B was saved and no one was needlessly hurt, say—the Giant did something reckless. And reckless actions are wrong. This is a theme to which we'll return.

LIKE THE PUSH OF A BUTTON?

Fernando Tesón proposes a Green Button test in chapter 2 for seeing whether interventions are morally justified. Suppose there were a magical Green Button, the pushing of which would bring an end to human rights violations elsewhere without causing any additional harm. (And suppose that, somehow, we know this.) Surely, Tesón thinks, pushing the button would be morally permissible.

We all agree with this, I'm sure. If such a button did exist, and we would be sure about what it would do, pushing it would be permissible (perhaps even required). But saying this is not all that interesting. What is interesting is what we might learn from this thought experiment. Tesón thinks his example shows that an intervention's consequences are where the action is. When interventions are like the pushing of a button—and actually bring about enough good overall—they are morally

international institutions, which at present aren't great. For discussion, see Allen Buchanan, "Institutionalizing the Just War," *Philosophy and Public Affairs* 34 (2006): 2–38, 6. See also chapter 11, this volume.

justified. Imaginary buttons or real life, in both contexts, the issue is essentially the same.[8]

But the Green Button test strips away much that is relevant. Most important, it strips away the circumstances of intervention and the *risks* that these imply. In Tesón's example, we are *guaranteed* that pushing the Green Button will do lots of good and no bad. But real interventions are quite literally never like that. They involve potentially destructive military force, they occur in highly unstable situations, and they are undertaken by fallible agents who are subject to incentives of their own. When we assume those things away, of course a permissible intervention is what remains. But the morality of intervention cannot safely assume those things away. The morality of intervention is *about* those things.[9]

Perhaps Tesón would say that we should construe an alternative thought experiment—one involving not a Green Button but, say, an Orange Button. Pushing the Orange Button would then be like deciding to intervene in real life. It means trying to bring about a humanitarian outcome, but at the same time taking significant risks of unjustifiably harming innocent people and even making things worse. Such a thought-experiment would be much more instructive, as it would simulate the actual decisions about intervention we face in real life. But whether such a thought-experiment still supports Tesón's favored interventionist policies is a much more difficult question. For once we introduce these risks and dangers, it becomes much more

8. For a similar argument, see Christopher H. Wellman, "Taking Human Rights Seriously," *Journal of Political Philosophy* 20 (2012): 119–130.
9. The point, then, is not *simply* that the circumstances of intervention are missing from the Green Button test. The lack of these circumstances is why the Green Button test is not relevant for us.

difficult to say that it's permissible to push the Orange Button. This will depend on just *how* risky pushing the button turns out to be. And pushing it would be very risky, indeed.

FAILURE IN REAL LIFE

Perhaps the most notorious example of just how risky pushing the Orange Button would be is the early 1990s Somalia crisis.[10] After a long period of conflict and civil war had severely weakened the state apparatus, Somalia had become increasingly more violent. Local authorities had lost the ability to subdue violence, and none of the rival groups vying for control was strong enough to take control. Between 15,000 and 40,000 people were killed from January 1991 to August 1992, when a drought hit, resulting in a famine that may have killed around 150,000 people.

These events took place as interventionism was at its peak. The French Foreign Minister affirmed a general "duty of intervention" in 1991,[11] and the United Nations had already authorized a number of humanitarian military operations. The first operation in Somalia had a mandate to monitor a ceasefire in the Somali capital Mogadishu, to provide security for UN personnel and equipment, and to escort the delivery of supplies. Their arrival led to a significant increase in food imports. However, the proportion of food that actually reached people in need plummeted, as UN forces were too weak to protect the

10. The following account largely follows Taylor Seybolt, *Humanitarian Intervention: The Conditions of Success and Failure* (Oxford University Press, 2008), 52ff; and Wheeler, *Saving Strangers*, chapter 6.
11. See Wheeler, *Saving Strangers*, 141.

incoming aid. The result was mainly to increase support for the warring parties.[12]

In response, a number of other military interventions were undertaken, the last of which, UNOSOM II, was the most ambitious. Its aim was to put a stop to the fighting, promote political reconciliation, and reestablish national and regional institutions, as well as civil administration in the entire country.[13] UNOSOM II was a disaster. General Aidid, the most powerful person in Somalia, saw the mission as a direct threat to his position and he attacked the interventionist forces. The UN Security Council responded by issuing a warrant for Aidid's arrest. As violence in Mogadishu intensified, UNOSOM II attacked Aidid's forces, opposing militias ambushed UN vehicles, helicopters were shot at, and many civilians were killed.

The violence climaxed in October 1993, when U.S. forces unsuccessfully attempted to capture Aidid. The operation led to a fifteen-hour firefight, now called the Battle of Mogadishu (made famous by the movie *Black Hawk Down*). According to official accounts, at least three hundred Somalis, eighteen U.S. soldiers, and one Malaysian soldier were killed. Most observers put the death toll much higher, though. The U.S. special representative Robert Oakley estimated that 1,500 to 2,000 Somalis were killed and wounded on that day alone.[14] Soon

12. This is not an isolated incident. The same happened, for instance, in Rwandan refugee camps in Zaire, where aid intended for refugees strengthened those responsible for perpetrating genocide; see Fiona Terry, *Condemned to Repeat?* (Cornell University Press, 2002).
13. UN Security Council Resolution 814, March 26, 1993.
14. See "Ambush in Mogadishu: Interview Ambassador Robert Oakley," *Frontline PBS*, at http://www.pbs.org/wgbh/pages/frontline/shows/ambush/interviews/oakley.html.

after, the United States withdrew its troops, which had made up by far the largest part of UNOSOM II.

The Somali intervention stands out as an unmitigated disaster. Political scientist Taylor Seybolt estimates that after March 1993, UNOSOM II troops killed or injured as many people as aid operations managed to save. Most were women and children.[15] Moreover, UNOSOM II made no progress toward meeting its lofty goals, but indeed ended up making things worse. From mid-1993 on, lawlessness and violence increased across the southern part of the country, and the country has effectively been in a state of war since.[16] Most disastrously, violence began to focus on relief organizations after the U.S. units withdrew from the country in March 1994.[17]

15. See Seybolt, *Humanitarian Intervention*, 59–60.
16. Ibid., 93.
17. Aid provided by these organizations had reportedly saved around 40,000 Somalis from starvation before UNOSOM II's military operations begun; see Seybolt, *Humanitarian Intervention*, 54ff. It's worth noting that others float far more optimistic numbers. The Refugee Study Group's report on the Somali relief operation, for example, estimates 110,000 people saved. But these numbers are problematic, since much of this decline in mortality happened in the period before the intervention; see Seybolt, *Humanitarian Intervention*, 56. Indeed, some others are skeptical that the intervention had any positive effects at all. As Alex de Waal writes, "[t]he evidence that the intervention had *any* impact on mortality in general is . . . extremely slender"; Alex de Waal, "Dangerous Precedents? Famine Relief in Somalia 1991–93," in *War and Hunger: Rethinking International Responses to Complex Emergencies*, ed. Joanna Macrae and Anthony Zwi (Zed Books, 1994), 158 (emphasis added). See also Alex de Waal, "African encounters," *Index on Censorship* 23 (1994): 13–31, 20.

While the Somali intervention was one of the worst cases of intervention failure, it's far from the only one. Consider two more recent misadventures. The 2003 U.S. invasion of Iraq was defended by many on humanitarian grounds,[18] but has had similar effects. According to the Iraq Body Count project, the war in Iraq has killed between 138,673 and 157,293 civilians alone.[19] Since this project uses a rather conservative method to estimate deaths, other observers claim the real number is much higher, up to well over a million.[20] At present, the country and indeed the entire region are threatened by the extremely violent fundamentalist group Islamic State.[21]

More recently, the United States intervened in Libya in order to depose Muammar el-Qaddafi. Despite—as always—initial high hopes,[22] Libya too is on a downward trajectory. The country now lacks a genuine central government. Amnesty International described the state of the country three years after the intervention as follows: "Armed groups and militias

18. See Tesón, *Humanitarian Intervention*, 402–403; Cushman, *A Matter of Principle: Humanitarian Arguments for War in Iraq*.
19. See Iraq Body Count, at https://www.iraqbodycount.org/.
20. See, e.g., Physicians for Social Responsibility, "Body Count of the 'War on Terror,'" March 2015, at http://www.psr.org/assets/pdfs/body-count.pdf.
21. See, e.g., Michael Knights, "Iraq War III Has Now Begun," *Foreign Policy*, June 11, 2014, at http://foreignpolicy.com/2014/06/11/iraq-war-iii-has-now-begun/.
22. See Ivo H. Daalder and James G. Stavridisoct, "NATO's Success in Libya," *New York Times*, October 31, 2011, at http://www.nytimes.com/2011/10/31/opinion/31iht-eddaalder31.html?src=tp&_r=0; Helene Cooper and Steven Lee Myers, "U.S. Tactics in Libya May Be a Model for Other Efforts," *New York Times*, September 28, 2011, at http://www.nytimes.com/2011/08/29/world/africa/29diplo.html?pagewanted=all&_r=0.

are running amok, launching indiscriminate attacks on civilian areas and committing widespread abuses, including war crimes, with complete impunity."[23]

I mention these examples not to deny that interventions can save lives. They can, and no responsible theory can ignore this. My point, instead, is to make vivid that interventions also pose grave dangers. The key question, then, is how likely interventions are to succeed or fail. And, as we'll see below, for every story about an intervention working out for the better, many more can be told where things turned out for the worse. No responsible theory can ignore this either.

23. See Stephen Kinzer, "The US Ruined Libya," *Boston Globe*, November 7, 2014, at http://www.bostonglobe.com/opinion/2014/11/07/the-ruined-libya/ZOSuLBCMzVhZ3tZJlHv2sL/story.html?event=event25. See also Alan J. Kuperman, "Obama's Libya Debacle: How a Well-Meaning Intervention Ended in Failure," *Foreign Affairs*, March/April 2015, at https://www.foreignaffairs.com/articles/libya/2015-02-16/obamas-libya-debacle. For discussion, see Christopher Kutz, "Democracy, Defense, and the Threat of Intervention," in *The Morality of Defensive War*, ed. Cécile Fabre and Seth Lazar (Oxford University Press, 2014), 232–233, 244.

8

Why Sovereignty (Still) Matters

IF THE MORALITY OF INTERVENTION is primarily about balancing internal and external threats to people's safety, theories of intervention can be differentiated in terms of how they strike that balance. That said, the morality of intervention is not just one thing. There are several dimensions along which questions about the ethics of intervention arise. One dimension is whether states, or sovereign states, enjoy rights against intervention and, if so, how extensive the protections afforded by these rights should be.

NEGLECTING INTERNAL THREATS

A good theory of sovereignty offers states the kinds of protections that strike an adequate balance between the internal and external threats to people's rights and safety mentioned before. The traditional (now largely abandoned) doctrine of state sovereignty holds that humanitarian military intervention is impermissible. Sovereign states must accept an absolute rule of nonintervention, meaning their internal affairs can be no legitimate cause for war. On this view, the only legitimate wars are wars of self-defense and, perhaps, wars that aid other countries in defense against foreign aggressors.

Historically, of course, the main impetus behind this view has been fear of the chaos that might result if countries are allowed to attack other countries when they judge their internal affairs unjust. The norm of nonintervention arose in lieu of the immensely destructive Thirty Years War, as part of the Peace of Westphalia of 1648. Since the Thirty Years War was fought by Lutheran and Catholic heads of state seeking to impose the true religion on one another, an absolute prohibition on intervention was thought necessary to avoid another war like this.[1]

Others have defended a similar view in more moralized terms. To them, outsiders should not interfere with domestic conflicts because doing so violates a people's right to self-determination. While not quite defending an absolute prohibition on intervention, Michael Walzer thinks the norm of nonintervention reflects "the right of a people 'to become free by their own efforts' if they can, and nonintervention is the principle guaranteeing that their success will not be impeded or their failure prevented by the intrusions of an alien power."[2]

Where the Westphalian argument considers nonintervention necessary to maintain international peace, the argument

1. This rule extended the principle agreed upon in the Peace of Augsburg in 1555, with minor exceptions. For discussion of the Peace of Westphalia and its lasting impact on international law, see Leo Gross, "The Peace of Westphalia, 1648—1948," *American Journal of International Law* 42 (1948): 20–41. For a brief defense of this view, see S. I. Benn and R. S. Peters, *Social Principles and the Democratic State* (George Allen & Unwin, 1959), 363.
2. See Michael Walzer, "The Moral Standing of States: A Response to Four Critics," *Philosophy and Public Affairs* 9 (1980): 209–229. See also Walzer, *Just and Unjust Wars*, 88. For a similar view, see, e.g., Kutz, "Democracy, Defense, and the Threat of Intervention."

from self-determination considers nonintervention necessary to protect the value of a society's internal political processes. But neither argument holds up. The Westphalian order has been significantly weakened since World War II. Current international legal doctrine recognizes that states do not enjoy absolute dominion over their internal affairs, but recognizes severe human rights violations as the limit of internal sovereignty.[3] Yet this weakening has not resulted in the kind of chaos or international aggression the Westphalian doctrine was said to be necessary to avoid. Indeed, some argue that the modern norm is not a weakening at all—the Westphalian doctrine never had that much sway to begin with.[4] But if it's true that a nonabsolute norm of sovereignty is not overly dangerous, it becomes difficult to see why further weakening would be.

Nor does Walzer's view support the traditional view of sovereignty. Even if internal self-determination is indeed morally valuable—a claim I will defend in limited fashion here—this simply does not rule out external intervention. For one, in cases where humanitarian intervention is a real issue, governments typically fail to act in ways that respect their people's self-determination. It's highly doubtful that whatever processes are going on under these circumstances are processes of valuable self-determination. After all, political self-determination itself will admit of moral limitations. Rulers, societies, or groups no more than individuals can violate human rights with morality on their side.[5] But if there is no necessary conflict between the

3. See United Nations 2005 World Summit Outcome, A/RES/60/1. See also Pattison, *Humanitarian Intervention and the Responsibility to Protect.*
4. See Stephen D. Krasner, *Sovereignty: Organized Hypocrisy* (Princeton University Press, 1999).
5. For a similar point, see Allen Buchanan, "Self-Determination, Revolution, and Intervention," *Ethics* 126 (2016): 447–473, 454.

two, the value of self-determination does not prohibit interventions where tyrants, war, or civil conflict get in the way of the people's self-rule.[6]

More generally speaking, both these arguments share an important flaw. For even though there certainly are dangers in allowing military interventions, and even though self-determination does have genuine moral value, it's simply not true that this is all that matters. And there are significant downsides to a strong doctrine of state sovereignty. A doctrine of strict nonintervention renders minority groups in states excessively vulnerable to the majorities alongside whom they have to live. Without at least some threat of outside intervention, majorities can violate the minorities' rights with impunity. For vulnerable minorities, the only genuine protection can come from without.

The problem runs deeper still. Absent external checks on domestic power, abusive regimes and groups not only enjoy free rein to oppress, exploit, and persecute their people, such a system gives these groups strong incentives to do so. Many abusive governments extract large amounts of wealth from their societies, through internal corruption and bribes, international loans, the sale of their countries' natural resources, and more.

Note that my claim is *not* that the right to self-determination can protect only things that are non-wrongful. That view ought to be rejected, I believe. My claim here concerns only that particularly grave kind of moral wrong involved in a human rights violation. See Bas van der Vossen, "The Asymmetry of Legitimacy," *Law and Philosophy* 31 (2012): 565–592.

6. Allen Buchanan has argued that the value of self-determination may even be a reason *for* intervention. As Buchanan puts it, "self-determination is compatible with much more extensive interventions"; see Buchanan, "Self-Determination, Revolution, and Intervention."

And many of those governments use that wealth to maintain their positions of power by paying off powerful factions in society.[7] In the absence of external checks on such behavior, already bad regimes are encouraged to become worse.

These problems are to a large extent due to the fact that the states and societies of our world are the result of messy and deeply unjust processes of conquest, oppression, war, and so on. These may be sins of the past (although to be sure they are still going on), but they are very much still part of our current world. As a result, states and societies often contain different groups, held together by force and violence. Indeed, they contain groups many of which might have good claims to self-determination themselves.

At a more theoretical level, then, the problem with the traditional doctrine of sovereignty is not just that it exaggerates the importance of states or societies as compared to groups and individuals—although it may do that. The problem is also that it exaggerates the moral importance of states or societies *as they currently exist*. In light of their history, composition, and current affairs, such a preference is simply unacceptable.

NEGLECTING EXTERNAL THREATS

By focusing so heavily, perhaps even exclusively, on the ways external forces can endanger societies and the people within

7. Daron Acemoglu and James Robinson, *Why Nations Fail: The Origins of Power, Prosperity, and Poverty* (Crown Business, 2013). See also Gary W. Cox, Douglass C. North, and Barry R. Weingast, "The Violence Trap: A Political-Economic Approach to the Problems of Development," SSRN, February 13, 2015, at http://ssrn.com/abstract=2370622 or http://dx.doi.org/10.2139/ssrn.2370622.

them, the doctrine of state sovereignty excessively downplays or overlooks the significance of dangerous internal threats to individuals and groups. In order to counterbalance these threats, human rights can limit state sovereignty and self-determination.

This insight, and it is a genuine insight, forms one of the main sources of attraction for the interventionist view. But there are different ways to take the insight into account. Some see intervention as permissible only if a state fails to adequately uphold the human rights of its subjects. When states are at least reasonably just, as measured by their human rights record, they enjoy rights of nonintervention. But as soon as a state falls below the threshold of legitimacy or adequate protection—as many states in our world clearly do—intervention becomes a live option.[8]

I will return to this possibility in detail, but first we should look at a more strongly interventionist position, one which goes beyond merely weakening the doctrine of state sovereignty to deny that states can enjoy protections against intervention at all. Fernando Tesón and Christopher Wellman argue that when concerns about sovereignty and human rights conflict, we should squarely side with the protection of people's human rights. As Wellman puts it, "even a legitimate state has no principled objection to outsiders' intervening in its internal affairs if this interference will prevent just a single human rights violation."[9]

8. See, e.g., Altman and Wellman, *A Liberal Theory of International Justice*. Note that Wellman himself has since defended the more radical view that even legitimate states have no rights against intervention; see Wellman, "Taking Human Rights Seriously."
9. See Wellman, "Taking Human Rights Seriously," 119. See also Fernando R. Tesón, "The Moral Structure of Humanitarian Intervention," in *Contemporary Debates in Applied Ethics*, 2nd ed., ed. Andrew I. Cohen and Christopher H. Wellman

On this view, state sovereignty or legitimacy has no independent moral weight. All that matters are the things that go into making a state legitimate in the first place—the protection of human rights. But when those things are absent, when human rights are being violated, the status of legitimacy or sovereignty cannot stand in the way of their protection. The upshot, Tesón and Wellman argue, is that the morality of intervention boils down to the question of whether a military intervention will actually lead to the better protection of human rights.[10]

By so downplaying the role of sovereignty or legitimacy, this interventionist view misses why these notions should play a role in international affairs in the first place. The international realm, even more than individual societies, is characterized by deep and extensive disagreement about justice. For any state or society, no matter how just or desirable one might find it, there are numerous others who judge it unjust or even evil. If decisions about intervention are left to the parties' judgments about the balance of harms and benefits they may cause, then

(Wiley-Blackwell, 2014), 391–403. David Luban suggests that "any proportional struggle for socially basic human rights is justified, even one which attacks the non-basic rights of others"; see David Luban, "Just War and Human Rights," *Philosophy & Public Affairs* 9 (1980): 160–181, 175.

10. See Loren Lomasky and Fernando R. Tesón, *Justice at a Distance: Extending Freedom Globally* (Cambridge University Press, 2015), chapter 8. Wellman's main argument comes in the form of a thought experiment similar to the Green Button test discussed in chapter 7, this volume. For further discussion, see Bas van der Vossen, "The Morality of Humanitarian Intervention," in *Contemporary Debates in Applied Ethics,* 2nd ed., ed. Andrew I. Cohen and Christopher H. Wellman (Wiley-Blackwell, 2014), 404–416.

very often there will be those who judge intervention worth the cost. As a result, this view will lead to many more interventions occurring than are desirable.

When states are judged to be sovereign or legitimate, and thus rights-protected against intervention, this problem is to some extent avoided because such judgments exclude the simple weighing of harms and benefits. Intervention in sovereign or legitimate states is impermissible, regardless of whether their internal affairs are judged to be unjust and easily fixable from the outside. And given that people who disagree about the justice of a society may nevertheless agree about its sovereignty or legitimacy, attaching a norm of nonintervention to the latter will help prevent the most problematic interventions.[11]

Of course, these problems of disagreement and the solution that state legitimacy can provide are frequently recognized in the domestic context. It's a common theme in justifications of the state or political authority that living together in peace with others who have significantly different views about justice requires a legitimate institution or body of rules that the disagreeing parties can use despite their several disputes. The problem with this interventionist view, then, is that it recreates the very same problems in the international context. By removing whatever few norms of legitimacy, sovereignty, and

11. See Joshua S. Goldstein and Jon C. Pevehouse, *International Relations,* 10th ed. (Pearson, 2014), 49ff. Ian Clark, *Legitimacy in International Society* (Oxford University Press, 2005), argues that a rule of nonintervention between states that are recognized as legitimate fosters not only peace but also decent internal behavior, thereby adding to the case against Wellman and Tesón. For a study on the role of legitimacy judgments in international law more generally, see Thomas Franck, *The Power of Legitimacy Among Nations* (Oxford University Press, 1990).

nonintervention there are, the problems of disagreement come to the fore again.

THE VALUE OF SELF-DETERMINATION

Traditionally, the most important reason given against intervention is the self-determination of the target country. Roughly speaking, the value of self-determination has to do with the value of self-government, or the idea that it's better for people to live under laws that are, in some way, based on their own will. Interventions upset self-determination, then, because they sever this link. They bring about the imposition of an outside will (or wills) on a population, turning them from citizens into subjects. As a result, the value of self-determination can prohibit an intervention, it is said, even if that intervention could correct or prevent real injustices.[12]

Anti-interventionist authors have often exaggerated the importance of self-determination. For instance, Michael Walzer thinks that the right to self-determination is so important as to prohibit intervention in all but the most extreme cases, such as when a regime permits or engages in genocide

12. For a particularly clear discussion of self-determination, see Altman and Wellman, *A Liberal Theory of International Justice*, chapter 2. My argument here follows the more detailed theory of self-determination I propose in Bas van der Vossen, "Self-Determination and Moral Variation," in *The Theory of Self-Determination*, ed. Fernando Tesón (Cambridge University Press, 2016), 13–31. The theory presented there draws on arguments about group agency offered by Christian List and Philip Pettit, *Group Agency: The Possibility, Design, and Status of Corporate Agents* (Oxford University Press, 2011).

or other forms of mass killing.[13] But even if there is some morally valuable kind of self-determination going on in societies containing oppressive regimes, its value may be outweighed by the (much greater) importance of undoing the oppression and accompanying human rights violations.

It's a mistake, then, to think that self-determination imposes a blanket prohibition on intervention. However, when critics like Tesón deny that self-determination contains any real value, and that the only things that matter are the autonomy and rights of individuals,[14] that too has to be a mistake. As we will see, collective self-determination (a process that happens at the group level) is genuinely possible, and when it happens it can be morally valuable. A theory of intervention neglects this at its peril.

Let's call a set of propositions about how a society ought to be organized that is endorsed by its holder a *political code*.[15] And let's call something a *group political code*, if such a thing is indeed possible, if it is the set of beliefs about how politics ought to be organized that is shared by a group. When different individuals form a group, their several political codes can combine into a new and separate group political code.

13. Walzer, "The Moral Standing of States," 225–226.
14. In his contribution to this book, Tesón holds that reasons of self-determination never count against intervention. Similarly, in his book *Humanitarian Intervention*, Tesón suggests that the only thing that matters morally is individual autonomy, not collective self-determination; see, e.g., Tesón, *Humanitarian Intervention*, 93–94.
15. No doubt this is to simplify considerably. The intuitive notion of a moral code may well include more than merely propositions, such as attitudes, affects, and so on. I set these complications aside for the sake of argument.

A group political code can be seen as the product of a process of collective self-determination when its content is based on the content of the political codes of the individuals who make up the group. Individual political codes can combine, or be aggregated, into a group code. There are a variety of ways in which this can be done, of course. Most obviously might be majority rule, by which the group code contains a certain proposition if the majority of its members' codes contains that proposition. But other aggregation methods are possible, and thus potentially consistent with self-determination, too.

Such group political codes cannot be simply reduced to individual political codes, however. Consider an example involving majoritarian decision making.[16] Suppose a group is facing a question about how to deal with different ideas about religious freedom that exist among its people. And suppose there is, within certain limits, some possible variation in terms of the different regimes that are morally acceptable. Let's further suppose that the individual members of the group base their views about religious freedom on their views concerning two other issues—or to put it differently, they treat their views about religious freedom as conclusions based on two premises. These premises are: (1) that the law should allow people significant freedom in important parts of their lives, and (2) that religion is among these parts.[17] Each of the group's members

16. The example here is a variation on a problem that can arise in legal contexts, first presented in Lewis A. Kornhauser and Lawrence G. Sager, "Unpacking the Court," *Yale Law Journal* 96 (1986): 82–117. List and Pettit, in *Group Agency*, discuss similar cases, which they call "discursive dilemmas."
17. Two points of clarification. First, as should be obvious, nothing for the present argument turns on this particular example. The assumptions in the text are only chosen for ease of exposition. If you strongly disagree with these points, you are free to insert

Table 8.1

GROUP BELIEFS ON RELIGIOUS FREEDOM

	Law should protect important freedoms	*Religion is an important freedom*	*Religious freedom legally protected*
P1	Yes	No	No
P2	No	Yes	No
P3	Yes	Yes	Yes
—	—	—	—
G	Yes	Yes	No

accepts that there exist basic logical connections between these two propositions and their views (conclusions) about religious freedom. That is, if one endorses both (1) and (2), then one also ought to endorse religious freedom.

Imagine that there are at least three persons in this group. Table 8.1 lists their views, as well as the views of the group based on the views of the majority. Note that each of the individuals has internally consistent beliefs about distributive justice (none of the persons endorses both premises of the argument without also endorsing the conclusion). However, the aggregate views of the group, based on the simple majority rule, are inconsistent in just this way. For while the majority of the group believes both that the law should protect important freedoms and that

your own favored issue. Second, and equally obvious, this example significantly understates the complexity involved. The propositions (1) and (2) are really not simple; rather, they are complex propositions, and people might take diverging views on each of their constituent parts. Note, however, that this complexity bolsters the result in the text, as well as its implications. That is, the more complex the issues involved, the stronger the current case for self-determination. For discussion, see List and Pettit, *Group Agency*, 77.

religion is important in this way, the majority also opposes the legal protection of religious freedom. Thus, the group's moral views are internally inconsistent even though none of its members' views are.

The result here, of course, is not a product of this particular issue. It can occur with any set of beliefs that have modest logical connections. Less obviously, the result is also not a feature of the majoritarian method of aggregating individual beliefs. Given a number of plausible conditions, this problem can arise for *any* method of aggregation (participatory, hierarchical, majoritarian, super-majoritarian)—with the only exceptions being very unattractive methods such as dictatorships.[18]

For obvious reasons, a group's political code really should be internally consistent. If the group is at the same time committed to premises that imply a conclusion, and the denial of that conclusion, it will not be able to come to any determinate views. Proponents of the conclusion will be able, and quite reasonably so, to point to the group's views about the premises. While opponents of the conclusion will be able, and quite reasonably so, to point to the group's view about the conclusion. Thus, without an internally consistent group political code, the group will lack the ability to arrive at determinate answers for certain cases—like the case of religious freedom.[19]

18. See Christian List and Philip Pettit, "Aggregating Sets of Judgments: An Impossibility Result," *Economics and Philosophy* 18 (2002): 89–110.
19. List and Pettit claim that this kind of consistency is a condition of group agency. Some people have challenged this thought; see, e.g., Robert Sugden, "Must Group Agents Be Rational? List and Pettit's Theory of Judgement Aggregation and Group Agency," *Economics and Philosophy* 28 (2012): 265–273, 269. But even if Sugden's challenge succeeds against the theory of group *agency*, the account of group *self-determination* I am offering here

This raises difficult questions. Groups face a choice between basing their views on the majority's views concerning the premises or the majority's views concerning the conclusion of a certain issue. It is a substantive moral issue which of the two will be the correct way to go, and this question lies beyond the focus of this essay. But the very fact that there is such a choice to be made shows something important. For, whichever way we go, it will be true that certain propositions need to be recognized as genuine elements of a group's political code, even though they are not directly reducible to the views of its members. Either the group adopts the majority's views on the conclusion—but then it will commit itself to beliefs about the premises that are contrary to the majority's views. Or it adopts the majority's views on the premises—at the price of ignoring the majority's views on the conclusion. Whatever the choice, the group will have adopted a position that is (directly) contrary to its views on one issue, even though it is (indirectly) based on its members' views about another issue. That is, in either case, the group will have a view that is genuinely formed at the group level. It follows that group self-determination is not reducible to individual political codes.[20]

survives. For my account relies on the very plausible assumption that *morality* should be consistent.

20. It is worth noting just how far-reaching this result is. For one, the beliefs of a group's members turn out to be both unnecessary and insufficient for particular group beliefs. In this way, the group can achieve views that are, in a sense, autonomous or self-standing. A group as a whole might endorse something even though each of its members does not endorse it. In fact, the group might endorse something that each of its members opposes. This, in turn, seems to violate certain other intuitive ideas about how rational groups should behave, such as that they allow Pareto-superior moves; see Robert Sugden, "Team Preferences," *Economics and Philosophy* 16 (2000): 175–204, 188.

Note that this account nicely explains both the "self" and the "determination" of self-determination. It is "determination" because groups, as such, can produce their own political codes, which can set their political course.[21] It is determination by the "self" because these processes occur on the basis of members' political codes. As a result, when group political codes are the result of self-determination, they become uniquely valuable. For one, they allow members of a single group who disagree with one another on issues like religious freedom to cooperate on a single determinate political code, without that code being simply imposed on them from the outside. Moreover, such a code is uniquely capable of solving people's disagreements. Because codes that result from self-determination are not readily reducible to any of the personal views of their members, group political codes are importantly impartial. They represent something other than either party to the conflict's insistence (or even any particular private individual's insistence) that they were in the right after all.

It can make sense, then, for people to value the processes of self-determination by which these group political codes come about. And it can make sense to expect others to respect these norms, including would-be interveners. The reason is the same throughout: the process of group self-determination provides people who would otherwise face real problems of disagreement with the possibility of living together on terms that are logically and morally consistent, impartial, and self-imposed in the sense that they are the result of their own views.

A few points are important to note. First, even though group self-determination is genuinely possible and valuable, it

For a different kind of argument, see Margaret Gilbert, *A Theory of Political Obligation* (Oxford University Press, 2008), 137.

21. Whether or when they do, of course, is a separate question.

is by no means a given that it happens in a society. Most obviously, self-determination will be absent when there is no clear connection between the wills of a society's members and the norms or laws by which they are governed. Thus, in societies ruled by oppressive or dictatorial elites, the value of (nonexistent) state self-determination cannot block the case for intervention.[22]

At the same time, it is important to be careful in the other direction as well. For even if it turns out that a society as a whole is not self-determining, it may still also be the case that certain subsets of that society are. That is, certain groups or communities might be organized around their own genuine political codes when the larger society in which they live is not.[23] But even if those forms of self-determination take place on a smaller scale, they are no less valuable. And since these forms of cooperation are still likely to be upset, their value offers, to that extent, a reason against intervention.[24]

Second, it is equally important to stress that even if self-determination can be valuable, this does not mean that any group political code that emerges from this will be morally acceptable, whatever its content. It is perhaps tempting to

22. Indeed, I believe that the chances of society-wide self-determination are exceedingly slim. For a more detailed argument, see Van der Vossen, "Self-Determination and Moral Variation," section 4.
23. Or, more accurately, certain parts of those groups of communities can—namely the parts consisting of the people whose wills are relevantly connected to the group political code.
24. Note that even if intervention were to replace an existing group political code with another, equally functioning one, the intervention will still destroy the value of self-determination. For it will have severed the connection between the group code and the wills of the individual members.

suggest that we should evaluate the acceptability of a group's code in terms of the underlying codes of its members, but that will not do. For even though the group's code is the product of its members' views, the two are importantly separate. As a result, it is possible for a group to develop a problematic collective code even if all its members' views are acceptable. (And, vice versa, it is also possible for people who have deeply unjust views to develop a morally acceptable code as a group.)

It follows that in order to distinguish between morally acceptable and unacceptable group norms, we need to appeal to something other than the views of group members. We need independent moral norms to make this judgment. And I can see no reason (other than potential bad consequences) why individual members ought to use a morally reprehensible group code instead of their own superior ones, or why outsiders should be thought to have to respect bad codes.

With those qualifications in place, then, the value of self-determination stands. And taking this into account, as well as the threat that interventions pose to it, means that the balance at which the morality of intervention aims will tilt toward non-intervention. In other words, the value of self-determination strengthens the presumption against intervention.

STRIKING A BALANCE

Suppose we place different theories of intervention on a spectrum. The Westphalian doctrine of sovereignty would occupy one extreme position, the strongly interventionist view would be at the other extreme. The faults of these views mirror each other. Whereas the traditional doctrine of sovereignty underestimates the importance of internal threats to people's rights and freedoms, the interventionist view underestimates the importance of external threats to people's rights and freedoms, as well as their collective self-determination.

We can make the same point from the opposite direction. Whereas the Westphalian argument mistakenly assumed that allowing any outside interference would lead to dangerous chaos, the opposite assumption by the strong interventionist—that we can remove the main bulwark against international violence without risk—is equally mistaken. At both extremes, in other words, we fail to adequately strike the balance at which the morality of intervention must aim.

A good theory of intervention ought to avoid these risks. The now dominant view of sovereignty and legitimacy, for instance, rejects the Westphalian doctrine without thereby accepting the position defended by Tesón and Wellman. Many now hold that states can be legitimate and therefore rights-protected against foreign military interventions, but only if they adequately protect and respect people's human rights. This view begins to balance the need to have failsafe protections for people's human rights in cases of extreme abuse through external interventions, and the real dangers to safety, peace, and self-determination that such operations pose.[25]

The norm of state sovereignty and noninterference, however, is but one among several norms constraining the international use of force. The threats that give rise to the call for intervention, as well the threats that go with undertaking an intervention in response, extend beyond those that surround the issue of state sovereignty. They form a separate dimension of their own. Thus, the moral and legal constraints on military intervention in countries where the protections of state

25. For a defense, see Van der Vossen, "The Asymmetry of Legitimacy."

sovereignty or legitimacy no longer apply also aim to strike this kind of balance.

In their attempt to loosen the norms of sovereignty and nonintervention, the International Commission on Intervention and State Sovereignty report on *The Responsibility to Protect* asserts that the permissibility of intervention should be evaluated "from the point of view of those seeking or needing support, rather than those who may be considering intervention."[26] Perhaps. But there is a serious mistake lurking here. The moral norms that apply to intervention are the norms that govern the permissible use of force. They specify the conditions under which outside forces can rightfully impose the external threats of intervention in an attempt to undo the internal threats to people's safety, rights, and freedoms. These are, at heart, questions about the permissibility of risk-imposition.[27]

In this sense, the ethics of intervention must (also) focus squarely on the position of the would-be intervener. And it follows, then, that even if states—even if *many* states—that would be the object of interventions lack the rights protections that sovereignty provides, the total set of moral constraints that weigh against intervention need not be weak, diluted, or taken less seriously. Indeed, it does not follow that we should be more open to intervention at all. Put bluntly, there may be many

26. International Commission on Intervention and State Sovereignty, *The Responsibility to Protect*, section 2.29, p. 17.
27. Put in these terms, we can reformulate the objections to the Westphalian doctrine of nonintervention, as well as its opposite extreme. Whereas the Westphalian view (mistakenly) holds that one is never justified in imposing the external risk of intervention (because of its associated dangers of instability and violence), the strongly interventionist view defended by Wellman and Tesón (mistakenly) ignores a crucial set of the risks posed by external interventions.

reasons that count against intervention other than state sovereignty. Indeed, oftentimes the argument against intervention may be overdetermined. A state's sovereignty might block it, but so too might other considerations. Removing the barrier of sovereignty thus need not open the road to intervention.

These other considerations, like the argument for state sovereignty, also capture the appropriate balance between the two competing considerations that govern the morality of intervention in general. This is the question on which I will focus for much of the remainder of this part of the book. I will ask when the imposition of external risks through military intervention is justifiable in order to stave off the internal risks to people's safety, rights, and freedoms.

The first step will be to develop an account of the *success condition* for justified military interventions. This condition is one among many conditions of just warfare, such as that interventions are proportional, measures of last resort, avoid using unacceptable weaponry, and so on. The success condition, as the name suggests, adds to these that a morally acceptable intervention must have a good enough probability of success.

After defending this condition as an appropriate constraint on the justified undertaking of military interventions, I offer an account of how it is best understood, and then apply it to the specific case of humanitarian interventions. Doing this, I will argue, makes clear why we should accept the presumption against intervention. In short, even when state sovereignty does not stand in the way, interventions are rarely justified because they rarely have a good enough probability of success.

9

The Success Condition

HUMANITARIAN INTERVENTIONS ARE PERMISSIBLE only if the risks they create for others can be permissibly imposed on them. Call the condition of such permissible risk imposition the *success condition*. The condition holds that morally justified interventions have a good enough chance of succeeding, thus rendering the dangers they impose, other things being equal, morally acceptable.[1]

If the success condition is sound, one part of the justice of an intervention is determined at the time it is undertaken. No matter what happens in the end, if the prospects of intervention are too poor at the time, military intervention is (at least to that extent) unjust. Accepting this condition thus implies accepting

1. The success condition is part of the traditional theory of *jus ad bellum*, the justice of initiating war. Surprisingly—to my mind, at least—the success condition has received relatively little attention in the now vast literature on the ethics of war. A few exceptions are Daniel Statman, "On the Success Condition for Legitimate Self-Defense," *Ethics* 118 (2008): 659–686. Suzanne Uniacke, "Self-Defence, Just War and a Reasonable Prospect of Success," in *How We Fight*, ed. Helen Frowe and Gerald Lang (Oxford University Press, 2013). See also Brian Orend, "War," in *The Stanford Encyclopedia of Philosophy*, Fall 2008 ed., ed. Edward N. Zalta, at http://plato.stanford.edu/archives/fall2008/entries/war/.

that the morality of a humanitarian intervention is not just a function of the actual outcomes it brings about.

As we will see, the prospects of actual interventions are almost never good enough to make them morally acceptable. As a result, perhaps, those who defend a more permissive stance on interventionism tend to criticize or debunk the success condition as a genuine requirement of just war.[2] This chapter and the next defend the success condition as an important part of *jus ad bellum*, and thus as a true necessary condition of justifiable humanitarian interventions.

"GETTING IT RIGHT THIS TIME"

Let's begin with a real-life example. In August 2014, President Barack Obama authorized airstrikes on Iraq aimed at stopping the fundamentalist group Islamic State (IS). As per usual, the justification for the airstrikes was put in glowingly humanitarian terms. IS had been conquering and brutalizing large parts of northern Iraq, killing and maiming tens of thousands of people in the process, and it aimed to establish an oppressive regime. America, President Obama urged, could not turn a blind eye.

2. See, e.g., Gillian Brock, *Global Justice: A Cosmopolitan Account* (Oxford University Press, 2009), 179–180. Altman and Wellman discuss the success condition—they claim it can be satisfied even when dealing with "a daunting foe"; see Altman and Wellman, *A Liberal Theory of International Justice*, 105. Even Walzer at times entertains the thought; see Walzer, *Just and Unjust Wars*, 70. Others, as we will see in the next chapter, claim that what matters is actual success at the end of the intervention, not its probability before.

Mr. Obama was the fourth consecutive U.S. president to authorize attacks on Iraq. Dating back to 1991, George H. W. Bush, Bill Clinton, and George W. Bush all attacked Saddam Hussein's Iraq. At first, airstrikes were undertaken to protect the Kurdish people in the north of the country. Later the aim became damaging Hussein's weapons capabilities and weakening his grip on the country so that he might be toppled.[3] When the change in regime did not happen by itself, President George W. Bush, now infamously, followed up with a full-scale invasion to force the issue.

The track record of these attacks has been poor, to say the least. The past two decades have seen enormous levels of death and destruction across the country. Iraq is now politically, ethnically, and socially unstable—and highly violent. Yet, despite this track record, the British magazine *The Economist* offered a strong endorsement of President Obama's decision to order the airstrikes in its August 16, 2014, cover story. If anything, the magazine argued, Mr. Obama was being too hesitant. *The Economist* wanted to see not only more robust action in Iraq but military operations in Syria as well.

The Economist was not unaware of the ignominious history of failed foreign interventions in Iraq. Much of the cover story discussed past failures and ongoing challenges, and indeed it emphasized that the probability that intervention would succeed this time around was very low. Nevertheless, it maintained that intervening would be the right thing to as long as the United States made sure that it was, finally, successful. The

3. See Philip Shenon, "Attack on Iraq; Mission Intended to Degrade Iraq Threat," *New York Times*, December 20, 1998, at http://www.nytimes.com/1998/12/20/world/attack-on-iraq-mission-intended-to-degrade-iraq-threat.html.

story's subtitle neatly summarized the main point: "Getting it right this time."

To anyone who takes the success condition seriously, this position is quite simply unacceptable. In light of that condition, one cannot simultaneously hold that the prospects of success for military intervention are extremely low *and* maintain that attacking would be the right thing to do. The success condition holds that a necessary condition of just intervention is that the chances of success are good. If we accept that condition, this alone would be sufficient to condemn the proposal.

EXCESSIVE RISK-TAKING

Should we accept the success condition? One way to see why the answer is yes is by thinking of the success condition as an application of the more familiar moral prohibition on the imposition of certain kinds of risk. At least at first pass, it seems that this moral prohibition is very plausible. As a result, its international application in the form of the success condition should look very plausible to us as well.

It's a truism that morally we cannot expose others to certain risks. Consider the stock example: playing Russian Roulette on unsuspecting passers-by is morally wrong, and it remains wrong if the gun doesn't fire. We owe it to others not to take that kind of a chance with their lives. The risks to which our actions expose others reflect the proportion of other factors than our wills determining whether or not certain benefits or harms will befall them as a result of what we do. The riskier an action, the more we choose to count on things outside ourselves to prevent those outcomes from befalling others. Risks are excessive when those others have a claim against us putting their fates in the hands of fortune this way.

What's not a truism is that the wrongfulness of risk-imposition doesn't just lie in the probability of a harm occurring. The reasons for which the probability is imposed matter, too. According to the National Safety Council, the average American has a 1 in 113 lifetime chance of dying from a car crash.[4] Let's say that it is morally acceptable for each of us to impose the corresponding risk of death on others when we get into our car. But if that's acceptable, it does not follow that exposing people to the same lifetime chance of dying from Russian Roulette would also be morally acceptable. Even if one were to play with a gun that imposed on others only a 1 in 113 lifetime chance of dying, the only acceptable option is to not play Russian Roulette on people at all. The probabilities are not all that matter.

It follows, then, that the morality of risk-imposition cannot be a matter of a simple expected utility calculation.[5] From such a standpoint, the two cases above are identical: both the harm (death) and the probability (approximately 9 percent) are the same. Other things than merely the probabilities and magnitude of harms matter, such as what the point is of creating the risk in question. In the case of Russian Roulette, the point of the action is a troubling kind of thrill seeking. In the case of driving, people have the legitimate purpose of transporting themselves and goods around the world.

The moral prohibition on risk-imposition, and by extension the success condition, must take this into account. Whether or not people have a claim against certain risks being imposed on them will depend on things like the magnitude of the harm

4. National Safety Council, *Injury Facts 2016*, at http://www.nsc.org/learn/safety-knowledge/Pages/injury-facts-chart.aspx.
5. See Thomas Hurka, "Proportionality and the Morality of War," *Philosophy and Public Affairs* 33 (2005): 37. I discuss Hurka's views in more detail later.

(if a harm is what is risked), its moral significance, and more. One way to approach this question is by thinking of the kind of overall combination of outcomes that would follow from adopting a certain rule about risk-taking. Prohibitions on excessive risk-taking in general, and the success condition in particular, can then be seen as limitations on actions that aim at bringing about an overall a mix of the good at which the risky action aims, and the bad that will predictably result from some of these risks materializing. For such a mix to be acceptable, the good must strongly outweigh the bad.

The success condition for military intervention, then, poses a rule that identifies a cutoff point for acceptable risks that these operations may impose, such that they will tend toward the overall acceptable mix of interventions that are successes and failures, undertaken and forgone. That is, it aims at an overall morally acceptable mix of successful interventions, failed interventions, interventions that are (unfortunately) forgone but would have been successful, and interventions that are (fortunately) foregone but would have failed. In this way, the condition operationalizes the balance between internal and external threats at which the morality of intervention aims in general.

Let's call an argument *teleological* if it aims to establish a certain rule or principle as justified because of its role in bringing about a morally desirable state of affairs. The argument just given, then, offers a teleological defense of the success condition as a moral requirement for justifiable interventions. This condition is not the only part of international morality, or for that matter morality in general, where such teleological arguments can be useful. Compare the theory of legitimacy discussed in the previous chapter, according to which states are legitimate only if they pass some morally important benchmark. Most theorists think that this benchmark includes things like the state's human rights record, whether it's democratic, and so on.

The reason to constrain the class of legitimate states in this way, we saw, is to better protect people overall.

It's a feature of teleological arguments that they can support rules that prohibit acts which would be beneficial in a particular instance because they are inconsistent with a (teleologically justified) rule that is beneficial in general. If such an act would be acceptable only under a rule that would be undesirable overall, such acts may be condemned as overly risky, say.

Compare again the case of state legitimacy. We could imagine an undemocratic state that (against the odds) offers near perfect protection of human rights. However, on a teleological view of legitimacy, this (imaginary) state is still illegitimate. Even if things go well in this case, counting such states as legitimate will *as a rule* encourage abuse and render people more vulnerable. After all, the norms of legitimacy apply around the world, not just to this one exceptional state. And we're all better off under a rule that does not recognize undemocratic states as legitimate.

The same is true with rules governing risk-imposition. As mentioned, the morality of risk-imposition is not simply a function of the harms that eventuate. Sometimes, risks can be impermissible even though they lead to no harm.

This is plausible, too. (Perhaps more plausible, even, than with legitimacy.) Consider a more extreme, imaginary analogue to *The Economist*'s proposal. Suppose that, instead of ordering airstrikes, the Obama administration had opted to send in its special forces to poison the Iraqi water supply and turn off the water only to innocent civilians, with the idea being to poison only members of IS. Obviously, this plan would be morally unacceptable, even if it were somehow (against the odds) successful. Allowing actions like this will much more often lead to indiscriminate and ineffectual deaths than would a discriminate and effective intervention, so we're better off with a rule that prohibits such actions outright. From a teleological perspective, the overall balance of benefits and harms would be unacceptable, thus ruling out any intervention using such risky methods.

That is not to say, of course, that it is *impossible* for the imaginary operation to succeed. We can imagine a case in which things worked exactly as planned (hoped). But the danger posed to ordinary Iraqis *ex ante* by this plan is simply morally unacceptable, no matter what the outcome. This is captured by the success condition for justified military intervention.

We would not take very seriously, I think, articles in imaginary magazines arguing that *if* this risky operation got things right, and if it would spare many more innocent lives, it would have been the right thing to do. But if that is so, and this imaginary plan clearly violates the success condition, it's at least an open question whether the actual intervention recommended by the actual *Economist* violated the success condition as well. As we will see, it did.

THE VALUE OF SUCCESS

The success condition avoids the problem of excessive risk-taking by allowing only those military interventions that have a good enough probability that they will succeed. This immediately raises two questions, of course. First, what counts as success? And second, what kinds of probabilities are involved? Let's take these in turn.

On the view I am sketching here, probabilities of success matter because they determine the proportion of morally valuable outcomes in the overall mix of outcomes that general adherence to the condition would bring about. Interventions are permissible, then, only if the value of this proportion is sufficient to outweigh the disvalue of the bad outcomes that will predictably also result from adherence to the condition. The probability of success that is necessary for an intervention to be justified will thus be sensitive to both the number and (dis) value of both the good and bad outcomes.

The point of the success condition is not merely that an intervention must have a good shot at achieving its ends. The success condition is more than simply the idea that it is better to do things efficiently rather than inefficiently.[6] The notion of success in play here is a moralized one. After all, risked successes can outweigh risked failures only if the former are indeed sufficiently good in light of the latter.

The problem with thinking about success in terms of mere efficiency (or, better, efficacy) is that it omits this moralized dimension. Doing so is plainly unacceptable. For a non-moralized condition of success (as efficacy) could help justify unjust wars as long as they were very well executed. Indeed, it would help justify them *for the reason that* they were very well executed. But that gets things exactly the wrong way around—evil is less bad when it's done poorly.

Because the idea of success is moralized, it will be sensitive to a variety of *jus ad bellum* requirements. Good humanitarian outcomes will not morally outweigh the use of violence and risked harms if those harms could have been reasonably avoided in bringing about the humanitarian result. And the good only outweighs the bad if there is enough of it—if the harms are not disproportionate to the humanitarian outcome. In this sense, the relevant notion of success presupposes that other conditions like necessity or proportionality are satisfied as well.[7]

6. See also Statman, "On the Success Condition for Legitimate Self-Defense," 660.
7. *Contra* Helen Frowe, who holds that the success condition refers only to proportionality; see Helen Frowe, *Defensive Killing: An*

The fact that the success condition makes reference to other *jus ad bellum* conditions explains why, as we have seen, the success condition's requirements cannot be captured by the product of only the probability and number of lives saved versus killed. And this is plausible, too. Suppose there is an evil dictator whom we are 90 percent sure is about to murder one hundred innocent people. And suppose that, other things being equal, this would be sufficient to justify killing him in order to save the innocents. Call the net value of saving the innocents V. It follows that an expected value of 0.9*V is sufficient for killing the dictator.

Compare this to a group of a hundred people, ninety of whom are each about to do the same as the evil dictator—that is, kill a hundred innocent people—while the remaining ten are innocent. Killing a person at random from this group would have the same expected value as 0.9*V, yet doing so might not be permissible. Or, at the very least, the two cases do not raise the same moral issues. Given that the success condition must reflect these moral issues if it is going to help justify interventions, again, it cannot be interpreted as a straightforward expected value calculation.

Since the point at which interventions become permissible is sensitive to the expected number and quality of outcomes, given the probability required by the success condition, there can be no single probability at which interventions are permissible. Generally speaking, it is true that the humanitarian good will outweigh the harms only when the value of the good is significantly greater than the disvalue of the harms. But when one's chosen means are less dangerous, a lower likelihood of the same good can suffice. If the water poisoning plan

Essay on War and Self-Defence (Oxford University Press, 2014), chapter 5. I discuss further problems with her view later.

exposed Iraqi citizens not to a risk of death but to the same risk of temporarily losing their hair, while still having the same probability of having the same beneficial results, one would feel differently. A different overall mix of outcomes can be acceptable in that case, leading to a different required probability of success.

Some philosophers think that this account of the success condition misconstrues the relation between success and other *jus ad bellum* conditions. According to Jeff McMahan "the requirement of 'reasonable hope of success' is subsumed by the proportionality requirement."[8] Thomas Hurka writes that "the *ad bellum* proportionality condition incorporates hope-of-success considerations."[9] According to McMahan and Hurka, then, success is a part of proportionality, not the other way around. Indeed, both McMahan and Hurka seem to think that this shows the success condition is not really an independent condition of just war.[10]

8. See Jeff McMahan, "Just Cause for War," *Ethics and International Affairs* 19 (2005): 5.
9. See Hurka, "Proportionality and the Morality of War," 37. See also A. J. Coates, *The Ethics of War* (Manchester University Press, 1997), 179. Altman and Wellman offer the same suggestion when they defend a *proportionality* condition in the following terms: "Subject to certain conditions, an armed intervention is permissible if the risk to rights is not disproportionate to the human rights violations that one can reasonably expect to avert"; see Altman and Wellman, *A Liberal Theory of International Justice*, 112, 105, 113.
10. The reasons for drawing this conclusion elude me. I'm not sure what's gained by settling whether conditions are *real* conditions of just war (at least if one agrees that they identify a dimension along which wars can be or fail to be morally acceptable), so I will set aside the matter. Suffice it to say that if there is a point to such discussion, the arguments in the text cast doubt on the

But this alternative suggestion has some highly implausible implications. For if the success condition is part of the proportionality condition, then it follows that in all cases where the use of force is proportional, it must also have a good enough probability of success. And this is plainly false. Suppose, for example, that I am threatening to punch you in the shoulder and you can only defend yourself by punching me in the shoulder first. It's clear that doing so would not be disproportionate. However, this says nothing about the likelihood that your attempt will actually succeed. If I'm a professional boxer, say, your chances of stopping me may well be very low. Obviously, this doesn't mean you are not permitted to defend yourself—you don't have to submit to me just because I'm a better fighter. It follows that the proportionality condition can be satisfied without the success condition being satisfied, *contra* McMahan and Hurka.

The difference here is due to the success condition governing lesser evil justifications, in which harms that would otherwise be unjustifiable can become acceptable because they are outweighed by a much greater good. Not so in cases of self-defense like the one just described. As a result of threatening you, I have forfeited my rights against your defensive force. No outweighing is necessary in that case, meaning that the success condition, but not proportionality, becomes inapplicable.[11] So, while Hurka is right when he writes that "[what] makes [a war] violate the reasonable hope of success condition, surely also

genuineness of the necessity and proportionality conditions (and perhaps others).

11. Another reason to reject McMahan and Hurka's view will become clear in the next chapter, where we will see a conflict in what I will call the *ex ante* and *ex post* versions of the proportionality condition.

makes it disproportionate,"[12] the relation goes in the opposite direction. Proportionality is part of the success condition, not the other way around.[13]

Helen Frowe offers an argument that might seem to cut against this view. Suppose, she writes, that we can make a war have a greater likelihood of success by using extreme violence. On the view just given, this seems to mean that doing so must also enhance the war's proportionality. But this is plainly false. After all, if a war is disproportionate at a certain level of force, it cannot be proportionate at a greater level of force, even if using disproportionate force would make it more likely to succeed.[14]

But this misconstrues the nature of the success condition.[15] As we've seen, that condition doesn't only track the likelihood of a war achieving the aims of the attacker—something which disproportionate violence might indeed make more likely. The success condition tracks the likelihood of a war achieving a humanitarian end sufficient to outweigh the harms that are caused in its process. Using disproportionate violence defeats that possibility. It is impossible for an intervention to be

12. Hurka, "Proportionality and the Morality of War," 37.
13. The ICISS Report on the *Responsibility to Protect* gets this right when it holds proportionality to be part of the success condition; see section 4.41, p. 37.
14. See Frowe, *Defensive Killing*, 150.
15. The relation between proportionality and the success condition is the source of much confusion. Frowe offers the argument as an objection to the McMahan and Hurka view. However, Frowe's argument fails as an objection to Hurka and McMahan's view because it assumes that wars that satisfy the success condition also satisfy proportionality. And that is precisely the reverse of the view proposed by Hurka and McMahan, who claim that if wars are proportional wars, then they also satisfy the success condition.

successful in the moralized sense when it is disproportional—much less *because* it is disproportional.

It's worth noting, then, that there are two points at which harms caused by interveners can be morally outweighed by humanitarian outcomes. On the one hand, these harms can be justifiable when and because they are proportional to a humanitarian outcome. At this point, the harms are (subject to other conditions) acceptable, if obviously regrettable, because of the role they play in saving the lives of many others. On the other hand, it can be acceptable to do things that may result in the imposition of harms (including harms that will not be acceptable in this first sense) because doing so is a practically unavoidable part of doing things that will end up actually saving lives. The success condition requires that the probabilities of this latter combination of outcomes represent an overall acceptable distribution of success and failure.

These really are two distinct points. The success condition considers the moral desirability of some interventions succeeding sufficient to accept the moral tragedy of some interventions failing. At this point, then, the harms and benefits of different interventions count in a single moral calculus. But this is true *only* about the success condition. A disproportionate intervention does not become acceptable because a previous intervention exceeded what was required by proportionality. At this point, the moral calculus remains wholly confined to a single operation.

THREE KINDS OF PROBABILITY

The second question about the success condition concerns the kinds of probabilities at work. There are at least three different kinds of probability that the condition might incorporate. First, the condition might refer to what we can call *objective probabilities*. Such objective probabilities refer to things in our world that occur in a random manner. The truth of a statement involving such an objective probability depends on the objective regularities in nature. Second, the condition might refer to *subjective probabilities*, which concern the degree of confidence that agents have in a certain proposition. The truth of such statements depends on whether they accurately report the agent's degree of belief. Finally, *evidentiary probability* occupies a space between the other two. This refers to the degree of confidence that an agent would be warranted or justified in having about a proposition in light of the evidence. The truth of this third kind of statement depends on the objective evidence the agent has in support of the proposition in question.[16]

To illustrate the differences between these kinds of probabilities, consider a simple example involving two people playing a game that involves rolling a die. Suppose both have high degree of confidence that the die they are using is loaded to come up on the number 3. And suppose they believe this even though all the evidence available to them indicates that the die is fair. Suppose finally that, contrary to both the evidence and their beliefs, the die is actually loaded to come up on the number 4. In that case, the subjective probability of the die coming up 3 would be more than 1 in 6. The evidentiary probability would be exactly 1 in 6. And the objective probability of the die coming up 3 would be less than 1 in 6.

16. See Alan Hájek, "Interpretations of Probability," in *The Stanford Encyclopedia of Philosophy*, Winter 2012 ed., ed. Edward N. Zalta, at http://plato.stanford.edu/archives/win2012/entries/probability-interpret/. Unfortunately, some commentators overlook this third possibility. See Hurka, "Proportionality and the Morality of War," 38.

While in principle the success condition of just war could be interpreted using any of these probabilities, it really should refer to the evidentiary probability that an intervention will succeed. In other words, interventions are permissible only if the intervening agent would be justified in believing that the intervention has a good enough probability of success, given the agent's evidence.[17]

In addition to the reasons discussed in the next chapter, the main reason for this is that it best fits the success condition's motivation. If the point of the condition is to avoid pointless—and therefore unjustified—harms, the most reliable way of doing so is by prohibiting irresponsible decisions to go to war. Basing the permissibility of intervention on objective probabilities may not further this end much since, as we've already seen, interventions can be reckless even when, objectively speaking, they will succeed. The imaginary plan of poisoning the Iraqi water supply might actually work, but that would not make it morally permissible.

On the other hand, tying an intervention's permissibility to the *mere* beliefs of intervening agents would be plainly unacceptable.[18] A strictly subjective version of the success condition

17. The attentive reader will have spotted an ambiguity in this evidentiary kind of probability. On the one hand, an intervention's probability of success could depend on the degree of confidence in success that one would be justified in having if one had fully availed oneself of all the *available* evidence. On the other hand, it could depend on the confidence one would be justified in having in light of the evidence of which one has actually *availed* oneself. The details of this issue go well beyond what matters for our discussion. For detailed discussion, and a defense of the latter option, see Michael Zimmerman, *Ignorance and Moral Obligation* (Oxford University Press, 2014), chapter 3.
18. As Nicholas Wheeler, for instance, seems to think. Wheeler writes that a necessary condition of justified intervention "is

could allow wars simply for the reason that the intervening agent had poorly supported but overconfident beliefs about the likelihood of success. It would allow the delusional, as well as those who simply do not care to investigate their beliefs any further, to wage war with justice. And it might prohibit wars by the overly careful. If anything, we would want things to be the other way around.

Reading the success condition along evidentiary lines removes this troubling subjectivity. There is a fact of the matter, independent of what any agent might think, about whether or not the evidence about a given intervention indicates that its chance of success is sufficiently good. Thus, the success condition understood along these lines is no less objective than it would be if understood as referring to objective probabilities.

IS THE SUCCESS CONDITION TOO DEMANDING?

The success condition, then, holds that justified interveners are warranted in believing that intervening has a high enough probability of justly bringing about a humanitarian outcome.[19] Some, however, doubt whether the condition is ultimately acceptable. For instance, Daniel Statman has argued that the requirement is counterintuitive, prohibiting what he thinks seem clearly permissible wars.

that decision-makers must believe the use of force will produce a humanitarian outcome"; see Wheeler, *Saving Strangers*, 37. Compare also Hurka, "Proportionality and the Morality of War," 37.

19. To say that a humanitarian outcome is achieved justly is to say that it is brought about in a way consistent with the (other) just-war requirements.

Statman offers the example of the Warsaw Ghetto Uprising of 1943.[20] When the Germans started deporting Jews from the ghetto to Treblinka, murdering around 300,000 of them within two months, those remaining took up arms against the German oppressors. The uprising had little to no chance of success, and was crushed by the Germans within a month. Yet, as Statman writes, if there ever were a justified case of self-defense, the uprising in the Warsaw Ghetto would be it. The success condition, then, seems to imply that faced with overwhelming opposition, the moral thing to do is to submit. But that's clearly counterintuitive.

Less clear, however, is whether this example puts much pressure on the success condition. Earlier we saw that the success condition primarily governs lesser-evil justifications of force—cases where the good one sets out to achieve is supposed to outweigh the (otherwise unjustifiable) harms one might cause. However, the Nazi attackers in Statman's example seem to plainly have forfeited their rights against defensive force. And when attackers act so as to forfeit these rights, resistance does not require a lesser-evil justification. It seems, then, that Statman's intuition that the Jews were justified in fighting, despite the small probability of success, does not challenge the success condition as it is defended here.

That said, things do become more difficult if the Jews' fighting in self-defense would risk harming innocent third parties. If, say, the Jews' fighting back against the Nazis would seriously threaten to kill a large number of other Varsovians—people who (we may suppose) did have a right not to be killed—the success condition becomes relevant again. In order for those harms to be justifiable, the Jews should have had a good enough

20. Statman, "On the Success Condition for Legitimate Self-Defense," 665ff.

prospect of success. Thus, on the view defended here, if the Jews' resistance to the Nazis were both dangerous to innocent third parties and indeed hopeless, this could render their fight impermissible after all.

Upon reflection, this strikes me as the correct verdict. Consider the opposite extreme from the stylized case that Statman considers. Suppose that the Warsaw Jews—technologically advanced at the time, let's imagine—had a nuclear bomb available and decided to "defend" themselves by blowing up the entire city, killing all Jews, Nazis, and all other Varsovians who would otherwise survive. Other things equal, surely those collateral harms are enough to render this strategy morally prohibited. Similarly, and a little less extreme, if the Jews had some tactical weapon available that would kill everyone in the city but them, that too, I believe, would be clearly impermissible.

Tragic though this can be, then, the rights of third parties can stand in the way of defending ourselves.[21] This is just what gives the success condition its force. It is because the harms that fighting will impose stand in need of justification that fighting must have a good enough chance of bringing about an end capable of providing that justification.

21. As Frowe writes: "It is concerns about harm to innocent people that explain why [Statman's view] . . . won't suffice to justify inflicting harms that have a low probability of success . . . collateral harms to innocent people must not only be proportionate but also the lesser evil"; see Frowe, *Defensive Killing*, 153.

10

Justice *Ex Post* or *Ex Ante*?

OUR QUESTION IS THIS: WHEN CAN an agent who is facing the decision whether or not to intervene permissibly do so? So far, I have argued that there are two kinds of moral restrictions to these decisions: interventions can be justified only when dealing with states that are not legitimate; and interventions can be justified only when they have a good enough chance of justly bringing about a humanitarian outcome (that is, success).

In earlier work, Fernando Tesón suggested that success indeed plays an important role in the morality of intervention. (He disagrees with the first restriction, of course.) But Tesón conceives of this role in a quite different way. As he sees it, "success is an integral part of the justification for war," but it is something that "can only be determined *ex post*."[1] Nicholas Wheeler suggests a similar view. According to Wheeler, "the legitimacy

1. Tesón, *Humanitarian Intervention*, 404; see also 407. For Tesón's more general *ex post* approach, see 103ff; compare also 155–156. Note that elsewhere Tesón seems to endorse the *ex ante* success condition. As I argue later, this suggestion is puzzling, too, as it allows one and the same condition to render contradictory verdicts.

of humanitarian intervention should be judged in terms of whether it produces a positive humanitarian outcome."[2]

The point here is the same as the one we saw *The Economist* make in the previous chapter. We should evaluate the justice of interventions not in terms of how likely they were to work out when the intervention was undertaken, but in terms of how they actually work out. Interventions, in other words, are justified if and only if we manage to get things right.[3]

In practice, there may often be little difference between judging interventions by their prospects or by their results. For, often, interventions are both unlikely to succeed and actually end up failing. Then again, sometimes long shots pay out. And in those cases, we're confronted with a choice: If the prospects

2. Wheeler, *Saving Strangers*, 107; see also 106: "the test of legitimacy becomes how far intervention rescues those in danger and creates the political conditions to safeguard human rights in the future." Compare 101–102, 141, 173, 188–200, 243, 284. Note that both Tesón and Wheeler elsewhere accept the traditional success condition, which may suggest a kind of hybrid account. I discuss such hybrid accounts, and their problems, in this chapter.
3. *The Economist* article, Wheeler, and Tesón are hardly alone in this view. See also, for example, Oliver Ramsbotham and Tom Woodhouse, *Humanitarian Intervention in Contemporary Conflict* (Polity Press, 1996), 72–76; Bruce Jones, "Intervention without Borders: Humanitarian Intervention in Rwanda, 1900-94," *Millennium: Journal of International Studies* 24, no. 2 (1995): 225–248, 238. Richard B. Miller discusses similar uses of this view in "Justifications of the Iraq War Examined," *Ethics and International Affairs* 22 (2008): 43–67. For a related issue, see Pattison's treatment of the "Extreme Instrumentalist Approach," in Pattison, *Humanitarian Intervention and the Responsibility to Protect*, 93–94.

were poor (or good) and the outcomes good (or poor), what should we think about the decision to intervene? Was intervention justified? Was it not? Was it justified *and* unjustified? (And does that even make sense?)

This chapter addresses the tension between these two ways of thinking about the morality of intervention.

CONFLICTING PERSPECTIVES

Let us call a theory *ex ante* if it judges the morality of interventions in the forward-looking manner exemplified by the success condition. *Ex ante* theories, then, see the justice of intervention as depending on facts as they were at the time of attack. The success condition counts as an *ex ante* condition because it sees the justice of interventions as depending on their likelihood of justly bringing about a humanitarian outcome.

By contrast, we will call a theory *ex post* if it evaluates the justice of intervention in a backward-looking manner. Such a theory focuses on facts about interventions as they work out in the end. *Ex post* theories, then, consider humanitarian interventions morally justified when they actually bring about a humanitarian end, when they used means that were actually proportionate to this end, when they were actually necessary, and so on.[4]

4. While in one sense *ex post* approaches evaluate the morality of intervention in terms of its results, they need not be consequentialist in nature. That is, *ex post* approaches do not entail the claim that the morality of interventions depends on their bringing about the greatest overall good, happiness, or what have you. The relevant outcomes can be identified in terms of the absence of rights violations, people's complying with deontological constraints, and so on.

Consider three ways of dealing with these contrasting approaches. First, we might think that the *ex ante* approach is exclusively correct. On this way of proceeding, a remark like Tesón's simply has to be mistaken. Success matters in a prospective sense, in a prohibition on excessively risky intervention. But the justice of intervention cannot depend directly on actual outcomes.

Second, we might take the opposite view, and side with the *ex post* approach. If that's right, the *ex ante* success condition I have been defending must be rejected. Here, what matters are not prospective probabilities but actual success in outcome. An intervention being risky at the time need not be irrelevant, but it would still be the right decision as long as things work out in the end (*because* things work out in the end).

I'll return to these two uncompromising options later. For now, let's first look at a third, more conciliatory possibility—combining both approaches into a single, unified view. On this third approach, the justice of intervention is mixed, with a part that takes an *ex ante* approach and another part that is *ex post*. Might such an approach work?

The conciliatory appearance of this mixed approach is attractive, of course.[5] It promises to honor the motivations behind each of the perspectives. And both motivations do track something real. On the one hand, we often don't care as much

5. This approach is very popular in recent theorizing about just war. Many authors try to combine so-called objective and subjective, or fact-relative and evidence-relative, standards of rightness in their theories. See, for example, Seth Lazar, "Risky Killing and the Ethics of War," *Ethics* 126 (2015): 91–117; Jonathan Quong, "Proportionality, Liability, and Defensive Harm," *Philosophy & Public Affairs* 43 (2015): 144–173; and Frowe, *Defensive Killing*. The arguments that follow strike against not only such mixed views of the success condition but also mixed views more generally.

about people's intentions or motivations as we do about the outcomes they bring about. We're right to care about this, too. It's of little solace to someone dying in Syria today who could have been saved that at least nothing reckless was done.[6] On the other hand, we also care about not being surrounded by people who would do reckless or irresponsible things, and especially when we're talking about recklessly or irresponsibly using military force. Again, we're right to care. Life among reckless political and military leaders makes our world less safe and less just.

However, this appearance of reconciliation is deceptive. Imagine that an intervention *ex ante* violated the success condition (in the sense defended earlier), but was undertaken anyway and actually worked out well in the end (thus satisfying the *ex post* sense of success). On a mixed approach, and other things being equal, this intervention would be both unjustified in the *ex ante* sense and justified in the *ex post* sense. But now we face an obvious question: What are we to make of that result? What are we to make of a situation in which the very same condition (of success) renders two contradictory verdicts? Should a would-be intervener, interested in doing the right thing, follow the *ex ante* or the *ex post* standard?[7]

One way to make sense of this answer would be to say that the two standards apply at different times. That is, maybe at t_1 the intervention was the wrong thing to do, but at t_2 it was the right thing to do. In that case, whether our would-be intervener should follow the *ex ante* or the *ex post* standard would depend on the time we're asking the question. If interveners

6. This seems to be Tesón's motivation for adopting an *ex post* approach. See Fernando Tesón, "Ending Tyranny in Iraq," *Ethics and International Affairs* 19 (2005): 1–20, 3ff.

7. Needless to say, the same question arises if things are the other way around and an intervention is *ex ante* justified but *ex post* unjustified.

find themselves at t_1, they should follow the *ex ante* standard. If they find themselves at t_2, then the *ex post* standard matters.

But that doesn't really help the case for a mixed approach. After all, if the intervention happens at t_1 and at t_1 intervening would be wrong, then it doesn't really matter much that at some other time t_2 it might have been the right thing to do. We're not at that time. We're at the time t_1, and there the justice of the intervention isn't mixed at all. It's *ex ante* wrong. Or, if we happen to be at t_2, the intervention is, again not mixed, but *ex post* right. This response, in other words, effectively abandons the mixed approach.

Might the idea be subtler than this? Perhaps the way things play out *ex post* can alter what was the right thing to do *ex ante*? This is quite the mysterious claim. For while it is plainly possible for an intervention that is at time t_1 morally prohibited, to become at a later point t_2 morally permissible, it cannot be the case that an intervention that is at time t_1 morally prohibited later at t_2 becomes *also* morally permissible *at* t_1. For now the original question reappears. If at t_1 the intervention is both permissible and impermissible, we don't know what to do anymore. If we're interested in doing the right thing, should we follow the *ex ante* or the *ex post* approach?[8]

A third possible suggestion would be that this is a false dilemma. Perhaps we can just live with this? Perhaps these are two different perspectives we take on the same condition, and we can simply accept that these perspectives sometimes render contradictory results.[9] In this case, the answer would be that

8. Might one say that the effect of the *ex post* standard is that the *ex ante* standard no longer applies at t_1? Perhaps. But if the *ex ante* standard doesn't apply at t_1, and (by hypothesis) doesn't apply at t_2, we've again abandoned the mixed approach.
9. Thomas Hurka suggests that the success condition is the prospective application of the proportionality condition, as it refers to

intervention is permissible in an *ex post* sense, but impermissible in an *ex ante* sense. And that, as they say, is that.

But this really won't do. Our would-be interveners are asking an important moral question—perhaps the most important moral question agents might in good faith ask.[10] They want to know what, as moral agents, they ought to do in their situation. When conscientious people ask that question, the mixed answer simply isn't an answer at all. "Don't intervene *ex ante*, but make sure you intervened *ex post*" isn't among their options. One cannot satisfy one part without violating the other.

Note that this is not to say that it is impossible to correctly describe acts at the same time as right and wrong. Perhaps there can be genuine moral dilemmas—cases in which doing one thing we're morally required to do rules out doing another thing we're also morally required to do. But even if there genuinely are such cases, surely this isn't one of them. The dilemma we're facing here is not one in which we have to choose between two genuine moral demands, only one of which we can comply with. Our dilemma here is a different one: Which is the real moral demand in the first place?[11]

an agent's subjective estimate that the proportionality condition will be satisfied; see Hurka, "Proportionality and the Morality of War," 37.

10. For important discussion on this, see Michael Zimmerman, *Living with Uncertainty* (Cambridge University Press, 2008); and Zimmerman, *Ignorance and Moral Obligation.*
11. It will not do either to say that interventions are permissible if and only if *both* standards are satisfied. As we will see in the next section, sometimes the evidence can conspire against us in ways that make it impossible to comply with both standards at the same time. This means once again that it is impossible for interveners to act permissibly.

We're no closer, then, to finding an acceptable mixed way of answering our question. And we really do need an answer if justice in intervention is to be possible. We really need to know, that is, whether the intervention is or is not the right thing to do. As a result, the mixed approach is to be rejected. We have to choose between the two perspectives—the justice of intervention is determined either *ex ante* or *ex post*.

INTERVENTION UNDER UNCERTAINTY

Suppose we abandon the mixed approach, then, and think about adopting a purely *ex post* theory of intervention instead. Of course, this means rejecting the arguments in favor of the success condition from the previous chapter. And, as a consequence, it means rejecting the view that risky acts can be morally wrong even though they ultimately worked out. These are not easy pills to swallow.

Indeed, in the end these problems are insurmountable. We really cannot do away with the prohibition on excessive risks or, by extension, the success condition. To see why, consider the way supporters of *ex post* theorizing typically respond to cases where the *ex ante* and *ex post* standards come apart. Consider the following stylized example involving a humanitarian emergency in a country called Krisistan.

> **Mistaken Intervention**
> You are the leader of a neighboring country and feel compelled to intervene in Krisistan, but only if doing so has a good enough chance of success. You consult your advisors, who are usually very reliable. They give you the following information: "According to our best intelligence, there are really only two ways to intervene in Krisistan. First, you can launch a limited campaign of airstrikes. Or, second,

> you can order a full-scale military invasion. In our estimation, airstrikes would very likely stop the crisis, while a full-scale invasion would make things worse." You choose the airstrikes. Unfortunately, your advisors were wrong and the violence escalates, making things much worse. Had you chosen the invasion, the intervention would have been a success.

It's safe to assume, I think, that anyone in your situation would have done the same. Of course, you were not *sure* that ordering the airstrikes would solve the problem, but then again we can never really be sure about what we do. Our best option is to follow the evidence and hope that things work out. And given your evidence, the airstrikes were the right thing to do.

Note, however, that saying all of this is not quite the same as saying that you did the right thing. And here the defender of a purely *ex post* standard will want to draw a distinction. It is one thing to say a decision was an understandable one, quite another to say it was the right one. The former may well be properly evaluated in *ex ante* terms—given your evidence, you did what anyone else would have done. But the latter, the question of the justice of the intervention, we should evaluate in strictly *ex post* terms—despite your evidence, airstrikes were not the right thing to do.

More precisely, we might distinguish between moral evaluations of certain acts and moral evaluations of the agents who undertake those acts. Since the objects of these two judgments are different, they can come apart. Sometimes people do the right thing insofar as the act goes, but do so culpably or negligently or in some other way of which we should disapprove. In those cases, we might say the person is blameworthy for acting the way he did, even though he did what he ought to have done. At other times, people make decisions in ways that make us judge them very favorably but end up doing the wrong thing, for instance because the evidence conspired against them.

This, then, is how we should think about Mistaken Intervention, according to the *ex post* approach. Launching the full-scale invasion was the right thing to do—the morally correct line of action to take—but that doesn't mean that we should positively evaluate agents who would choose that option, given your evidence. Given the evidence you had available, no conscientious agent would reasonably choose to do that. And if one did, our moral judgment of the person should be one of condemnation. He would be blameworthy for going against the evidence, even though he ended up doing the right thing.

The distinction on which this response rests is sound, of course. There really is a difference between judgments of agents—as blameworthy or not—and judgments of acts—as right or wrong. And these judgments do come apart. At times the evidence can conspire against us, and at times we try to do the right thing but end up doing something that's wrong. This much everyone ought to accept.[12] But what's not clear is whether this also means that we must adopt an *ex post* approach to the justice of intervention. For such an approach runs into very serious problems of its own.[13]

Consider another stylized example, again involving the ongoing humanitarian emergency in Krisistan. Your (still

12. Which is not to say that everyone accepts it. In his criticism of Tesón's view, Richard B. Miller claims that we cannot really distinguish between people's intentions and the acts they undertake because intentions are oriented towards acts; see Miller, "Justifications of the Iraq War Examined," 63. I confess to not fully understanding Miller's argument. Even if intentions are oriented toward actions, it does not follow that there is no difference between the action one actually undertakes and the action one intends to undertake. And given this difference, it seems perfectly possible to evaluate the two independently.
13. In discussing these problems, I follow and have been strongly influenced by Zimmerman, *Living with Uncertainty* and Zimmerman, *Ignorance and Moral Obligation*.

generally reliable) advisors tell you that you're facing the following situation.

> **Uncertain Intervention**
> Our best intelligence suggests that an evil warlord in Krisistan is about to bomb a town of more than a hundred innocent people. Should you decide to intervene, there are three things you can do:
>
> *Option 1*: Launch a missile that will definitely kill the warlord, but will also kill ninety of the innocent civilians.
>
> *Option 2*: Launch a missile that will kill the warlord in a way that will also kill five of the innocent civilians.
>
> *Option 3*: Launch a missile that will kill only the warlord.
>
> Your advisors explain that, "While we're sure that these are our options, we're unfortunately not sure about how to take each of them. We know how exactly to take option 2—this is an old and trusted missile. But options 1 and 3 each use newly developed missiles, and at the moment we can't tell which is which. And there's no time to wait and figure out which is which, as the warlord is about to launch his attack."

As before, this situation involves uncertainty. However, where in the previous case you had no choice but simply to do the best you could *ex ante*, in this case you do have a choice. For you can choose to deal with the uncertainty of this situation in an *ex ante* or *ex post* manner. And by making this choice, you find out which of the two approaches is ultimately the one that matters.

On an *ex post* standard, we said, the right thing to do is whatever brings about the best humanitarian outcome. In Uncertain Intervention, this means killing the warlord without killing any of the innocent civilians, or option 3. However, since you do not know how to choose option 3 other than by taking a 50 percent chance of taking option 1, it follows that on an *ex post* approach the right thing to do in Uncertain Intervention is to take that chance (if taking the chance works out). Perhaps the defender of the *ex post* approach may want to condemn any intervening agent as blameworthy for taking this chance, but that, we say, they consider a different question. When we ask what you ought to do, the answer is: take the gamble.

But this is a serious problem. For it is plainly *not* right to say that you, or any other conscientious moral agent facing this choice, would consider the gamble the right thing to do. Taking the gamble is a horrible decision, even if it works out. Just as no reasonable person would choose to launch the full-scale invasion in Mistaken Intervention, no reasonable person would do this in Uncertain Intervention, either. Plainly, the right thing to do is to take option 2, and it's not particularly close.

Taking option 2, of course, is what the *ex ante* standard requires, and what the *ex post* standard condemns. And we *are*, here, talking about what is the right thing to do. The distinction between evaluating actions and agents won't help. For it is not enough to say only that there is no reason to blame you, as an agent, if you don't choose to take the gamble—and there is reason to blame you if you do. While that's obviously correct, it doesn't go far enough. For it doesn't remove the truth that taking the gamble would also be, quite simply, the wrong thing to do. Whatever standard we apply to acts, in other words, should prohibit these kinds of terrible gambles. And the *ex post* standard doesn't just fail to prohibit them, it may actually require them.

Earlier, we could avoid this conclusion by pointing out that we did not know that the full-scale invasion would be the right thing in *ex post* terms. But that response isn't available here. For in Uncertain Intervention, the one thing we *do* know for sure is that taking option 2 means not bringing about the best humanitarian outcome. That is, by taking option 2 we accept that the *ex post* standard is not the right one to live by. And again, it's not particularly close.

This is a grave problem. For if it can be true that doing the right thing means purposely violating the *ex post* standard, then it follows that the *ex post* standard doesn't correctly identify what's the right thing to do in Uncertain Intervention. And if it doesn't correctly identify what's the right thing to do, then the *ex post* approach also cannot correctly identify the standards of justice in intervention, including the success condition.

Note that this is not the result of some unusual or unique feature of Uncertain Intervention. The conclusion that morally right action must be identified with reference to our evidence follows from the fact that we are uncertain about what outcomes we will bring about. But this is *always* the case (and it is especially the case for judgments about the likelihood of success in military intervention). These operations are fraught with risk, unpredictability, and uncertainty. We never know for sure whether they will succeed, what unintended consequences they will have, whether our means will turn out to be proportionate, whether some other, less violent means were available, or what the consequences would be of the available alternatives. If *ex post* theories fail whenever a situation involves uncertainty, they fail whenever a situation involves intervention.[14]

THE *EX ANTE* JUSTICE OF INTERVENTION

Consider once more Uncertain Intervention. Facing a decision to either take a 50/50 gamble between the worst (option 1) and

14. It is popular to suggest that the *ex ante* approach functions only as a heuristic or decision-rule, while the *ex post* approach captures rightness. See, e.g., Allen Buchanan, "A Richer *Jus Ad Bellum*," in *The Oxford Handbook of Ethics and War*, ed. Seth Lazar and Helen Frowe (forthcoming). But this won't do for the reasons stated in the text. Again, it's simply not true that taking excessive risk is the right thing to do.

the best (option 3) outcomes, or take the option that definitely ranks second best in *ex post* terms (option 2), the right thing to do is clearly the latter. This fits the *ex ante* version of the success condition, of course. The former option involves a 50 percent chance of killing almost all the civilians—far too low a probability of justly bringing about a humanitarian outcome. But since the collateral harms on the five civilians can be justifiable given the intervention's humanitarian aim, option 2 does have an acceptable probability of success. The *ex ante* standard thus correctly picks out the right thing to do.

A purely *ex ante* standard might seem problematic, however. One obvious worry is that it can consider actions the right thing to do even though they lead to very bad outcomes. We've seen this in Mistaken Intervention. But while the fact that such tragic mistakes are possible is definitely disconcerting, it cannot be an objection to the case for adopting a purely *ex ante* standard. After all, the very *point* of adopting this approach is to not base the justice of intervention on *ex post* outcomes. As we saw in Uncertain Intervention, that leads to the kind of horrible decisions even the staunchest supporter of an *ex post* approach can't endorse.

Here's one way of summarizing the idea I'm proposing: the decision to intervene is justifiable only if doing so is morally acceptable in terms of the evidence available to the intervener at the time. As a rule of thumb, we might say that interventions are morally acceptable only if they pose a good enough moral bet—at the time of intervening, in light of the intervener's evidence.[15] This is what was meant in the previous chapter when I said that the relevant kind of probability for the success condition is evidentiary probability.

15. The idea of a good bet is discussed in detail by Zimmerman; see *Living with Uncertainty* and *Ignorance and Moral Obligation* throughout.

We've come full circle. If the justice of interventions depends on these *ex ante* facts, and we can (therefore) be sometimes required to do things that may not bring about the best possible outcomes, it follows that the *ex post* idea of success (endorsed by Tesón and others at the beginning of this chapter) must be rejected. But this does not mean rejecting the central motivation behind that *ex post* approach. It's not to say, that is, that we shouldn't care about actually protecting or saving lives in the end. After all, it sees success in terms of justly bringing about a humanitarian end.

The difference between the *ex ante* and *ex post* approaches, then, concerns how those values affect the justice of interventions. A moral rule leading to the best outcomes overall need not be the same as the moral rule that leads to the best outcomes in each particular instance. Indeed, as we've seen, a moral rule that tries to lead to the best outcomes in each particular case will predictably lead to worse outcomes overall.

The *ex ante* approach sides with the former of these options. It affirms the importance of success overall by identifying a benchmark of probability in terms of what would be a morally acceptable distribution of successes and failures, in interventions undertaken and those foregone. But the significance of the benchmark derives from the significance of the outcomes toward which it tends to lead.

That said, these arguments are revisionary. For one, it seems difficult to restrict the relevance of the arguments to just the success condition. After all, the problem posed by Uncertain Intervention is perfectly general. If it applies to the success condition, it will by the same logic apply to other conditions as well. Indeed, since the success condition invokes a moralized sense of success, as justly achieving a humanitarian end, it refers to those other conditions of just war, like proportionality or necessity. If it won't do to combine the *ex ante* and an *ex post* versions of the success condition in one theory, it also won't do to combine the *ex ante* version of the success condition with *ex post* versions of those other conditions. The result, then, may very well be that we ought to adopt a thoroughly *ex ante* approach to the justice of interventions.[16]

EX ANTE STANDARDS AND ADVICE

To some, this may seem too much. Consider the following objection. Suppose we accept, for now, that the justice of intervention in Uncertain Intervention depends on the evidence available at the time of acting. And suppose that you now come to me asking me for advice about what to do, given your peculiar situation. What ought I to say? If I know all and only what you know, it's clear that I should tell you to take option 2. That much is not problematic. But suppose that I *do* know which of the two new missiles is which, so I can tell you how to take option 3. Now what should I tell you?

16. Frowe argues that (a) the *ex ante* success condition entails proportionality, and (b) the proportionality condition is insensitive to *ex ante* probabilities (that is, *ex post*): "we have a success condition that entails, but is distinct from, the proportionality condition"; see Frowe, *Defensive Killing*, 152–153. Also, "when we ask whether a war would be *ad bellum* proportionate, we are asking, 'Would war, fought with the means at our disposal, be a proportionate way of securing the just cause?' That is, we build an *assumption* of success—of securing the just cause—into our calculation. The calculation cannot, therefore, also be sensitive to the *probability* of success"; Frowe, *Defensive Killing*, 152 (italics in original). Frowe attributes the same view to McMahan; see McMahan, *Killing in War*, 20.

Note that your question is not: Which of these missiles brings about the best outcomes? You're asking, being the good *ex ante* theorist that you are, what you ought to do, in light of your evidence. And in light of your evidence, it's true (*ex hypothesi*) that you ought to take option 2. But now it seems to follow that I should tell you that you ought to take option 2. And that's clearly crazy. I should tell you to take option 3 and save five lives. The *ex ante* perspective thus seems to have an unacceptable implication of its own.[17]

This objection is mistaken owing to an ambiguity in the example. It's true that the *ex ante* justice of your intervening depends on your evidence, and it's also true that, given your evidence in the second example, option 2 is the right thing to do. But what is ambiguous is whether my giving you advice about what to do itself counts as more evidence. When we're explicit about whether my advice constitutes evidence for you, the objection disappears.

Consider the following exchange:

YOU: Hey, Bas, I'm really stuck here in Uncertain Intervention; what ought I to do?

ME: Given your evidence, you ought to take option 2. But I know something you don't. I know that option 3

17. This objection is inspired by a somewhat different argument offered by Jonathan Quong, who roundly rejects *ex ante* theorizing. The form of this objection is offered in many places. For detailed discussion, as well as a version of the answer I offer in the text, see Zimmerman, *Ignorance and Moral Obligation*, chapter 3, objection 11. For a more direct response to Quong's argument, see Van der Vossen "Uncertain Rights Against Defense."

is the one that will kill the warlord and spare all the civilians. So you ought to take option 3.

YOU: Really? How do you know this?

ME: I helped design these missiles. I'd recognize option 3 a mile away.

Unless you have reason to think I'm lying, this conversation provides you with new evidence. Before I gave you my information, it was true that you ought to take option 2. And that's exactly what I started out by (truthfully) saying. But after I told you about option 3, it's no longer true that the right thing for you to do is take option 2. Our conversation changed your evidence and, as a result, what is right for you to do. After all, now that you know that option 3 is the best option, you plainly ought to take option 3, as I told you after I gave you the extra information. The objection misfires.

Of course, our conversation need not have the effect of giving you additional evidence. Consider the following, alternative conversation:

YOU: Hey, Bas, I'm really stuck here in Uncertain Intervention; what ought I to do?"

ME: Take option 3.

YOU: Wait, are you sure? How do you know I should take option 3?

ME: My horoscope this morning said good things come in threes.

This conversation, of course, doesn't give you reliable information about which option is which. And as a result, your evidence hasn't changed. Here, the *ex ante* approach entails that what you ought to do can't change, either. And this is clearly the correct result. For if we ask what you ought to do after this second conversation, clearly the answer is still option 2. Again, the objection above doesn't land.[18]

The seeming force of the objection, then, relies on the ambiguity about whether our conversation conveyed new evidence to you. Only when we assume that my telling you to take option 3 does not convey new information, but also assume that you ought to take option 3, can any problem arise. But as we saw, when my telling you to take option 3 conveys no new evidence, you remain in the situation of Uncertain Intervention. And in that case, you ought not take option 3, as the *ex ante* standard implies. As soon as we allow my giving you advice to convey new information, the *ex ante* standard yields the (correct) result that option 3 is the right thing to do.

THE ROLE OF OUTCOMES

Most people I know are uncomfortable with a purely *ex ante* view. I used to be, too. However, the arguments just given strike

18. You might think the second conversation silly. Consider, then, a third version:

    YOU: I'm really stuck here in Uncertain Intervention; what ought I to do?
    ME: Take option 3.
    YOU: Wait, are you sure? How do you know I should take option 3?
    ME: Can't say; just take option 3.

    Here, it's not clear whether this conversation adds to your evidence. If you have no idea who I am or what I might know, this conversation is similar to the one involving a horoscope. If you have reason to trust me, it's similar to the first conversation. In both cases, the results will follow those from the cases discussed in the text.

me as inescapable. (And as these things go, once I began accepting the view, my discomfort started waning, too.)

My sense is that at least some of this concern is due to the deeply rooted intuition that in the end it is outcomes that matter most. And in obvious ways they do. It's only when things go wrong, for example, that there can be a case for making the victims of our failures whole. The *ex ante* approach might seem to obscure this from view. After all, if one does the (*ex ante*) right thing and things go wrong anyway, what grounds for complaint might there be, on this view?

However, nothing in this discussion implies that outcomes do not matter. It does not follow from saying that person A did the right thing that person B, who is negatively affected by person A's actions, has no claim for restitution or assistance. (It does follow, of course, that person B has no claim against person A that person A do something differently, but that's a different point.[19]) Perhaps person B doesn't deserve to be made worse off in this way, and perhaps that's enough to justify making person B whole. Or perhaps there is a kind of injustice that emerges from how person A's actions interact with the also permissible actions of persons C, D, . . . In all these cases, the outcomes our actions bring about (even inadvertently) may be of real moral concern.

Outcomes may have other roles to play in our thinking about intervention, too. It is possible, say, that the law should take them into account in ways that aren't directly grounded in morality. Perhaps the law cannot do better than go with the (observable) outcomes, for example. It's important, then, to keep in mind exactly what the question is that we are dealing with here. The question we're asking, I've said, is when an

19. See Van der Vossen, "Uncertain Rights Against Defense," for a detailed argument.

agent, who is facing the decision whether or not to intervene, can permissibly do so. And for *this* question, the *ex ante* perspective is the only acceptable approach.[20]

20. For the same reason, attempts to sidestep these arguments are likely to fail. Richard B. Miller suggests that we can judge actions from either a first-personal or a third-personal point of view, and that the first-personal perspective concerns whether we did the right thing and the third-personal concerns whether our actions were right; see Miller, "Justifications of the Iraq War Examined," 63. In a similar vein, a reviewer of this book's manuscript suggested that the *ex ante* approach concerns only people's decisions, not their actions.

    I find both distinctions rather obscure. But what suggestions like this have in common is, again, the idea that the *ex ante* approach captures only part of the truth—the part that is about our actions or decisions. But note that this *is precisely the part that matters* when we confront decisions about intervention. If the *ex ante* approach governs only our decisions (and, somehow, not our actions), or if the *ex ante* approach governs only what we do (and, somehow, not our actions), it remains true that when we intervene, or decide to intervene, the *ex ante* success condition must be satisfied.

11

Three Structural Problems

INTERVENTIONIST AUTHORS ARE OFTEN OPTIMISTIC about the chances that intervention will succeed. Andrew Altman and Christopher Wellman assert that:

> [T]here are many cases in which the modest use of military force had very little prospect of producing an escalating and uncontrollable spiral of reciprocal violence, cases in which it was clear from the outset that a modest use of force could accomplish the goal in question.[1]

To their minds, intervention rarely poses a threat of significant failure because:

> Many of the worst human rights abusers in recent years have been undisciplined forces mainly interested in what they can gain personally by joining in the atrocities. When confronted with substantial firepower, such abusers are not likely to put up the kind of resistance that would lead to an escalating cycle of violence.[2]

1. See Altman and Wellman, *A Liberal Theory of International Justice*, 102–103.
2. Ibid., 103.

Similarly, in a recent commentary on the Syrian crisis, Fernando Tesón writes:

> I am more optimistic about the ability to implement a just end . . .. It might require the Coalition to occupy Syria and Iraq longer than the public would currently stomach, and it certainly requires the cooperation of indigenous forces and populations. But none of this is impossible or unachievable. Victorious just warriors have faced such difficulties before, and have managed to resolve them.[3]

But this kind of optimism is simply unfounded. In the most rigorous empirical study of interventionism around, political scientist Patrick Regan finds that interventions in general succeed to reduce violence and loss of life in only about 30 percent of the cases. Under the most favorable circumstances,[4] interventions manage to reduce violence and loss of life in about 50 percent of the cases.[5]

At the other end of the spectrum, when circumstances are least favorable, interventions succeed to reduce violence and loss of life only around 15 percent of the time.[6] Finally, and

3. Fernando Tesón, "ISIS and Just War Theory," *Lawfare*, December 19, 2015, at https://www.lawfareblog.com/isis-and-just-war-theory.
4. Most favorable, meaning interventions undertaken unilaterally by major powers in intense conflicts on behalf of the existing government.
5. See Regan, *Civil Wars and Foreign Powers*, 29–31. Taylor Seybolt finds a similar result. Writing about interventions aimed at protecting aid delivery, which rank among the easier missions, Seybolt concludes that "Half of the operations examined here that were intended to protect aid made a bad job of it"; see Seybolt, *Humanitarian Intervention*, 176.
6. Meaning multilateral interventions on behalf of minorities or opposition groups.

most tragically, when interventions do not make things better, they typically end up making things worse.[7] Perhaps the worst outcome is when interventions attract counterinterventions on behalf of one of the parties. These almost always drastically lengthen and worsen the conflict.[8]

"In general," Regan summarizes, "outside interventions contribute to the prolonging of the conflict."[9] This chapter discusses three structural reasons why the likelihood of success in intervention is generally very low. These reasons are not exhaustive of the problems that beset intervention. They are significant, however, and together make for a strong case against intervention.

CONFLICTING AIMS

Humanitarian interventions typically consist of two missions at once. While they must aim to end the ongoing violence as quickly as possible, they also aim to put into place the preconditions for a lasting and just peace. Unfortunately, these missions require very different things. Indeed, they are frequently in tension with one another.

In the short run, interveners aim to end the fighting as quickly as possible in order to relieve the suffering of the victims of conflict. The violence that is part of humanitarian

7. See Regan, *Civil Wars and Foreign Powers*, 30. See also Patrick M. Regan, "Understanding Civil War," *Journal of Conflict Resolution* 46 (2002): 55–73, 56; and Frederick S. Pearson, "Foreign Military Interventions and Domestic Disputes," *International Studies Quarterly* 18 (1974): 259–289.
8. See Regan, "Understanding Civil War," 70–71.
9. See Regan, *Civil Wars and Foreign Powers*, 31. See also Seybolt, *Humanitarian Intervention*, 278.

crises leads to large-scale displacement, hunger, sickness, and other kinds of harm. But it also obstructs efforts to relieve these problems. If humanitarian aid is to be effectively delivered, interveners must bring an end to the fighting. As a result, one of the most important short-term goals of interveners is to coax the fighting parties into negotiations about a ceasefire, pressure the sides to reach an agreement, and help enforce its terms.

However, and in addition to this short-term goal, interveners are now widely expected to take on a broader task as well. Just interventions, we are told, achieve not only a temporary reduction in violence but they also put their target societies on a path toward recovery, reconstruction, and reconciliation. What is needed are the building blocks of a just and durable peace.

As a result, interveners are now expected to reconstruct (or build anew) their target country's broken social and political institutions. In the terms adopted by the *Responsibility to Protect*, interveners—and the global community at large—have a "responsibility to rebuild."[10] The United Nations created its Peacebuilding Commission specifically for this purpose.[11]

Consider the different challenges that these two tasks pose. Since the effectiveness of aid delivery requires the maintenance of a ceasefire, interveners must avoid being seen as aligned with one side or another. Such a position requires a strong sense of impartiality among aid agencies and interveners. And traditionally, aid agencies have adhered to such a doctrine in order to make sure aid will reach the most vulnerable people. Their creed has been to protect people and deliver aid on the basis of

10. See International Commission on Intervention and State Sovereignty, *The Responsibility to Protect*, chapter 5.
11. See the mission statement of the UN Peacebuilding Commission as described at http://www.un.org/en/peacebuilding/.

need, not on grounds of ethnicity, religion, ideology, or what side they are on.

By contrast, here's how the ICISS Report describes the task of the long-term rebuilding effort:

> To avoid a return to conflict while laying a solid foundation for development, emphasis must be placed on critical priorities such as encouraging reconciliation and demonstrating respect for human rights; fostering political inclusiveness and promoting national unity; ensuring the safe, smooth and early repatriation and resettlement of refugees and displaced persons; reintegrating ex-combatants and others into productive society; curtailing the availability of small arms; and mobilizing the domestic and international resources for reconstruction and economic recovery.[12]

This is a wholesale reconstruction of society. In order to succeed at this, and put the society on the path to development and stability, intervening forces must get extensively and deeply involved with their target societies. It means creating, substituting, and renovating basic state institutions, monitoring and organizing elections, supervising public security, creating a new civilian police force, controlling the civil administration, undertaking democratic education, and more.[13]

Such efforts are impossible to carry out in an impartial, nonpartisan manner. Societies that call for humanitarian intervention are almost invariably unstable and oppressive, ruled by elites that use their political and social power to

12. See International Commission on Intervention and State Sovereignty, *The Responsibility to Protect*, section 5.6, p. 40.
13. For an (even) more extensive summary of intervenors tasks, see Michael Doyle, "The New Interventionism," *Metaphilosophy* 32 (2001): 212–235, 229.

extract resources to build and maintain their armed forces, buy judges, rig elections, and so on.[14] Under such conditions, when interveners promote political inclusiveness, they are directly attacking the position of these elites. When interveners promote national unity, they are thereby directly opposing possible secessionist groups or minorities. When interveners begin reintegrating and disarming past combatants, they are thereby deeply altering previous social hierarchies. And so on.

Undertaking this second, long-term task (of rebuilding), then, means that interveners undercut their ability to successfully undertake the first, short-term task (of delivering aid), and vice versa. The result is that the probability of success for one of these tasks of intervention is inversely proportional to the probability of success for the other.[15] (It should come as no

14. For a detailed exposition of these dynamics, see Acemoglu and Robinson, *Why Nations Fail*, 343, 83–91, and chapter 12. For a supporting, if different analysis, see Cox, North, and Weingast, "The Violence Trap: A Political-Economic Approach to the Problems of Development." See also Seybolt, *Humanitarian Intervention*, 265; Thiemo Fetzer and Samuel Marden, "Take What You Can: Property Rights, Contestability and Conflict," SERC Discussion Paper 194 (April 2016), Spatial Economics Research Centre, London, at http://eprints.lse.ac.uk/66534/1/__lse.ac.uk_storage_LIBRARY_Secondary_libfile_shared_repository_Content_LSE%20Spatial%20Economic%20Research%20Centre_Discussion%20Papers_2016_April_sercdp0194.pdf. Also, Hannes Mueller and Agustin Tapsoba, "Access to Power, Political Institutions and Ethnic Favoritism," Barcelona GSE Working Paper Series Working Paper 901 (April 2016), at http://www.barcelonagse.eu/sites/default/files/working_paper_pdfs/901.pdf.
15. Altman and Wellman cite the (short-term) protection of the Kurds in northern Iraq as one of the best examples of successful intervention. To be sure, many lives were saved. However, see Seybolt, *Humanitarian Intervention*, 51, for discussion of the

surprise, then, that the combination of the humanitarian and rebuilding tasks is an issue of significant controversy within the humanitarian aid community.[16])

Over the course of the last century, the success rates for these tasks haven't been great. Measuring success in terms of saving lives, interventions have the best prospects when they focus only on the short-term goal of aid delivery. Interventions that are limited in this way (as well as some other ways) tend to save lives approximately half the time.[17] The track record of

long-term failure of Operation Provide Comfort to offer political stability for the Kurds. See also Wheeler, *Saving Strangers*, 170; J. E. Stromseth, "Iraq," in *Enforcing Restraint: Collective Intervention in Internal Conflicts*, ed. L. F. Damrosch (Council on Foreign Relations, 1993), 99; L. Freedman and D. Boren, "'Safe Havens' for Kurds," in *To Loose the Bands of Wickedness*, ed. N. S. Rodley (London: Brassey's, 1992), 81.

16. See, e.g., David Rieff, *A Bed for the Night* (Simon & Schuster, 2003); Mark Duffield, *Global Governance and the New Wars: The Merging of Development and Security* (Zed Books, 2001); Didier Fassin and Mariella Pandolfi, eds., *Contemporary States of Emergency: The Politics of Military and Humanitarian Interventions* (Zone Books, 2013); Conor Foley, *The Thin Blue Line: How Humanitarianism Went to War* (Verso, 2010); Michael Barnett, *Empire of Humanity: A History of Humanitarianism* (Cornell University Press, 2011).
17. As Seybolt puts it, "reasonable prospect of success is the most difficult criterion to meet. Half of the operations examined here that were intended to protect aid made a bad job of it"; see Seybolt, *Humanitarian Intervention*, 176, 133, 265–266, 279. Patrick Regan breaks down the success rate of different interventions, finding that the 50 percent success rate applies only to interventions undertaken unilaterally by major powers in intense conflicts on behalf of the existing government. By contrast, intervention on behalf of minorities or opposition groups

interventions that include rebuilding efforts is worse.[18] A recent study of U.S. interventions during the twentieth and twenty-first centuries found that the majority of rebuilding efforts have failed. Measuring at five-year intervals after the intervening forces left, research found that 29 percent of the target states counted as democratic after five and ten years, 39 percent of the time after fifteen years, and only 36 percent of the time after twenty years. The remaining cases had virtually no positive effects at all—many experienced negative effects.[19]

INFORMATIONAL PROBLEMS

Consider again a possible humanitarian intervention in our fictional country Krisistan. Suppose that the crisis in Krisistan is due to an ongoing and recently escalated civil war. How *exactly* is intervention going to stop the violence?

Before we can answer that question, we need to know a number of things: Who are the fighting parties? What is driving them to fight? How might we, as outside interveners, change their incentives so that continued fighting becomes less attractive than a ceasefire or peace? Is there a way of changing these incentives that is acceptable to all parties involved? Can all parties accept peace without seeming to accept defeat? Can outside forces offer them a route to this peace? Might the parties change as a result of the conflict or as a result of intervention?

succeed only around 15 percent of the time; see Regan, *Civil Wars and Foreign Powers*, 29–31.

18. Note that Tesón sees nation-building as a just cause for intervention; see Tesón, *Humanitarian Intervention*, 402–403.
19. Christopher J. Coyne, *After War: The Political Economy of Exporting Democracy* (Stanford University Press, 2007), 12–19.

Are foreign fighters being drawn in at the moment? Would an intervention have the result of drawing them in? And so on.

Perhaps the first of these questions is easy to answer (although that's definitely not always the case). But the remainder are all extremely nebulous. The true causes and dynamics of conflict are very difficult to understand. They depend on complex historical and current processes, which outsiders usually only partially know and comprehend. And these processes interact in ways that are often genuinely difficult, if not impossible, to predict.

That is not to say, of course, that one cannot become intimately familiar with other societies and their power relations, social hierarchies, traditions, and prevailing beliefs. Clearly, one can. But situations that call for intervention are hardly conducive to the kind of prolonged and detailed investigation that doing so requires. Interveners rarely will have the time it takes to acquire all this information, as they must work under extreme pressures of time, safety, feasibility, and scarcity. Military and civilian officials of intervening countries are typically strangers, who spend the vast majority of their time in heavily guarded green zones, travel in armored vehicles protected by security details, typically do not speak the language, do not get clearance to interact with locals, and so on.[20] Nor do they have the time to learn about the country, as much of the staff consists of short-term international consultants who have to work extremely long days.

Rory Stewart, a former member of the British Parliamentary Foreign Affairs Committee, describes these difficulties during his stay in Afghanistan from 2008 to 2010. Stewart relates that it was nearly impossible to get security clearance for American,

20. See Rory Stewart and Gerald Knaus, *Can Intervention Work?* (W. W. Norton, 2011), 14–17.

British, or Canadian civilians to visit even a small historic neighborhood in the center of Kabul, despite the fact that it had no record of attacks or violence, and was only a hundred yards from the door of the Finance Ministry and three hundred yards from the presidential palace. One senior official who did make it to the site was given twelve foreign bodyguards and fifty members of the Afghan police and security department as protection. He was allowed to remain exactly six minutes in the area before being "extracted." If they could not visit a safe neighborhood in central Kabul, it was out of the question, of course, to visit a Pushtun village.[21]

The depth and difficulties of these informational problems mean that interveners are more often wrong than right in their predictions about intervention.[22] Consider again the case of the early 1990s U.S. intervention in Somalia. While this quickly turned into a violent and infamous affair, at the time

21. Stewart describes the typical tasks of personnel as follows: "dealing with emails from their capitals, writing cables, and preparing press tours and official visits. Development officials are absorbed in coordination meetings with 'major donors,' writing 'strategic plans' and 'feasibility studies,' submitting reports, and ensuring the proper processing of 'contracts, invoices and receipts.' Their main responsibilities include maintaining 'multilateral diplomacy,' accounting, human resources, and 'global policy' concerning things like climate change, trade, or heritage"; see Stewart and Knaus, *Can Intervention Work?*, 14–17.
22. For studies of just how frequently and deeply predictions about war are mistaken, see Dominic P. Johnson, *Overconfidence in War: The Havoc and Glory of Positive Illusions* (Harvard University Press, 2004); Barbara W. Tuchman, *The March of Folly* (Random House, 1984); Daniel Ellsberg, *Secrets: A Memoir of Vietnam and the Pentagon Papers* (Random House, 2003); Fred Ikle, *Every War Must End*, rev. ed. (Columbia University Press, 2005), chapter 2.

it was widely considered relatively risk-free. The U.S. National Security Council judged that it could be carried out with little or no risk to soldiers' lives. General Colin Powell thought a forceful ground operation could overwhelm Somali opposition and minimize casualties.[23] Diplomat Lawrence Eagleburger describes the prevailing sense at the time as follows: "we could do this . . . at not too great a cost and, certainly, without any great danger of body bags coming home."[24]

Similarly, interveners frequently don't know enough about the conflicts they are dealing with to solve them. During the Rwandan genocide, much of the killing was done by loosely organized thugs who did not enjoy the support of the army. Had outsiders known this, a fast-and-light intervention force might have saved many lives.[25] But this, of course, is precisely the problem. If outsiders can only guess about whether the army will back the thugs, sending in a light force may be unacceptably dangerous.[26]

23. See J. L. Hirsch and R. B. Oakley, *Somalia and Operation Restore Hope: Reflections on Peacemaking and Peacekeeping* (United States Institute of Peace, 1995), 42–43; and Ioan Lewis and James Mayall, "Somalia," in *United Nations Interventionism 1991-2004*, ed. Mats Berdal and Spyros Economides (Cambridge University Press, 2007), 124.
24. Quoted in Wheeler, *Saving Strangers*, 181.
25. See Seybolt, *Humanitarian Intervention*, 214–215.
26. For more on the tricky balance intervenors must strike, see Suzanne Werner and Amy Yuen, "Making and Keeping Peace," *International Organization* 59 (2005): 261–292, esp. 271; and Pearson, "Foreign Military Interventions and Domestic Disputes." See also Regan, *Civil Wars and Foreign Powers*, 29–31; Kyle Beardsley, *The Mediation Dilemma* (Cornell University Press, 2011); Dan Reiter, *How Wars End* (Princeton University Press, 2009).

If a lack of information makes imposing peace difficult, it makes reconstruction efforts nearly impossible. It is a common observation about nation-building that the only way people can achieve living together peacefully and prosperously is by adopting the right kinds of institutions, including democracy, the rule of law, private property and freedom of contract, and so on. But it's equally clear that interveners cannot easily duplicate the relatively successful cases. Institutions cannot simply be transplanted.

The problem is that institutions don't come in a vacuum, and they certainly don't operate in one. They must be adapted to the informal norms, customs, and beliefs prevailing in a particular society. The institutions required for stability, the rule of law, and democracy need the broad support of people across society. For such institutions to have a chance to work and survive, they need to align with complex networks of formal and informal rules, norms, and shared expectations in the society. People must accept the constraints that these institutions impose on the pursuit of their private ends, respect the state's claimed monopoly on violence, avoid attempting bribes and coercion, and so on.

These background norms, perhaps even more than formal legal checks, are what actually prevent people from abusing power. In their absence, as John Stuart Mill long ago observed, "the government which it has given to itself, or some military leader or knot of conspirators who contrive to subvert the government, will speedily put an end to all popular institutions."[27]

27. Mill, "A Few Words on Intervention." There are many serious problems with Mill's position and arguments, many of which I do not endorse. For critical discussion, see Van der Vossen, "The Morality of Humanitarian Intervention," 411ff.

At the same time, as Mill also saw, these norms are virtually impossible for outsiders to create. Detailed and accurate information about the society's norms, customs, and beliefs is nearly impossible to acquire from the outside. Knowing how to adjust these norms to fit with the required institutions, and how to calibrate those institutions to fit the norms as they arise, is even harder to achieve.

Of course, it is never up to outsiders to create and impose institutions by themselves. Or, at least, it ought not to be. The building of domestic institutions should be done primarily by the local people and their representatives. But if this seems to mitigate some of the informational problems we've been discussing, that benefit comes at a steep price. Revolutions are coercive, minority control affairs for the most part. And the parties—and their representatives—involved with rebuilding will typically seek to create institutions that protect their several interests. The process that results will rarely be the same as building the kind of inclusive institutions that foster peace, stability, development, and justice.

MISALIGNED INCENTIVES

Let's imagine that, somehow, you actually know how to stop the fighting in Krisistan. And suppose that, amazingly, you also know how to transform it into a stable and prosperous society. We're assuming that you are the political leader of a country yourself, and being generally decent, the country is democratic. Given that position, would you actually be able to carry out the intervention in the right way?

Since democratic leaders are accountable to their voters, the political system in which they operate is designed to skew their decisions toward the best interests of their people. Generally, of course, this is a good idea, as it protects people against the use of political power for the private interests of the leaders. But the system does not just steer decisions away from the private interests of politicians; it steers them away from the interests of anyone to whom the decision makers are not accountable. This includes, of course, the citizens of countries that are the target of military interventions.

Unfortunately, the interests of the people (and interest groups) of intervening countries are generally not well aligned with the interests of the people whom the intervention is supposed to help. The voters in intervening countries have a strong interest in limiting potential casualties among their own armed forces, in limiting the financial cost of intervention, and in avoiding a lengthy military presence in the target country. Each of these interests moves interventions away from what is required for a good chance of success.

One place where this becomes visible is with decisions about where to intervene. As Patrick Regan has shown, interventions are more likely to succeed if the violence it aims to stop is more intense. However, as the intensity of violence goes up, and the dangers of intervention are most salient in the eyes of the intervener's domestic population, the likelihood that countries actually intervene goes down. In other words, countries "select" themselves out of interventions that actually have a chance of justly bringing about a humanitarian outcome.[28]

These political dynamics are terrible. Roméo Dallaire, the leader of the UN mission in Rwanda that was charged with implementing the Arusha accords, describes the following episode, which happened during the first week of the Rwanda genocide: As calls for early intervention mounted, a group of

28. See Regan, *Civil Wars and Foreign Powers*, 131, 141–142. Intensity here is understood as the number of casualties that occur in a given period of time.

bureaucrats from the governments that would be involved in an intervention visited Rwanda in order to assess the situation. Dallaire showed them around and explained why, in his opinion, a relatively small intervening force could have a very beneficial impact. When the tour was done, Dallaire was told that the liaisons would recommend to their governments not to intervene. Asked why, they responded: "the risks are high and all that is here are humans."[29]

In politics, the lives of foreigners have almost no value. And so the same dynamics plague political decisions about how to intervene. Interveners choose their strategies primarily with an eye toward maintaining domestic support, not toward optimizing the chances of success. Since the main goal is to minimize casualties on one's own side, interventions often depend heavily on air power. But while this kind of engagement minimizes the domestic political costs, it is rarely strategically optimal. Committing ground troops is often a better strategy, yet one that is too tough to sell to voters back home.[30]

Airstrikes can work, of course. As interventionist are happy to point out, the no-fly zone over northern Iraq during the early 1990s was relatively successful. But whereas the main threat to the Kurds was Saddam Hussein's airpower, thus making a no-fly zone effective, in other cases a reliance on airpower may be ill advised. During the Bosnian intervention, the 1999

29. Roméo Dallaire, *Shake Hands with the Devil: The Failure of Humanity in Rwanda* (Da Capo Press, 2004), 6. See also Regan, *Civil Wars and Foreign Powers*, 65.
30. See, e.g., Timothy Hildebrandt et al., "The Domestic Politics of Humanitarian Intervention: Public Opinion, Partisanship, and Ideology," *Foreign Policy Analysis* 9 (2012): 243–266. Note that during the run-up to the most recent U.S. intervention in Iraq, President Obama categorically ruled out the deployment of ground troops.

NATO bombings of Serbia, and the 2011 U.S. intervention in Libya, airstrikes were strategically much less well suited to the needs of intervention. And politically motivated strategic choices plague interventions in other areas, too. Infamously, the interventions in Somalia and Rwanda partly failed because domestic political pressures precluded the requisite military commitments.[31]

Finally, and equally damagingly, intervening governments can almost never offer credible commitments that they will see their interventions through to the end—and this is especially true for democratic governments. Once news stories about massacres and violence disappear, or news stories about casualties on the side of the interveners appear, domestic support for intervention typically wanes and a continued military presence abroad is no longer in the interest of the intervening governments. Their voters will have to bear the burdens of these long-term commitments, and often they grow weary of the mission long before it is completed.[32]

On standard accounts of conflict resolution, it is a precondition for ending violent conflicts in a lasting manner that belligerent parties consider peace in their several interests. One thing this typically requires is a credible threat by the intervening powers to coerce the sides to maintain the peace, if need be. This threat gives the various parties assurance because it means that each will consider the option of continued fighting costlier

31. For discussion of how the selection of methods in conflicts such as Somalia, Bosnia, or Rwanda has been sensitive to domestic political pressures and not military needs, see Wheeler, *Saving Strangers*, 268; Seybolt, *Humanitarian Intervention*, 77, 214–215.
32. Indeed, in anticipation of this, political leaders usually under-commit to interventions in the first place. See, e.g., Wheeler, *Saving Strangers*, 175. See also Aidan Hehir, *Humanitarian Intervention After Kosovo* (Palgrave, 2008), chapter 5.

than keeping peace. When the sides know that the intervening forces are under-committed, this again significantly lowers the likelihood of success.[33]

ENDOGENOUS VERSUS EXOGENOUS VARIABLES

When Dallaire tells his chilling story, he uses it to make his case for a more extensive interventionist policy. He wants to illustrate just how tragic the decision *not* to intervene can be. To him, a lack of political will doesn't mean that intervention is unjustifiable. It shows that politicians (and their voters) aren't ready to do the right thing. His aim, commendably, is to strengthen political will in order to overcome at least some of the problems mentioned.

Philosophically, one might try to generalize this thought. Perhaps the points just made don't strike against intervention as the right thing to do, but only that doing the right thing can be difficult, that politicians (and voters) often can't muster the will to do the right thing, and so on. Those issues might be real, it might be said, but they are external to the justice of intervention. What we need to do is encourage people to do what's right, not change our view about whether intervention can be

33. See Regan, *Civil Wars and Foreign Powers*, 73, 148–149; Paul Pillar, *Negotiating Peace: War Termination as a Bargaining Process* (Princeton University Press, 1983); Werner and Yuen, "Making and Keeping Peace"; Beardsley, *The Mediation Dilemma*; Barbara Walter, *Committing to Peace: The Successful Settlement of Civil War* (Princeton University Press, 2002); and Michael W. Doyle and Nicholas Sambanis, "International Peacebuilding: A Theoretical and Quantitative Analysis," *American Political Science Review* 94 (2000): 779–801.

justified. And if that's so, then the arguments of this chapter are beside the point.

In one way, there can't be much disagreement about this. If General Dallaire was right that everything pointed to a Rwandan intervention having a good chance of success, it is clear that the governments involved should have thought the imperative to save lives good enough reason to intervene. The position that natural resources or strategic value warrant intervention but that people (and African people, in particular) do not—the view that Dallaire ascribes to them[34]—is truly heinous. There can be no reasonable disagreement about this.

However, if the point is supposed to be that problems of information or lack of political will do not affect the morality of intervention, then we are dealing with a real disagreement. When asking whether intervention would be the right thing to do, we simply can't answer in the affirmative without considering the circumstances (and then blame those circumstances for getting in the way). Those circumstances are part of the environment in which an intervention is to take place. They are endogenous variables; they are part of the question.

Again, this is not to say that we can't condemn those governments that refuse to commit troops to solve a humanitarian crisis because "all that is here are humans." We should, and in the sharpest terms possible. But when we ask whether a given intervention is morally permissible, we cannot close our eyes to the reality that our ability to see things through as they ought to be seen through depends not just on our own will, determination, or desires; it also depends on other people (often good, sometimes rotten) and other things, too.

Of course, this is in many ways a deeply depressing point. We live in a deeply depressing world. The good news is that

34. Dallaire, *Shake Hands with the Devil*, 6.

this need not always be so. Some of the points made earlier depend on the problems caused by the institutional environment in which interventions take place. This environment is not static or immune to change. Perhaps in a different world, populated with different institutions, some of these problems might be overcome. The question of how to improve this part of our world is extremely important.[35] But until we do improve it, the presumption against intervention will stand.

35. Allen Buchanan has recently developed a number of intriguing proposals in this direction. See, for instance, Buchanan, "Institutionalizing the Just War."

12

Looking for Exceptions

THE 1990S BEAR THE HIGH-WATER mark of interventionism. It's still visible in most studies of the subject. Pick up a book on intervention, and you'll likely read about the same examples: Kosovo, Bosnia, the northern Iraqi no-fly zone, Rwanda, Somalia, perhaps East Timor.

But the history of intervention is much longer and more widespread.[1] Still, focusing on those few 1990s cases, one might think that failure is rarer than it is. Perhaps Somalia went wrong, but weren't the others pretty successful? And can't we expect our governments to learn from failures like Somalia and do better next time, thus boosting the probability of success even more?

ON INTUITIONS

In this chapter, we look at whether these examples ought to make us feel optimistic about the prospects of intervention.

1. In his empirical study, Patrick Regan looks at 174 cases of foreign military intervention between 1946 and 1994; see Regan, *Civil Wars and Foreign Powers* and "Understanding Civil War"; see also Seybolt, *Humanitarian Intervention*. There is, then, a real methodological problem of selection bias when one focuses on only these few salient cases. This should give one pause when attempting to draw reliable conclusions about the *ex ante* probability of success of intervention in general.

But first it's important to note that we really ought to be careful about drawing conclusions on the basis of intuitions like these.

As a rule, we significantly overestimate the likelihood that endeavors like military interventions will succeed. We're psychologically predisposed to be overoptimistic about our abilities and plans, and the circumstances of intervention exacerbate this tendency. This overoptimism results from the interplay of a number of well-known psychological biases. Daniel Kahneman and Amos Tverski discuss how we tend to exaggerate our abilities to bring about good outcomes.[2] Most of us think we are above average in terms of positive qualities—we think we're smarter than average, have better leadership abilities, better morals, and so on. What's more, we do the opposite with others, especially when we can classify them as members of a certain group (which we can then see as inferior). We tend to underestimate other people's abilities and character, as well as the likelihood that they will resist our efforts.

Kahneman and Tverski discuss how these biases make our plans and expectations be unrealistically close to best-case scenarios. Because we focus on our own goals and the things we are going to do (and how well we can do them), we neglect the plans and skills of others, as well as the relevant base rates of variation. This means we tend to lose sight of what are the true probabilities of success. We focus on what we know and neglect what we do not know, thus overlooking the role of randomness and luck, especially when rare but catastrophic. But those random events are usually where the action is.

2. Daniel Kahneman and Amos Tversky, "Intuitive Predictions: Biases and Corrective Procedures," *TIMS Studies in Management Sciences* 12 (1979): 313–327. See also the discussion in Daniel Kahneman, *Thinking Fast and Slow* (Farrar, Straus and Giroux, 2013), 250–256.

In the context of military operations, this overoptimism leads to inflated views of our own military capabilities and deflated views of the likelihood that interventions will fail or meet resistance, thus creating an exaggerated sense that the likelihood of success is high.[3] And the more optimistic groups are, the more likely they are willing to use violence.[4]

Examples abound, of course. Readers will recall the hubris with which the George W. Bush administration invaded Iraq, and we've seen another example in the previous chapter with the case of Somalia. But those are not isolated cases. Instead, overoptimism is the rule. As many studies have shown, countries tend to become embroiled in conflicts that last longer than they expect, for which they do not plan with sufficient detail, and they confidently undertake military operations even when the evidence indicates that failure is likely.[5]

Our own intuitions, as students of intervention, about the feasibility of intervention are likely not much better. To be sure, psychological biases can be corrected, but doing so takes time, energy, and effort. People typically correct their biases when

3. See Johnson, *Overconfidence in War*, 18ff., and the many references therein. For an accessible overview and introduction, see Kahneman, *Thinking Fast and Slow*, part III.
4. See Roy F. Baumeister and J. M. Boden, "Aggression and the Self: High Self- Esteem, Low Self-Control, and Ego Threat," in *Human Aggression*, ed. R. G. Geen and E. Donnerstein (Academic Press, 1998), 115.
5. See, e.g., Johnson, *Overconfidence in War*. For similar findings, see Tuchman, *The March of Folly*; Ellsberg, *Secrets*: Ikle, *Every War Must End*. See also Roy F. Baumeister, "The Optimal Margin of Illusion," *Journal of Social and Clinical Psychology* 8 (1989): 176–189, esp. 181; Dan Lindley and Ryan Schildkraut "Is War Rational? The Extent of Miscalculation and Misperception as Causes of War," working paper, at http://www3.nd.edu/~dlindley/IWR/IWR%20Article.htm#_ftn1.

there are strong feedback loops that might inform them about their mistakes, and when they have a significant personal stake in their decisions being correct. Under those conditions, we are less prone to overoptimism because being overoptimistic is costly.[6]

Unfortunately, none of these conditions are present in thinking about intervention. When we, as students of intervention, consider the feasibility of these operations, we lack direct feedback. Interventions are extremely complex, and success depends on the interplay of a host of factors. Responsibility tends to be diffused, and it takes years before success or failure can be established. As a result, bad outcomes can always be attributed to a host of other factors, other people, and unforeseen problems—a good idea that got derailed this time. (Success, of course, can still be attributed to our efforts.) Moreover, we rarely experience any effects of either the successes or the failures. The costs of interventions are almost entirely externalized. When violence continues or intensifies, it is soldiers and especially foreigners who pay the price. We move on with our day.[7]

There are further psychological forces that push us in the direction of the interventionist position. In many circles, including the ones in which students of intervention tend to move, there is significant social pressure to be seen supporting the victims, the downtrodden, and the oppressed. In those circles, taking a stand against intervention—never mind writing a book against it—means opening oneself up to charges of callousness, selfishness, and the like. In those circles, that is, there are rewards (psychological and otherwise) for adopting the interventionist position. Doing nothing is unacceptable,

6. Compare Kahneman, *Thinking Fast and Slow*, 250ff.
7. See also Seybolt, *Humanitarian Intervention*, 61.

complacent, or (heaven forbid) conservative.[8] This affects the reliability of our views: the greater the expected rewards for biased opinions, the less accurate one's views tend to be.[9]

We should not base our thinking about the feasibility of military force on intuitions, anecdotes, or a small sample set of cases, then. When we think about intervention in these terms, when we see it as something that happens (or not) only in cases like Kosovo, Rwanda, and northern Iraq, we are setting ourselves up for mistake. We will focus on the success cases, forget about the failures, underestimate the role of luck, and so on.

8. Elsewhere, I have expressed my concern about these broader dynamics. See Bas van der Vossen, "In Defense of the Ivory Tower: Why Philosophers Should Stay Out of Politics," *Philosophical Psychology* 28 (2015): 1045–1063.
9. See Philip E. Tetlock, *Expert Political Judgment: How Good is It? How Can We Know?* (Princeton University Press, 2005). The same is found in a range of areas, including financial specialists, the medical field, economics, and so on. See, e.g., Itzhak Ben-David, John R. Graham, and Campbell R. Harvey, "Managerial Miscalibration," *Quarterly Journal of Economics* 128 (2013): 1547–1584; Dan Lovallo and Daniel Kahneman, "Timid Choices and Bold Forecasts: A Cognitive Perspective on Risk Taking," *Management Science* 39 (1993): 17–31; Daniel Kahneman and Dan Lovallo, "Delusions of Success: How Optimism Undermines Executives' Decisions," *Harvard Business Review* 81 (2003): 56–63; Manju Puri and David T. Robinson, "Optimism and Economic Choice," *Journal of Financial Economics* 86 (2007): 71–99; Arnold C. Cooper, Carolyn Y. Woo, and William C. Dunkelberg, "Entrepreneurs' Perceived Chances for Success," *Journal of Business Venturing* 3 (1988): 97–108; Pat Croskerry and Geoff Norman, "Overconfidence in Clinical Decision Making," *American Journal of Medicine* 121 (2008): S24–S29; and Kahneman and Tversky, "Intuitive Prediction: Biases and Corrective Procedures."

None of this means, once again, that intervention is never justifiable. The presumption against intervention is just that—a presumption. As such, it can be overcome. When we really do have good evidence that an intervention is an exception, and has a good enough chance of success, intervention may be on the table. But we should be skeptical when presented with such a case. After all, we are predisposed to see exceptions where there are none.[10]

IS OUR BEST GOOD ENOUGH?

Operation Allied Force, the NATO campaign in Kosovo, is typically cited as one of the most efficient and successful recent interventionist campaigns. Allied Force is said to have killed around 5,000 Serb combatants and 500 civilians.[11] And while

10. Unfortunately, most studies of intervention are rather unhelpful for this purpose. Spotting true exceptions is difficult, but it's even harder in the absence of firm decision-rules for spotting them. Books on intervention are often disappointing in this respect. A typical recommendation, for instance, is that the type of intervention must be well suited to the nature of the conflict, but almost none provide any generalizable rules for how interventions might be made to suit different kinds of conflicts. Thank you very much. For an example, see (the otherwise excellent) Wheeler, *Saving Strangers*. The main exception I've found, again, is Regan, *Civil Wars and Foreign Powers*.
11. The extent of civilian casualties is disputed. The number in the text follows the number of people who were verifiably killed by the intervention. However, other estimates, which include deaths that have not been verified, range from 1,200 to 5,700. See, e.g., Human Rights Watch, "The Crisis in Kosovo," at https://www.hrw.org/reports/2000/nato/Natbm200-01.htm. As we will see,

there is some controversy about the numbers of lives saved,[12] most estimates put the number at several thousand.[13]

Suppose, then, that we are dealing with an intervention that has roughly these prospects—would that be good enough? That is, if we're dealing with a country that is about as good at intervening as we can reasonably expect, and a crisis that is about as good a candidate for intervention as we might reasonably expect, would the presumption against intervention be overridden?[14]

Let's say, for the sake of argument, that the "several thousand" people saved were 3,000 people. And let's say that, for the sake of argument, of the total number of 5,000 Serb combatants killed, 4,000 were liable to be killed. By saying that they were liable we're saying that they had lost their rights against being killed by a humanitarian intervention like Allied Force (perhaps because of their role in the conflict, perhaps because of their complicity in the killing of Albanian Kosovars, or perhaps because of something else). Assuming further that those

these higher estimations of the civilian death toll are more in line with the way wars in general tend to harm civilians.

12. Some dispute that *any* were saved. Ken Booth, "The Kosovo Tragedy: Epilogue to Another 'Low and Dishonest Decade'?", *Politikon* 27 (2000): 5–18.
13. See, e.g., Seybolt, *Humanitarian Intervention.*
14. Another example of success that is often cited is East Timor. However, strictly speaking, East Timor is not a case of intervention as the operation happened with the consent of the Indonesian government. Moreover, East Timor is highly unusual. In addition to Indonesia's consent, local militias were unusually weak, the territory was small and isolated, the population was supportive, and a legitimacy-conferring political process preceded the operation; see Seybolt, *Humanitarian Intervention*, 261.

who are liable to be killed in pursuit of a humanitarian end don't count against the use of military force (and assuming other conditions of just war are respected as well[15]), that leaves 1,000 combatant deaths and 500 civilian deaths as the price of saving 3,000 innocent people.[16]

Would such a prospect be enough? There are two important issues here. First, while there exists an enormous literature on the ethics of warfare, I'm not aware of anyone who has taken a stand on the ratio of lives saved versus people killed that would be required for an intervention like this to be morally justifiable. Generally, however, it seems that ratios like saving five lives at the expense of one is deemed acceptable. If that's where we draw the line, our imaginary intervention clearly falls short of what is required. At two lives saved for every one person killed, we're not even close.

Of course, the numbers might be different. Perhaps the required ratio is significantly lower, perhaps something like 3:1? Or perhaps it really is 5:1, but we can (thankfully) expect our most promising operations to save 7,500 people.[17] (Then again, if things are really different, they might be different in the other direction, too.[18])

15. Which was not the case during the Kosovo intervention.
16. Assuming, of course, that the civilians are non-liable.
17. Or, perhaps, *all* Serb combatants were liable? Some believe—mistakenly, in my view—that all combatants lose their rights against being killed, simply by virtue of being combatants.
18. Taylor Seybolt, himself fairly friendly to intervention, discusses how claims about the effectiveness of intervention are frequently purposefully inflated. In the cases of Kosovo and East Timor, numbers have been inflated by up to a factor 10; see Seybolt, *Humanitarian Intervention*, 89–93.

Suppose that our evidence tells us that the imaginary intervention will likely bring about a certain ratio R_1 of people saved versus non-liable people killed. And suppose that, as a matter of general moral principle, and subject to various constraints and conditions of just war theory, a ratio equivalent to R_1 is morally acceptable. It still doesn't follow that this intervention would be justifiable. For a probability (even a high probability) of an intervention bringing about R_1 is not the same as the intervention actually bringing about R_1.

This is the second point. If interventions are to be acceptable and satisfy the success condition, they must bring about outcomes such that the balance between lives saved and non-liable people killed is morally acceptable over time. Let's label the minimum ratio that helps make up this latter outcome R_2. Since the expected ratio of any particular intervention is given by R_1 times the probability p of R_1 being brought about, and since $p < 1$, it follows that $R_2 > R_1$. The evidence, in other words, must indicate that the intervention will likely do significantly better than a ratio equivalent to R_1.[19]

It's worth remembering here that, in general, the toll of war in real life is usually far worse than our imaginary case. Political scientists Dan Lindley and Ryan Schildkraut find that the probability of success of powers initiating armed conflict has gone down over the course of the twentieth century.[20] And, in general, the harms of war disproportionally

19. Assuming that the expected outcome of the intervention not bringing about R_2 is not significantly better than R_2. As we'll see, this is generally a very safe assumption.
20. Lindley and Schildkraut conclude: "miscalculation and misperception now dominate the foreign policy process in decisions for war"; see Lindley and Schildkraut, "Is War Rational? The Extent of Miscalculation and Misperception as Causes of War."

affect ordinary citizens. The most optimistic observers estimate that war kills about equal numbers of civilians and combatants (excluding casualties that result from war-related famine and disease).[21] More pessimistic estimates, such as the European Union's European Security Strategy, go up to 90 percent of casualties in war being civilian.[22]

It is quite unlikely, then, that even the more efficient and successful cases of intervention satisfy the criterion of justifiability. For even those interventions rarely promise to bring about a sufficiently good humanitarian end. As Patrick Regan puts it, "overwhelmingly *any* intervention tends to increase the expected duration of a conflict."[23]

If the presumption against intervention is to be overcome, then, it will likely be in cases of the most egregious humanitarian crises. These are cases where intervention can save exceptionally large numbers of people from death and harm—thus making the risk of failure more acceptable. And these are cases where success, the saving of life, is easier to obtain as fewer of the problems we saw in the previous chapter will obtain.[24]

21. See W. Eckhardt, "Civilian Deaths in Wartime," *Security Dialogue* 20 (1989): 89–98; Adam Roberts, "Lives and Statistics: Are 90% of War Victims Civilians?", *Survival* 52 (2010): 115–136.
22. See Javier Solana, EU High Representative for Common Foreign and Security Policy, *A Secure Europe in a Better World: European Security Strategy* (European Union Institute for Security Studies, 2003), 5, at http://www.iss.europa.eu/uploads/media/solanae.pdf. The 90 percent number is also listed by Paul Collier et al., *Breaking the Conflict Trap: Civil War and Development Policy* (World Bank, 2003), 17.
23. Regan, *Civil Wars and Foreign Powers*, 71, emphasis in original.
24. These tend to be focused more clearly on achieving peace and humanitarian relief, and suffer from fewer informational and incentive problems. The salience of these conflicts, as well as

Thus, the now discredited view that interventions are justified only in cases of supreme humanitarian emergencies is much closer to the truth than the interventionist alternative.[25]

their limited time horizon, make these interventions more feasible and enables a credible commitment of the requisite resources; see Regan, *Civil Wars and Foreign Powers*, 131, 141–142; Seybolt, *Humanitarian Intervention*, 176, 220. This is true especially if the conflict is relatively new, as this means there is a greater chance of outside forces readjusting the balance of forces needed for the violence to stop; see Regan, *Civil Wars and Foreign Powers*, 73, 94, 97, 148–150. Cf. Pillar, *Negotiating Peace*.

25. For instance, interventions on behalf of groups that want to secede from larger states will likely be impermissible. First, interventions against existing governments are among the least likely to succeed; see Regan, *Civil Wars and Foreign Powers*, 29–31, 138. Second, and additionally, these interventions often provoke violent resistance by the existing government; see Seybolt, *Humanitarian Intervention*, 119–120. Once this happens, Regan shows, the probability of success dangerously approaches zero.

13

Humanitarian Nonintervention

INTERVENTIONISTS OFTEN COMPLAIN THAT A policy of nonintervention means doing nothing. And in the face of so much human suffering, surely that's unacceptable. Surely, we simply can't stand by idly? We've got to do something.

I agree, of course, that the kind of suffering that is going on in our world is unacceptable. (Every decent person does.) But that's really not the question. The question is what the morally right response is to this unacceptable state of affairs. Or at least, that should be the question.

In most discussions, humanitarianism and nonintervention are posited as opposites. Nonintervention, we're told, means supporting sovereignty, self-determination, statism, the legalist paradigm, a Hegelian Myth, or what have you. Humanitarianism, we're told, represents a care for the lives, freedoms, and rights of individuals. And humanitarianism, of course, means intervention.

But this is an imaginary opposition. Most of the time, the truly humanitarian thing to do, the thing that really respects human life, is to refrain from using military force. Most of the time, interventions are simply too risky, imperiling innocent life, to count as genuinely humanitarian.

A DUTY TO INTERVENE?

One might go beyond merely saying that we ought to *respect* life, of course. Often, supporters of expanded interventionism assert a duty to *protect* life as well. They assert that there a moral duty to intervene in case of crisis.[1]

I say "assert" rather than "argue," because the claim is rarely backed up. One way one might try to back it up would be to invoke an argument by Peter Singer. According to Singer, there is a general moral duty to help those in need. Indeed, most of us are already committed to this idea, Singer thinks. Of course, Singer's discussion concerns humanitarian aid and redistribution, not military intervention, but his arguments are easily extended that way.

Consider the following application of Singer's argument:

1. Suffering, and death from a lack of food, shelter, and medical care are morally bad.
2. *The Singer Principle (Weak Version):* If it is in our power to prevent something bad from happening, without thereby sacrificing anything of moral significance, we ought, morally, to do it.[2]
3. *The Empirical Claim*: We can prevent suffering and death by supporting foreign military interventions.
4. Therefore, we ought, morally, to support military interventions.

1. See, among others, Oberman, "The Myth of the Optional War: Why States Are Required to Wage the Wars They Are Permitted to Wage."
2. Peter Singer, "Famine, Affluence, and Morality," *Philosophy and Public Affairs* 1 (1973): 229–243, 231. Note that this reflects the weaker of two principles Singer discusses.

Note the neat separation of facts and principles. Morality demands that we help those in need. How we help is an empirical question. The two are different issues, and one does not affect the other.

Most people who find Singer's principles plausible find them plausible because of a famous thought experiment:

> **One Drowning Child**
> Suppose you are walking past a shallow pond and see a child drowning in it. You can wade in and pull the child out, even though this means getting your clothes muddy. But this is insignificant compared to the death of the child.[3]

To Singer, this thought experiment illustrates the application of the more general principle just given. The only difference between One Drowning Child and the case of intervention is the empirical part. What is the same is a general moral duty to help those in need.

I agree, of course, that you ought to wade in and help the child in One Drowning Child. But this does not mean accepting Singer's general principle. For while it is true that there are important empirical differences between One Drowning Child and the circumstances of intervention, it's false to think the differences in the one case do not affect the other case.

Consider the following variation of One Drowning Child, offered by David Schmidtz:

> **One Drowning Child–II**
> A baby is drowning in the pool beside you. You can save the baby by a process that involves giving the thug who threw the baby in the pool a hundred dollars. If you do not save the baby, the baby will die. You save the baby. A crowd

3. Ibid., 231.

> begins to gather, including several more thugs carrying more babies. Seeing what you have done, the thugs throw a few more babies into the pool. The babies will drown unless you give each of the thugs a hundred dollars. More thugs begin to gather, carrying even more babies, waiting to see what you do.[4]

Schmidtz's point is not that this alternative thought experiment better reflects the world we live in. Nor is his point that helping people will immediately turn our world into this. Rather, the point is that the actions we choose will have consequences, and those consequences matter. Or, more precisely, the *principles* we choose will have consequences, and those consequences matter—including for what principles are acceptable in the first place.

A duty to intervene is a standing principle to intervene whenever we can alleviate need. We don't need thought experiments to know the consequences this might this have. During the late 1990s Kosovo crisis, the Kosovo Liberation Army (KLA) sought independence from Serbia.[5] The Albanian minority in Kosovo had long been discriminated against by the Serbian authorities. In 1991, the Democratic League of Kosovo, under leadership of Ibrahim Rugova, organized a referendum in which an overwhelming majority of voters supported independence from Serbia. Rugova proposed a tactic of peaceful negotiation with Serbia in order to work toward secession out of fear for a Serbian backlash against the Albanians.

When Rugova's peaceful strategy failed to mobilize international support for Kosovar independence, more radical

4. David Schmidtz, "Separateness, Suffering, and Moral Theory," in his *Person, Polis, Planet* (Oxford University Press, 2008), 148–149.
5. The discussion here follows Wheeler, *Saving Strangers*, 257ff. and the references therein. See also Seybolt, *Humanitarian Intervention*, 81.

groups came to prominence, including the KLA, which openly advocated the use of violent means. Because the KLA lacked popular support and was weak compared to the Serbian authorities, they settled on a strategy of deliberately provoking Serbian police and Interior Ministry attacks on Albanian civilians. Their aim was to increase civilian casualties in order to draw international attention and support, and eventually a military intervention. As Dugi Gorani, a Kosovar Albanian negotiator, said: "Every single Albanian realized that the more civilians die, intervention comes nearer."[6]

During February 1996, the KLA started a campaign of bombing against Serb targets, which lasted until 1998, when Serbian forces attacked the KLA with heavy weapons and air support. The Serb forces burned villages and drove hundreds and thousands of Kosovars from their homes. These attacks were quickly condemned by the Clinton administration. U.S. Secretary of State Madeleine Albright stated in March 1998 that "we believe that in 1991 the international community stood by and watched ethnic cleansing [in Bosnia] . . .. We don't want that to happen again this time."[7] The message was clear: this administration would not allow the human rights of Kosovars to go violated like this again.

The violence continued, leading to the NATO campaign's Allied Force. Once the campaign commenced, Serbian forces

6. A. Little, "Moral Combat: NATO at War," *BBC 2 Special*, March 12, 2000, transcript at http://news.bbc.co.uk/hi/english/static/events/panorama/transcripts/transcript_12_03_00.txt. Hashim Thaci, a KLA leader, openly admitted that "any armed action we undertook would bring retaliation against civilians. We knew we were endangering a great number of civilian lives." See also discussion in Seybolt, *Humanitarian Intervention*; and Hehir, *Humanitarian Intervention After Kosovo*, 111.
7. Cited in Wheeler, *Saving Strangers*, 258, following J. Steele, "Learning to Live with Milosevic," *Transitions* 5 (1998): 19.

intensified their assault on the ethnically Albanian population in Kosovo, with significant casualties, large numbers of refugees, and thousands of additional civilian deaths as a result.[8]

Singer might object that none of this impugns his proposed moral principle. But that would be to miss the point of One Drowning Child–II. If a proposed moral duty of intervention encourages thugs to sacrifice innocent lives so as to promote their political agendas, that fact counts against the proposed moral duty. The duties of help that we end up endorsing, if we do end up endorsing them, better actually help the people who need it the most.[9]

Singer seems to think that if we accept that there is a duty to save the child in One Drowning Child, then we must also accept a duty to save the child in One Drowning Child–II. And, by extension, we must accept the duty in cases of intervention. Indeed, Singer thinks we have a duty to assist anyone around the world who needs our assistance, even if this means bringing down our own living standards by a lot. (Possibly to the

8. See Seybolt, *Humanitarian Intervention*, 82. See also Alan T. Kuperman, "Mitigating the Moral Hazard of Humanitarian Intervention: Lessons from Economics," *Global Governance* 14 (2008): 219–240, offering additional evidence about Kosovo and similar dynamics more recently in Sudan.
9. It's worth noting that, in earlier cases, the international community has been quite sensitive to this issue. For example, during the imposition of a no-fly zone in northern Iraq, it was made quite clear that independence for the Kurds was off the table, since as Wheeler puts it, "any proposal along these lines would have sent shock waves through those governments in the region that had large Kurdish minorities. Moreover, legitimating secession would have established a dangerous precedent that would have placed at risk the constitutive rules of sovereignty, non-intervention, and territorial integrity in the society of states." See Wheeler, *Saving Strangers*, 158.

point where the marginal disutility of giving help is greater than the marginal utility of the help itself.)

But note that this is an *additional* claim. And it's one that doesn't follow from saying that there is a duty to save the child in One Drowning Child. It's a risky claim, too. After all, if we cannot choose between saving the child in One Drowning Child and saving all the vulnerable people in the world, we will be forced to choose between having to save everyone and having to save no one. And in that case, we may be forced to choose no one. That would be an even greater tragedy.

PEOPLE AND PLACES

If interventionism isn't humanitarian, that doesn't mean any kind of nonintervention is humanitarian. No policy exists in a vacuum, and what we surround it with matters. Humanitarian nonintervention has to be made that way.

The aim of the interventionist is to bring peace and stability to places where people are forced to live under conditions of oppression, conflict, and war. But there are two variables to this equation: the people and the places in which they live. Unfortunately, the quality of the institutions that govern places is highly inert. Bad institutions incentivize political and social elites to keep them bad. Their extractive ways of life depend on it. And there isn't much that we as outsiders can do about it.

Fortunately, the people living in these places are not so inert. They can and often are willing to move. And we, as outsiders, can make it much easier for them to do so. The truly humanitarian response to suffering and oppression around the world, then, is not to try and fix other countries through the use of violence. The truly humanitarian response is to make it as easy as possible for those who are forced to live in these countries to leave for better places.

Unfortunately, in our world, few people have the opportunity to improve their lives in this way. Every safe and prosperous country in our world tries its best to keep immigrants out. They put up fences and walls, and post them with armed guards. They patrol their coastal waters, monitor airports, and so on. Millions who nevertheless see themselves forced to flee their homes in places like Syria, Iraq, and Sudan end up spending years in camps, in legal limbo while their asylum applications are pending, and so on.

A policy of humanitarian nonintervention is not a policy of maintaining the status quo. It requires significant and deep changes to politics as usual. But this does not tell in favor of more intervention. After all, intervention *is* politics as usual. The fact that this has not reduced conflict, disorder, and misery around the world is no reason for wanting more of it. Quite the opposite.

The real tragedy is the combination of this impermissible stance on intervention with the also impermissible position of keeping immigrants out. Indeed, I find it difficult to think of a more atrocious combination of policies than, on the one hand, an overly interventionist foreign policy, exporting violence in order to silence our conscience while on the other hand, doing one's best to trap the victims of this violence where it hurts the most.[10]

10. Of course, there is just as much political opposition to freer immigration as to long-lasting nation-building. However, and contrary to intervention, immigration *does* have a history of success. So, while I see no reason to think that governments will become willing to support long-lasting foreign nation-building, the prospects for more open immigration policies may be better.

INDEX

Made in United States
Orlando, FL
26 August 2023